Diverse Voices
in Modern US
Moral Theology

Diverse Voices

in Modern US

Moral Theology

CHARLES E. CURRAN

Georgetown University Press
Washington, DC

Library of Congress Cataloging-in-Publication Data

Names: Curran, Charles E., author.
Title: Diverse Voices in Modern US Moral Theology / Charles E. Curran.
Other titles: Diverse Voices in Modern US Moral Theology
Description: Washington, DC : Georgetown University Press, 2018. | Includes
    bibliographical references and index.
Identifiers: LCCN 2018004912 (print) | LCCN 2018006840 (ebook) |
    ISBN 9781626166332 (ebook) | ISBN 9781626166325 (pbk.: alk. paper) |
    ISBN 9781626166318 (hardcover : alk. paper)
Subjects: LCSH: Christian ethics—Catholic authors. | Christian ethics—United States. |
    Theologians—United States. | Catholic Church—Doctrines.
Classification: LCC BJ1249 (ebook) | LCC BJ1249 .C81724 2019 (print) | DDC
    241/.0420973—dc23
LC record available at https://lccn.loc.gov/2018004912

19 18   9 8 7 6 5 4 3 2 First printing

Printed in the United States of America.
Cover design by Martha Madrid.

In gratitude to all those who over the years have helped to prepare my manuscripts for publication. They are too numerous to mention but too important to forget.

Contents

Preface

This volume discusses the method and approach of twelve significant figures in Catholic moral theology in the United States beginning with John C. Ford (1902–89) and continuing down to the present. In addition to Ford, this book explores the approaches of Bernard Häring; Josef Fuchs; Richard A. McCormick; Germain G. Grisez; Romanus Cessario; Margaret A. Farley; Lisa Sowle Cahill; Ada María Isasi-Díaz; Bryan N. Massingale; the New Wine, New Wineskins movement; and James F. Keenan.

Some comments about those included in the volume are in order. Bernard Häring and Josef Fuchs were both Germans who taught for a long time in Rome, beginning in the 1950s. These two were major international figures, but they also made a significant impact on Catholic moral theology in the United States because of their writings and their teaching and lecturing in this country. Häring and Fuchs were teaching at a time when the home of moral theology was in seminaries and the theologates and the theologians themselves were priests. There were very few publishing US moral theologians at this time.

In the United States, the home of moral theology in the late 1970s and especially the 1980s began to shift to colleges and universities. Some of the newest moral theologians were female religious, such as Margaret Farley, but they were followed by laypeople, such as Lisa Sowle Cahill. Today the majority of moral theologians in the United States are laypeople. Since the late 1970s, there has been a tremendous growth in the quantity and quality of moral theologians writing in this country. In addition, as we come closer to the present time, theologians teaching in Rome no longer have the influence or the reputation of Häring and Fuchs.

All the approaches discussed here deal with individual moral theologians, except for the treatment of the New Wine, New Wineskins movement. The approach of this movement, which came to the fore in the first decade of the twenty-first century, is significant both because of its distinctive approach to moral theology and the fact that almost all of those writing in this movement were laypeople, thus showing how dramatically the face of Catholic moral theology in the United States has changed.

This book deals with those who have contributed different methods or approaches to moral theology in general.[1] In an earlier volume, I discussed the different approaches to Catholic social ethics. The theologians discussed here are not necessarily the most important voices in modern Catholic moral theology. Jean Porter, for example, who has an endowed chair at the University of Notre Dame and is a fellow of the American Academy of Arts and Sciences, has made a noteworthy contribution to moral theology with her work on the history of the natural law and Thomas Aquinas. Her work, however, does not fit into the category of diverse methods and approaches to moral theology that is discussed here.

This book has three aims or purposes. The first aim is to make available to the interested reader the approaches and method of some major figures influencing moral theology here in the United States. Even those who are professional moral theologians might not be aware of all these different authors and how they have developed their approaches. In this context, I decided I would not offer any in-depth critique of the different authors. I have spelled out my own approach to moral theology in my many writings and see no need to do that again in this volume. In this book I have endeavored to let the individual authors speak for themselves with only occasional observations and comments from me.

The second aim is to try to foster a dialogue among all those who do Catholic moral theology. In this country there is a serious division between what has generally been called the conservative and liberal approaches to moral theology. There is comparatively little or no dialogue and great divisions between these two groups. One illustration of the division is the fact that the groups generally belong to different academic societies. The liberals belong to the Catholic Theological Society of America. To its credit, this society has made some efforts toward dialogue, but it has been hard to sustain. The more conservative theologians belong to one or both of two other societies. The Fellowship of Catholic Scholars came into existence in 1977 after the negative reactions to *Humanae vitae*, the Land O'Lakes Statement calling for academic freedom for Catholic higher education, and the publication of a book on human sexuality commissioned by the Catholic Theological Society of America. The purpose of the Fellowship of Catholic Scholars is to redirect Catholic scholars "toward a more friendly approach to the teaching authority of the Church."[2] The Academy of Catholic Theology, which had its first annual conference in 2008, has the principal purpose of fostering theology faithful to God's revelation "authoritatively interpreted by the Magisterium."[3] In addition, each group tends to publish in journals friendly to its approach.

These divisions are very deep and rooted in the divisions within the contemporary Roman Catholic Church and thus are very difficult to overcome. One comparatively insignificant volume such as this is not going to overcome these divisions. But by including all different approaches representing the full spectrum of Catholic moral theology, perhaps it might remind all of the breadth of Catholic moral theology and the need for some dialogue among scholars who profess to belong to a church that is catholic with a capital *C* and a small *c*.

The third and perhaps most important aim of this book is to show the significance of *Sitz im Leben* influencing the approach of individual moral theologians. Sitz im Leben refers to one's historical situation and circumstances—one's "setting in life." Each author's Sitz im Leben is explained to show how it has affected his or her approach to moral theology.

Looking back, as this book does, it is evident how Sitz im Leben has played a significant role in how the authors developed their approach to moral theology. Not only history but also the very understanding of the discipline of moral theology recognizes the influential role of Sitz im Leben. Moral theology strives to serve three publics: the Church, the academy, and society. Each of these publics develops over time, and moral theology must deal with this continuous evolution. From the perspective of the academy, moral theologians have been in dialogue and even building on different philosophical and theological approaches. Thomas Aquinas used Aristotle; some contemporary theologians have used Karl Marx. Contemporary Catholic moral theologians are in dialogue with a multiplicity of philosophical and theological approaches. The Church itself, one of the three publics, is a pilgrim church and is always on a journey. The early chapters in this book show the influential role that Vatican II and *Humanae vitae* played in Catholic moral theology. Moral theology also deals with the changing social, political, and cultural realities of our world. The chapters on Ada María Isasi-Díaz and Bryan Massingale well illustrate how moral theology often evolves in light of the new historical realities—in the case of Isasi-Díaz, the role of Latinas in United States society; in the case of Massingale, the reality of racism. The final chapter discusses the work of James F. Keenan. Keenan, like all the others, is affected by his Sitz im Leben, but he differs from the other approaches by his greater concern for the discipline of moral theology as such.

Sitz im Leben has not only strongly influenced Catholic moral theology in the past, but it will continue to do so in the future since moral theology is always dealing with the three publics mentioned above. As a result, there will never be a perennial moral theology, but it will continue to grow and evolve in the light of these publics that it serves.

I will end this preface with a personal reflection. I have been privileged to know all the persons I have discussed in this volume. John Ford was a considerate and gracious senior colleague in my first year teaching at the Catholic University of America. Bernard Häring and Josef Fuchs were my teachers and mentors whose personal friendship and support over the years I will never forget. Richard McCormick was my closest colleague and friend. We coedited the multiple volumes of the series of Readings in Moral Theology published by Paulist Press beginning in 1979, and I edited a Festschrift in his honor in 1990.[4] Margaret Farley, Lisa Sowle Cahill, and James Keenan have been dialogue partners and friends in our mutual journey of doing moral theology. Ada María Isasi-Díaz and Bryan Massingale were friends even before they finished their doctorates. The younger scholars in the New Wine, New Wineskins movement have shared conversations and friendly dialogue with me in many different venues, often in my room at various meetings.

My own approach and position have differed most from those of Germain Grisez and Romanus Cessario. Germain and I in the late 1960s and 1970s were often on opposing sides, but both of us have made attempts to recognize that we share a common faith and journey. I was greatly touched when Grisez recently referred to "Curran, whom I have always found to be fair-minded."[5] Romanus Cessario is the only author discussed here who ever took a class from me. Despite our differences, we have always shared friendly conversation over the years. At the 2017 meeting of the Society of Christian Ethics, he volunteered to be the convener of a discussion of my latest book.

In this book I have tried to be fair and objective in presenting the different approaches by these significant figures in the field in the last seventy-five years.

I am grateful to all those who have assisted me in my research and writing in general and especially of this volume. Since 1991, I have been privileged to hold the Elizabeth Scurlock University Professorship of Human Values at Southern Methodist University. My students and colleagues, the librarians of the Bridwell Library, and the university administration have made Southern Methodist University a very hospitable and challenging home for me. I remain ever grateful to the late Jack and Laura Lee Blanton, who endowed the professorship that I hold. This manuscript never would have seen the light of day without the extraordinary contributions of my associate, Leslie Fuller. She has been more helpful than anyone else in the writing of this book.

This is the ninth volume that I have contributed to the Moral Traditions series of Georgetown University Press. I remain ever grateful to Richard

Brown, the former director of the press; to Hope LeGro, the interim director; to James F. Keenan, the founding editor of the Moral Traditions series;
and to the present editors of the series, David Cloutier, Kristen Heyer, and
Andrea Vicini. In addition, the staff of the press has always been most helpful.
Once again, my friend Ken Himes has helped me with his careful and critical
reading of the manuscript.

Notes

1. Charles E. Curran, *American Catholic Social Ethics: Twentieth-Century Approaches*
(Notre Dame, IN: University of Notre Dame Press, 1982).

2. Fellowship of Catholic Scholars, https://catholicscholars.org/aboutus.php.

3. Academy of Catholic Theology, www.academyofcatholictheology.org.

4. Charles E. Curran, ed., *Moral Theology: Challenges for the Future: Essays in Honor
in Richard A. McCormick* (New York: Paulist Press, 1990).

5. Germain Grisez, "Residual Entities," First Things, https://www.firstthings
.com/web-exclusives/2015/06/residual-entities.

1

John C. Ford

John Ford's *Sitz im Leben* very much influenced his approach to moral theology. In the pre–Vatican II period of the 1940s, 1950s, and early 1960s, moral theology was identified with the manuals of moral theology. The purpose of these manuals was to train future priests for their role in the confessional to know what acts were sinful and their degree of sinfulness—mortal or venial sins. The method was casuistic. Authoritative papal teaching had a primary role, and such a teaching provided guidance and answers to particular problems within these parameters. Ford was a leader in moral theology in this country and abroad. He strenuously defended the papal teaching condemning artificial contraception and in the 1960s also worked behind the scenes to maintain the condemnation.

John Cuthbert Ford, SJ (1902–89), was a Jesuit (Society of Jesus) priest recognized by many as the leading Catholic moral theologian of his generation. Despite some illness, he was ordained a priest in 1932 and shortly afterward was sent to obtain a doctorate in moral theology at the Pontifical Gregorian University in Rome run by the Jesuits. In 1937, he defended his dissertation on the validity of virginal marriage, which brought together canonical and sacramental aspects of theology as well as moral theology. He began teaching at the Jesuit theologate in Weston, Massachusetts, where he had been a student, and taught much of his academic life there, with a stint as professor of moral theology at the Catholic University of America from 1958 to 1966. He resigned from teaching at Weston in 1969 and died twenty years later.[1]

Ford never wrote a systematic moral theology textbook, but he began publishing the article "Notes on Moral Theology" in the new Jesuit publication *Theological Studies*, which since its beginning in 1940 has generally been acknowledged as the leading Catholic theological journal in the United States. To this day, *Theological Studies* still publishes "Notes on Moral Theology" every year. From 1941 to 1956, Ford and his friend Gerald Kelly, SJ, who taught at St. Mary's, the Jesuit theologate in Kansas, were responsible for "Notes on Moral Theology." Ford and Kelly then decided to reorganize, greatly expand, and develop the matters and issues treated in "Notes" as well as the issues that came afterward.[2] They published in 1958 *Contemporary Moral Theology*, volume 1: *Questions in Fundamental Moral Theology*, and, in 1963, *Contemporary Moral Theology*, volume 2: *Marriage Questions*.[3] Both volumes were very well received. The two authors worked very closely together in agreement, so what I will call Ford in this chapter is often Ford and Kelly. (Kelly's major contribution was in the area of medical ethics, but he died before the discussions about Vatican II and *Humanae vitae*.) These volumes constitute Ford's most academic contribution, but he also published many articles and small books on other topics, such as alcoholism and how religious superiors use psychiatry and psychological testing in relation to the rights of their subjects.[4]

John Ford as a Manualist

John Ford's Jesuit vocation was to teach seminarians and priests how to administer the sacrament of penance, in those days commonly called confession. Confession played a very significant role in Catholic life in the pre–Vatican II times. In his teaching, Ford followed the manualistic approach of his Jesuit predecessors, and by his publications he played a leading role in moral theology in the United States and even outside the country. He was looked on as a significant reformer for his contributions to the discipline.[5]

Although Ford never wrote a textbook or manual of moral theology, he used a manualistic approach in his understanding of the discipline. This Jesuit professor strongly agreed with the focus of the manuals as preparing priests and future priests for hearing confessions. *Contemporary Moral Theology* speaks of the apostolate of the confessional and recognizes that the historical evolution of the science and the principal goal to which it is directed explained to some extent the necessary emphasis on mortal sin and its limits.[6] Traditional Catholic moral theology recognizes mortal sin as a serious violation of the law of God, which separates the person from God's love and is ultimately deserving of eternal damnation. The very nature of mortal sin underlies the importance of discussing what is mortal sin and what is not. Venial sin is a lesser sin that does not break the relationship with God and result in eternal damnation if not repented before death.

An Illustration of the Emphasis on Determining Sinfulness

An illustration from *Contemporary Moral Theology* shows Ford's great concern of establishing what is mortal sin and distinguishing it from venial sin.

The specific issue concerns determining the degree of sinfulness in the case of avoiding occasions of sin (1:147–57). An occasion of sin is an external circumstance involving an impulse or allurement to sin with a consequent likelihood or danger of sinning, which would not be present or would be greatly diminished if the external circumstance were avoided. The manuals distinguish between proximate and remote occasions. Another important distinction concerns necessary and voluntary occasions. Theologians agree that, given an occasion of serious sin, which is voluntary and truly proximate, there is a grave obligation to remove it or avoid it. Not to do so would itself be a mortal sin objectively. (The distinction between objective and subjective mortal sin will be discussed later.)

For a good number of moral theologians, an occasion is proximate when the danger of sinning is truly probable, even though it is equally probable that, in spite of the occasion, the sin will be avoided. Thus, mortal sin is objectively committed each time one exposes oneself to this probable danger without a proportionate cause. Putting oneself in such a danger would be a serious violation of the virtue of prudence.

Contemporary Moral Theology opposes this thesis that it is objectively a mortal sin to voluntarily expose oneself to the danger of probably committing an objective mortal sin. The authors do not maintain that no sin is involved but only that it is not necessarily gravely or mortally sinful. A number of reasons prove this point. First, a duty under pain of mortal sin must be proved, and the burden of the proof rests on those who assert the obligation. The degrees of the danger of sin are indefinitely numerous, extending from certain to mostly certain, to highly probable, more probable, equally probable, probable, less probable, hardly probable, to even degrees of possibility. There is a gradually diminishing malice as one goes down in this scale so that at some stage all would agree there is no grave malice involved. Here we are talking about a prudential judgment, and other theologians propose different degrees of probability. Arthur Vermeersch, SJ, Ford and Kelly's professor in Rome, draws the line that the danger of sinning has to be more probable than not sinning, while others maintain that it must be highly probable or morally certain. Consequently a formula based on probable danger is too rigid.

In addition, just as there are degrees of certitude and probability, there are also degrees of the seriousness of mortal sins, admitting of degrees of gravity from an internal thought, a solitary external act, a sin that offends one or a few others, sins that damage the bodies or souls of others, to sins that damage the public good of the community or of the Church. Since prudence is the ultimate criterion, it is very difficult to propose a universal criterion when the danger of sinning becomes grave in the light of all these indefinite considerations.

Another argument against the universality of the stricter view is that the person who enters an occasion of sin where the danger of sinning is probable might have some reason for so entering the occasion of sin even if it is not proportionate to the danger. The distinction between free and necessary occasion is theoretically clear but very murky in practice. Necessity, like probability, admits of an infinite number of degrees.

It is fascinating that Ford himself does not propose any universal formula (e.g., equiprobable, more probable). Without his explicitly saying so, his reason apparently is that the very complexity involved makes it difficult to come up with a rigid universal norm. In his words, the judgment to decide when the penitent has a grave obligation not to expose oneself to the danger of sinning has to take into account the degrees of the probability of sin, the degrees of the gravity of the sin in question, and the degrees of necessity that may exist for entering occasions of sin. In light of all these factors, he does not propose his own universal norm but simply disagrees with the proposed norm that grave guilt is universally present whenever the probable danger of sinning is entered.

In addition, this illustration also shows Ford's significant use of the method of casuistry, which was the method frequently employed by the manuals of moral theology. Critics of the manuals of moral theology show a pronounced dislike for casuistry, but Ford insists there is no really practical moral theology without good casuistry (1:141–42). This example also shows that Ford is a good casuist. A good casuist uses careful analysis to determine what are the most important considerations involved and does not get bogged down in what is peripheral. Good casuistry requires a broad knowledge of moral theology, which the casuist thus brings to bear in analyzing the particular issue or case. This example also shows why Ford at the time was considered to be a liberal Catholic theologian, arguing against the opinions of others that he judged to be too rigorous.[7]

Three other aspects of Ford's writings also show that he was in the manualist tradition of moral theology. First, manualists followed a deontological or law model of ethics. Law was the objective norm of moral theology. Ford, like the manualists, insists on the primacy of law, duty, and obligation as the primary aspects of moral life. The first chapter in *Contemporary Moral Theology*, volume 1, is titled "The Church and the Moral Law" (1:3–18). He defines sin as the violation of a law that obliges in conscience (1:254). Opponents of a manualist approach decry the centrality of law, but Ford maintains it is dangerous "to decry a morality of duty, of law, and of obligation, because in the last analysis there is no other" (1:92). If all people would only obey the commandments of God, the combined interior beauty of those souls would be indescribable and the world itself would be a paradise (1:96).

Second, Ford sees a close relationship between moral theology and canon law. The manuals emphasize the connection between the two disciplines. The treatise on the sacraments in moral theology is almost totally canonical.[8] His doctoral dissertation on virginal marriage included many canonical considerations.[9] Ford's first article in *Theological Studies* in 1941 was titled "Current Moral Theology and Canon Law" and was the precursor of "Notes on Moral Theology." In this overview, Ford devotes twenty-six pages to canon law, covering the specific topics of canon law and civil law, law for religious, and matrimonial law.[10] Under the heading of moral theology, he treats from a broader perspective "the Sacraments, Holy Eucharist, Penance" for five pages.[11] In 1953, he wrote a brief book on the norms for fasting before receiving communion.[12] The chapter in *Contemporary Moral Theology*, volume 1, "Juridical Aspects of Subjective Imputability," includes a consideration of canonical norms of criminal imputability (1:253–59).

Part 1 of *Contemporary Moral Theology*, volume 2, deals with the ends of marriage and frequently refers to canonical considerations. Ford insists that "a divorce between canonical and theological principles would be intolerable, especially in the case of marriage, which is a society, and therefore essentially an entity of the juridical order" (2:56).

Third, and also in accord with the legal model, is the use of probabilism, which has already been mentioned somewhat in the discussion of occasions of sin. What happens when one is doubtful whether there is a law or obligation in a particular case? Among Jesuit theologians and many others, the theory of probabilism provided the answer. In case of a doubtful law or obligation one can follow, except in a certain few cases, an opinion proposing freedom from the law, provided it is truly probable even if the opinion in support of the law or obligation is more probable. The word "probable" is a translation of the Latin *probabilis* and means provable rather than probable. There are two kinds of probabilism. Intrinsic probabilism is based on the strength of the reasons given for the position. Extrinsic probabilism is based on the authority of the authors who hold such a position. It was generally accepted that six reputable authors would constitute a probable opinion but that one author of outstanding excellence, such as Thomas Aquinas or Alphonsus Liguori, could make an opinion probable.[13]

Ford appeals to probabilism when there is a doubtful obligation. Like other manualists, he also consults other authors to see if there are sufficient authors to make an opinion extrinsically probable. One controversial issue discussed in *Contemporary Moral Theology*, volume 2, is the removal of a woman's uterus that is weakened and in danger of rupturing in a future pregnancy. Many authors claim that the problem comes not from the uterus itself but from the pregnancy and therefore is a condemned direct sterilization. Ford claims there is intrinsic probability in this case because such a uterus is in a pathological condition because it cannot fulfill its function even though there would be no danger without a pregnancy. In addition, there is solid extrinsic authority for maintaining this position as an acceptable, indirect sterilization (2:333). In the light of this extrinsic probability, no confessor can impose a grave obligation on the penitent (2:429).

Explicit Defense of the Manualist Approach

In addition, John Ford has explicitly defended the manualist approach. In fact, three of the chapters in *Contemporary Moral Theology*, volume 1, deal with modern criticisms of moral theology, new approaches to moral theology, and the author's response to these developments. As an accomplished academic, Ford was aware of these criticisms and newer approaches, almost all of which were written in languages other than English. In these chapters, he summarizes the approaches of over ten different moral theologians (1:42–103). The critics of moral theology generally agree that a Christian morality should be Christocentric, recognizing the primacy of love and growth in the virtues, which are concrete expressions of the twofold commandment of love of God and neighbor (1:42–79).

Ford, the open-minded moralist, admits that a great deal of the criticism of the seminary course in moral theology is justified. Too often the professor is looked on as a lawyer for the defense who gets people out of obligations. Critics often refer to the professor of moral theology as the one who takes away the sins of the world! The moral professor and textbooks should recognize the ascetical aspect of the Christian life and encourage confessors to urge their penitents to a deeper and fuller Christian existence. But one cannot put all of ascetical theology or dogmatic theology into the moral textbook or course. The moral course will always have to put primary emphasis on what is sinful and the degree of sinfulness, but it should also show that Christian living calls for more than that. Ford hopes that there will be textbooks in the future that take such an approach, but there are none at the present time (1:96–103).

The Primary Role of Papal Teaching

For Ford the primary and most important aspect in Catholic moral theology is the authoritative papal teaching office. The earlier manuals obviously recognize this important aspect, but they do not give it the centrality and overwhelming importance found in *Contemporary Moral Theology*. The reason for this is that as the twentieth century developed, the centrality of the papacy and its role in moral teaching greatly increased, and the number of authoritative papal teachings on moral matters multiplied immensely.

The first and last pages of volume 1 insist on the importance of the authoritative papal teaching for moral theology. On the first page, moral theology is pointed out as being different from ethics: "Reason is the supreme argument in ethics; authority is the sovereign guide of the theologian." Authority is described as revelation and the teaching of the Church, but throughout the volume revelation plays a very minor role (1:3). The last page summarizes what is in the book. There is an objective moral order, and the Church is the authoritative teacher of that order (1:352).

The very first chapter of volume 1 insists on the necessity of the papal magisterium. The chapter spends one page on the necessity of revelation and twelve pages on the necessity of the magisterium (1:4–18). In proving the necessity of the magisterium, *Contemporary Moral Theology*, volume 1, begins with what papal documents themselves have said. In addition, errors and ignorance about God's moral law abound outside Catholic parameters. "To state all the basic errors of unguided intellectuals . . . would require volumes" (1:7).

Both volumes clearly show the centrality and ultimate importance of authoritative papal teaching. As a general rule every chapter, except those of a historical nature, begins with a quite long section on what the popes, especially Pope Pius XII, have taught on such issues. The volumes also frequently cite the documents coming from the Roman Curia, especially the Holy Office—the predecessor of the Congregation for the Doctrine of the Faith and the successor of the Inquisition.

Contemporary Moral Theology, volume 1, recognizes that with Pius XII there was a massive increase in papal documents. Pius XII wrote no encyclical letters directly dealing with morality, but unlike any previous pope he gave many addresses both in person and on the radio. Pius XII wrote more than a thousand documents, the vast majority dealing with faith and morals. It is not mere facetiousness to say that even if the pope had said nothing in the next ten years, theologians would have had plenty to do in classifying and evaluating the theological significance of his public statements. These documents thus play a most important role in the life and work of the moral theologian (1:20–21).

Ford, however, is no fundamentalist when it comes to interpreting papal documents. Here he uses the same careful analysis as he does in his casuistry. The interpreter must study and pay attention to the words, the content, and the intention of the pope. The words themselves are very important, but they are not the ultimate criterion since they can be obscure and admit of reformulation. Popes themselves have gone out of their way to clarify or restrict their earlier teachings. Consequently there is nothing disloyal when a theologian supposes that other papal statements may need clarification or restriction or rephrasing (1:28–32).

The most important question concerns the authoritative nature of these teachings and statements. According to *Contemporary Moral Theology*, although a few papal teachings on moral issues may be infallible, in general the papal teaching on moral matters has been given in encyclicals and especially in radio messages and allocutions, which are normally the ways in which the pope proposes his authentic but not infallible teaching. (More will be said later about the condemnation of artificial contraception.) Pope Pius XII himself in the 1950 encyclical *Humani generis* discussed the authoritative nature of such papal teachings. Such teachings belong to the ordinary magisterium to which it is true to apply the biblical words that "he who hears you hears me." If the supreme pontiffs, in their official documents, purposely pass judgment on a matter debated until then, it is obvious to all that the matter, according to the mind and will of the same pontiff, cannot be considered any longer a question open for discussion among theologians (2:22–25).

Does this apply to addresses and discourses to smaller groups and not only those documents that are addressed to the universal Church? Pope Pius XII himself in a 1952 document made it strikingly clear that even addresses to small groups can contain an authoritative teaching destined for the whole Church. Ford and Kelly feel sure that the pope himself would agree that the decisive character of the teaching must be evident (1:22–32). However, they never give an example of a papal teaching on a specific moral issue that does not have this decisive character. *Contemporary Moral Theology* explicitly recognizes that theological controversies affecting the whole Church, such as the nature of the sin of putting oneself in a probable danger of committing grave sin, can be authoritatively settled by the pope (1:157).

Particular Issues

This first part of the chapter has analyzed the basic approach and method used by John C. Ford in his moral theology. The second part will discuss his approach to some particular issues and their relationship to this basic approach.

Contraception and the Ends of Marriage

Without doubt the primary issue receiving the most attention was artificial contraception for spouses. *Contemporary Moral Theology*, volume 2, is subtitled *Marriage Questions*, but for all practical purposes the volume is focused on the meaning of the sexual faculty and act and the sin of contraception.

One chapter does deal with marriage as a Christian vocation (2:143–65). The volume itself is divided into two parts: "The Ends of Christian Marriage" and "The Christian Use of Marriage." The first part includes many theoretical aspects, but the very first chapter shows that the primary concern is contraception. This first chapter deals with Protestant views on the ends of marriage. The chapter traces the change in Protestant teaching beginning especially with the Lambeth Conference (Anglican) in 1930. Protestants today do not accept that procreation is the primary end of marriage and thus accept contraception for spouses. What has brought about this change? The general reasons for this change are the Protestant acceptance of situation ethics and "the lack of an infallible teaching authority." Among the more immediate causes is the Protestant failure to recognize "the natural marriage act" as the criterion of sexual morality (2:1–15).

According to *Contemporary Moral Theology*, volume 2, there are five ends of marriage. Ford recognizes two primary ends of marriage: procreation and the rearing of children. In enumerating the secondary ends of marriage, he follows the terminology of Pope Pius XI in the 1930 encyclical *Casti connubii* that condemned artificial contraception: mutual help, the remedy of concupiscence, and the fostering of conjugal love. Some want to give a more positive understanding to the remedy of concupiscence and call it the sexual fulfillment of the partners, but *Contemporary Moral Theology*, volume 2, prefers to stay with Pius XI's terminology of the remedy of concupiscence (2:47–48).

What is an essential end of marriage? An essential end is one that is intrinsic to the institution of marriage itself without which marriage cannot exist. But there is an obvious problem. Procreation, for example, sometimes cannot occur, so how can it be an end of marriage? Using careful analysis and casuistry, Ford maintains that the marriage bond gives the spouses the right to acts by which the ends are attainable (2:50–51). He later takes great pains to show there is a fundamental right but not a proximate right to these acts by which the ends are attained (2:57–74).

Contemporary Moral Theology, volume 2, first proves that the secondary ends are truly essential. The fundamental right involved in the conjugal bond is the right to acts by which the mutual help of the spouses, the remedy for concupiscence, and conjugal love are achieved. Ford proves each of these assertions with reasons heavily based on papal teaching and canon law. Ford admits that moral and canonical manuals have not always done justice to the essential end of conjugal love, and hence he wants to recognize conjugal love as truly an essential end of marriage (2:75–126).

The next logical step is to show that the secondary ends are subordinate to the primary ends. *Contemporary Moral Theology*, volume 2, clearly explains what "primary" does not mean. The secondary ends are not less essential than the primary ends. Nor does it mean that the secondary ends have value and legitimacy only as means to achieve the primary ends, which actually was the position of Saint Augustine. Spouses do not have to choose procreation as the primary end. They need only intend the institution of marriage as it is and respect the obligations that go with it. The primary ends are more important and more fundamental. The secondary ends depend on and are subordinated to the primary ends in a way in which the primary ends do not presuppose or depend on the secondary ends (2:127–31). In the practical order, the subordination of the secondary to the primary ends has its most common application in the condemnation of artificial contraception. The spouses cannot directly deprive the sexual faculty and act of their procreative character (2:136).

The above has briefly summarized the understanding of the ends of marriage developed in much greater depth and precision in *Contemporary Moral Theology*, volume 2. This discussion of the ends of marriage well illustrates the characteristics of Ford's general approach to moral theology—the primacy given to papal teaching, the frequent use of canon law, and the close reasoning, analysis, and casuistry as seen in the many distinctions that are made.

Contraception

In keeping with Ford's basic approach, the primary reason why contraception is wrong comes from the authoritative teaching of the Church, beginning with Pius XI's encyclical *Casti connubii* in 1930, which obviously was responding to the Anglican change in teaching and including a number of documents and addresses of Pius XII. *Contemporary Moral Theology*, volume 2, insists that the teaching condemning artificial contraception is unchangeable and irrevocable. Since this teaching on a point so profoundly and intimately connected with the salvation of millions of souls has been the same over such a long period of time, the inevitable conclusion is that the teaching is true and unchangeable. Otherwise, the church that God entrusted to interpret the moral law and guide souls to salvation would be failing in its mission (2:258). Ford and Kelly's own opinion is that the teaching is infallible by reason of the ordinary and universal magisterium of the Catholic Church as something taught for a very long time by all the bishops of the Church together with the pope. However, in light of some other opinions, they conclude that the teaching is "at least definable doctrine." It is definitely unchangeable (2:263–71). In a 1978 article in *Theological Studies* coauthored with Germain Grisez, Ford maintains the teaching is infallible by the ordinary magisterium of the Church according to the conditions for infallibility in the Vatican II document on the Church.[14]

Contemporary Moral Theology, volume 2, analyzes the papal texts condemning artificial contraception. According to these texts, God has written a certain definite plan into the nature of the human generative process, and human beings are not free to change it. The conjugal act by God's design must be per se apt for generation, and human beings cannot interfere with its physical integrity. Those who deny this logically have to admit that anal and oral intercourse are justified if they have relational value, and such a position is also open to accept homosexual relations. The papal texts stress the immorality of contraception because it violates the marriage act as procreative, but *Contemporary Moral Theology*, volume 2, also sees it as violating the love union aspect because it is not a total and complete giving of the spouses to each other. Thus, the contraceptive act goes against both the primary and the secondary ends of marriage (2:286–91; 305–14).

Anyone familiar with the Catholic tradition wonders why *Contemporary Moral Theology* pays little or no attention to the natural law, which has been so central and important a part of the Catholic tradition and the method of Catholic moral theology in the pre–Vatican II Church and in the documents of the popes. Any book on fundamental moral theology should have had a long and detailed chapter on the natural law, but volume 1 has no such chapter. Even more surprising is the fact that *Contemporary Moral Theology*, volume 2, recognizes that there are some shortcomings and even problems with the natural law argument against artificial contraception. Some do not easily see how the understanding of the marital act as an act per se apt for generation applies to naturally sterile conjugal intercourse. One could also accept this understanding of the marital act and still defend many forms of contraception that do not interfere with the sexual act itself. Catholic scholars have the challenge of further completing and elucidating the natural law arguments against artificial contraception so that the obscurities in the truth of what is known by the magisterium may shine ever more brightly. The debate about contraception and its rejection by the vast majority of Protestants shows the moral necessity of the magisterium for an adequate knowledge of the natural law (2:311–12).

John Ford was appointed to what was popularly called the Papal Birth Control Commission, which Pope John XXIII brought into existence with a small group of six members in 1963. A few additional members were appointed for the second and third meetings in 1964. Pope Paul appointed many more members, including Ford, before the fourth meeting in 1965. For the sixth meeting in 1966, fourteen new cardinals and bishops were appointed to form the official commission members.[15] Throughout this time, Ford was a staunch supporter of no change in the teaching.

In 1965, Ford urged Pope Paul VI to intervene so that the Vatican II Pastoral Constitution on the Church in the Modern World would clearly condemn artificial contraception, and he even wrote part of the papal intervention to the commission drafting the document. Until then there existed a general understanding that there would be no condemnation of contraception in the document, since the papal commission was studying the issue. However, after opposition from the commission drafting the constitution, the pope accepted some changes in his proposal. The final document, by referring both to *Casti connubii* and the existence of the papal commission, did not directly condemn artificial contraception. Even after the last meeting of the commission in 1966, Ford with the help of Cardinal Alfredo Ottaviani continued to lobby the pope to condemn artificial contraception.[16]

In the work of the commission, he was the leading voice against any change in the teaching. Ford was the primary author of the working paper at the commission, which at times was mistakenly called the Minority Report.[17] In this paper, Ford reiterated his reasons why the condemnation of artificial contraception could not be changed. If there were clear and cogent arguments from reason, the very commission would not exist. The Church cannot change its teaching, because this teaching is true. It is true because the Catholic Church, instituted by Christ to show people the secure way to eternal life, could not have so wrongly erred during all these centuries of history.[18]

Ford also gave a greater role to the magisterium than was the norm in the tradition of Catholic moral theology. A strong influence here was the unprecedented number of addresses and documents coming from Pope Pius XII. As illustrated throughout both volumes of *Contemporary Moral Theology*, the first and primary role of the moral theologian is to understand, explain, and interpret papal teaching. The emphasis on papal teaching was closely related to the lack of attention paid to the natural law.

Ford insisted that papal teaching could intervene to condemn artificial contraception, even though the reasons for such a condemnation were not certain. In this regard, Ford seems to deny the traditional Thomistic and Catholic insistence that morality is intrinsic. Something is commanded because it is good. Authority does not make something good. Authority must always conform itself to what is good.[19]

John Ford must have felt elated and vindicated when Pope Paul VI in late July 1968 promulgated his encyclical *Humanae vitae*, reiterating the condemnation of artificial contraception. His jubilation, however, was short-lived. *Humanae vitae* set off a huge debate in the Catholic Church, which has continued and grown down to the present about papal teaching on sexuality and the role of dissent from such papal teaching. Also, Vatican II's approach sounded the death knell of the manualist approach to moral theology. In 1969, Ford resigned as professor of moral theology at Weston. Among his reasons were some health problems, his opposition to the move of the theologate to Cambridge in cooperation with Protestant institutions, and the realization that the manualist approach was no longer acceptable to the Jesuit seminarians. He died twenty years later in 1989.[20]

Subjective Culpability

John Ford's most significant contribution to the moral theology of the manuals was his discussion of subjective culpability. A human act may be objectively wrong, but the person performing it may not always be culpable, or culpability can be diminished. In their general treatment of human acts, the manuals discussed the obstacles or impediments to a free human act. Some of the later manuals added a recognition of some contemporary psychiatric and psychological conditions and problems.[21] But in their discussion of specific human acts, the manuals generally do not bring up the issue of subjective culpability. The requisite freedom for a human act is presumed. Ford with his concern for the work of the confessor considered subjective culpability in some depth.

Alcoholism was Ford's first entrée into the issue of subjective culpability. He wrote extensively on alcoholism and its treatment in the 1950s, discussing the treatment of alcoholics both inside and outside the confessional and strongly supporting the work of Alcoholics Anonymous. Only near the end of his life did Ford reveal that he himself was an alcoholic and had been treated for it in the 1940s. His superiors at that time asked him not to reveal this fact since it might have a negative effect on his own work with alcoholism and alcoholics. Ford was a pioneer among Catholics with his theoretical and practical work with alcoholism.[22]

The chapter on alcoholism in *Contemporary Moral Theology*, volume 1, presents a systematic understanding of Ford's approach. He agrees with the formula that alcoholism is a triple sickness of body, of mind, and of spirit (1:283). Notice here the typical Catholic "both-and" approach rather than "either-or." Alcoholism cannot be reduced either to just a sickness or a moral problem. Yes, it is a sickness, but the Twelve Step recovery program of Alcoholics Anonymous involves moral and spiritual rejuvenation (1:288). As for moral culpability, Ford concludes that subjectively not many alcoholics are mortally guilty as far as the addiction itself is concerned. The alcoholic's responsibility for the drinking itself is generally diminished to a considerable extent, frequently beyond the point of mortal sin (1:294). Notice again the concern of the manualist with what is mortal sin and what is not, but also recognize Ford's judicious approach to what in practice is mortally sinful.

With regard to the broader question of freedom and responsibility under stress, *Contemporary Moral Theology*, volume 1, proposes a general rule: "Subjective disabilities and impediments excuse the average man and woman from mortal guilt much more frequently than a reading of moral theology manuals might leave one to suppose" (1:239).

In his study of alcoholism and subjective culpability, Ford became familiar with psychological and psychiatric findings. The role of the moral theologian is to incorporate new psychological findings into the manualistic treatise on human acts and the obstacles to freedom and responsibility (1:200). The manuals spoke about full deliberation and consent in order to commit a mortal sin, but they really meant sufficient deliberation, consent, and freedom. All recognize there can be degrees of freedom and that perfect freedom probably never exists. The problem is obscure and baffling (2:243); only God knows the exact answer (1:210). *Contemporary Moral Theology*, volume 1, again proposes a moderate position between two extremes. The degree of psychological freedom that is required for mortal sin should not be so high as to negate the fundamental moral responsibility of the average man and woman, but confessors should judge much more leniently than we have in the past a great many individual cases of human misconduct and frailty (1:201–47).

Obliteration Bombing and Innocent Persons

The most famous article Ford wrote was his 1944 *Theological Studies* article "The Morality of Obliteration Bombing."[23] In fact, one can safely say that no article written by an American Catholic moral theologian has been cited more in the academic literature than Ford's article. The context helps to explain the article's importance. In the midst of a very popular war, which Ford himself supported, he challenged and condemned the Allied strategy of obliteration bombing of German cities as a means to win and end the war sooner. In the first installment of what became "Notes on Moral Theology" in *Theological Studies* in 1941, he signaled his interest in this question. In reviewing the literature on war, he remarked that direct killing in war is the most pressing moral issue.[24]

Obliteration bombing is the opposite of precision bombing, which aims at a specific military target such as military encampments and airfields but also munitions factories and railroad bridges. Obliteration bombing aims at a large area, even an entire city that also contains many residential areas. The basis of his argument is the right of a majority of citizens (those who are noncombatants) to be immune from direct killing and violence. Obliteration bombing violates these rights of innocent civilians. There is some discussion and disagreement about who are noncombatants. Ford admits that munitions workers are probably considered combatants. Also, there are obviously some gray areas where there is legitimate debate, but at least three-quarters of the people in any city are noncombatants—most of the women and older men (except munitions workers), as well as all the children.

Some have argued that the good of ending the war is intended and not the killing of noncombatants. Also, the good to be obtained constitutes a proportionate reason to excuse the evil that is done. Ford refutes both of these arguments. The article marshals many statements from political and military leaders of Britain and the United States that clearly show they intended to do such obliteration or saturation bombing. One of their goals was to terrorize the enemy population and to break down its morale. Ford also cites casualty figures of the bombings of German cities such as Cologne and Hamburg. If one intends the end of terrorizing the citizens, one logically has to intend the principal means that achieve the end—the killing and wounding of civilians. You cannot target innocent people and then claim you are not intending to kill them.

What about the existence of a proportionately grave cause to excuse the evil that is done by the obliteration bombing? Even if the intention argument is not valid (a point that Ford totally disagrees with), obliteration bombing would still be wrong because there is no proportionate reason to justify the evil created by it. The proportionate reason proposed was military necessity and thus shortening the war and preventing more evil. The evil wrought by obliteration bombing is certain death and injury to thousands in the here and now; the ultimate good to be achieved is speculative, future, and problematical. Many times in the past, military necessity did not turn out to be such. Even if the short-term goal of winning this war were to be achieved by obliteration bombing, the long-term effect would be appalling. Once such a policy is accepted, there are no limits on what can be done to win a just war. Thus, we would have what is called "total war."

The final section of the article contains references to over nine addresses and documents of popes in defense of the right of innocents and condemning the indiscriminate air bombardment of civilians, as well as the increasing ferocious and immoral practices of total war. In Ford's opinion, these utterances truly and strongly condemn obliteration bombing. Earlier in the article, however, Ford admitted that the popes never directly mentioned obliteration bombing as such and therefore did not put a clear, direct burden on the conscience of Catholics to condemn the new reality.[25]

Rights of Individuals

Ford based his argument condemning obliteration bombing on the rights of innocent persons. He frequently defended the rights of the individual in his work. In his 1941 *Theological Studies* review of writings on war, he defended the right of Catholic individuals to be conscientious objectors.[26] In later personal correspondence, he argued for the state to recognize the right to selective conscientious objection.[27] A 1941 article disagreed with the late US Supreme Court justice Oliver Wendell Holmes Jr., whose totalitarianism meant he did not respect rights of individuals, as illustrated in some of his court rulings. For example, Holmes opposed the rights of a child after birth to sue for injuries suffered in the womb. Holmes also upheld the Virginia statute that required enforced compulsory sterilization for the mentally retarded.[28]

Throughout his life, Ford was concerned about the rights of individual religious subjects in their relationship with their religious superiors. Early on, he distinguished between the paternal forum and the judicial forum. In the paternal forum, the superior deals with the subject as a father for the good of the subject. In the judicial forum, the superior acts primarily for the good of the religious community, the common good, and disciplines the individual for the sake of the community. However, no information shared with the superior in the paternal order can ever be used in the judicial order.[29] In a long paper given originally at the meeting of the Catholic Theological Society in 1962, Ford developed his position on subjects and superiors in light of their relationship with the psychiatrist or psychological testing. The subject retains his [*sic*] right to psychic privacy in his dealings with his psychiatrist. Psychological testing for a candidate for religious life is understood by all to be used in determining whether to admit the candidate to religious life, but such knowledge after admission can be used only with the permission of the religious subject involved. Ford also opposed obligatory testing of all religious without seeking the permission of those involved.[30]

Ford consistently defended the freedom of the individual Catholic conscience when certitude is lacking. Such is the basic approach of probabilism. Obligations must be certain; a doubtful law does not oblige. If there is no certitude, no confessor can impose a position on a penitent (1:155–57). Ford recognized that he cannot impose his own position if the matter is not certain, as in the case of obliteration bombing. The confessor, including Ford, should absolve the bombardier who participates in obliteration bombing.[31] In theory, however, such a position of probabilism has the problem of seeing freedom and obligation in opposition to each other. Most Catholic moral theologians today would not want to affirm that opposition. Although

Ford insisted on the freedom of the individual conscience in these cases, he strongly maintained that whenever the pope speaks on an issue, the matter is certain and all Catholics are bound to follow what the pope has said.

We have to recognize that John Ford contributed greatly to the academic nature of moral theology and to the approach of the manuals of moral theology. He himself recognized, however, that Vatican II spelled the end of the manualist approach. For some in the Church, Ford was a prophetic voice in defense of the Church and the papal teaching on artificial contraception.[32] The majority of Catholic moral theologians disagreed with Ford's defense of the manuals and his position on artificial contraception while still recognizing him as an important figure in the history of moral theology.

Notes

1. For biographical information on John Ford, see Eric Marcelo O. Genilo, *John Cuthbert Ford, SJ: Moral Theologian at the End of the Manualist Era* (Washington, DC: Georgetown University Press, 2007), 1–4; and Germain Grisez, "About John C. Ford, SJ," www.twotlj.org/Ford.html.

2. John C. Ford and Gerald Kelly, *Contemporary Moral Theology*, vol. 1, *Questions in Fundamental Moral Theology* (Westminster, MD: Newman, 1958), v–vi.

3. John C. Ford and Gerald Kelly, *Contemporary Moral Theology*, vol. 2, *Marriage Questions* (Westminster, MD: Newman, 1963).

4. John C. Ford, *Man Takes a Drink: Facts and Principles about Alcohol* (New York: P. J. Kenedy & Sons, 1955); John C. Ford, *Religious Superiors, Subjects, and Psychiatrists* (Westminster, MD: Newman, 1963). For a complete bibliography, see Genilo, *John Cuthbert Ford*, 201–4.

5. William P. Fischer, "John C. Ford, SJ: A Mid-Century Reformer Revisited, 1937–1969" (PhD diss., Catholic University of America, 2004), 287–93.

6. Ford and Kelly, *Contemporary Moral Theology*, vol. 1, 97–99. Subsequent references to these two volumes will be made in the text with the volume number and the page number (e.g., 1:97–99).

7. Fischer, "John C. Ford," 69–114.

8. Marcellinus Zalba, *Theologiae Moralis Summa*, vol. 3, *Theologia Moralis Specialis: De Sacramentis et Poenis* (Madrid: Biblioteca de Autores Cristianos, 1958), 3–751.

9. John C. Ford, *The Validity of Virginal Marriage* (Worcester, MA: Harrigan, 1948).

10. John C. Ford, "Current Moral Theology and Canon Law," *Theological Studies* 2 (1941): 556–71.

11. Ibid., 539–43.

12. John C. Ford, *The New Eucharistic Legislation* (New York: P. J. Kenedy & Sons, 1953).

13. Marcellinus Zalba, *Theologiae Moralis Summa*, vol. 1, *Theologia Moralis Fundamentalis* (Madrid: Biblioteca de Autores Cristianos, 1952), 279–311.

14. John C. Ford and Germain Grisez, "Contraception and the Infallibility of the Ordinary Magisterium," *Theological Studies* 39 (1978): 259–312.

15. Robert McCrory, *Turning Point* (New York: Crossroad, 1995), 189–90.

16. Genilo, *John Cuthbert Ford*, 51–59. For the most complete account of Ford's work of opposition to contraception in the 1960s, see Fischer, "John C. Ford," 115–285.

17. For the role of Ford in the commission, see Grisez, "About John Ford."

18. Robert G. Hoyt, "The State of the Question," in *The Birth Control Debate*, (Kansas City, MO: National Catholic Reporter, 1968), 34–37.

19. Thomas Aquinas, *Summa Theologiae* (Rome: Marietti, 1952), Ia IIae, q. 94. For my understanding of Aquinas on this matter, see Charles E. Curran, *The Development of Moral Theology: Five Strands* (Washington, DC: Georgetown University Press, 2013), 31–42.

20. Genilo, *John Cuthbert Ford*, 196.

21. Zalba, *Theologiae Moralis Summa*, vol. 1, 703–48.

22. Ford, *Man Takes a Drink*. This volume was published in paperback with a new title in 1961: John C. Ford, *What about Your Drinking?* (Glen Rock, NJ: Paulist, 1961). For a complete bibliography of his other writings on alcoholism, see Genilo, *John Cuthbert Ford*, 201–2. For an in-depth discussion of Ford's work for and with alcoholics, including the fact that his superiors told him not to tell others that he himself was an alcoholic, see Oliver J. Morgan, "'Chemical Comforting' and the Theology of John C. Ford, SJ: Classical Answers to a Contemporary Problem," *Journal of Ministry in Addiction and Recovery* 6, no. 1 (1999): 29–66.

23. John C. Ford, "The Morality of Obliteration Bombing," *Theological Studies* 5 (1944): 261–309.

24. Ford, "Current Moral Theology," 555.

25. Ford, "Obliteration Bombing," 269.

26. Ford, "Current Moral Theology," 551–52.

27. Genilo, *John Cuthbert Ford*, 167–69.

28. John C. Ford, "Totalitarian Justice Holmes," *Catholic World* 159 (1944): 114–22.

29. John C. Ford, "Paternal Governance and Filial Confidence in Superiors," *Review for Religious* 2 (1943): 146–55.

30. Ford, *Religious Superiors, Subjects, and Psychiatrists*.

31. Ford, "Obliteration Bombing," 268–69.

32. In 1988, the Fellowship of Catholic Scholars presented the Cardinal O'Boyle Award for the Defense of the Faith to John C. Ford. The full text is found at www.twotlj.org/Ford.html.

2

Bernard Häring

Bernard Häring did not want to teach moral theology. He ardently desired to leave his native Germany and be a missionary in Brazil. In fact, he totally disliked the moral theology course he took as a student.[1] In 1954, however, he published in German the most significant book in moral theology in the twentieth century, *Das Gesetz Christi: Moraltheologie dargestellt für Priester und Laien* (*The Law of Christ: Moral Theology for Priests and Laity*). The original German was published in one volume, but the translations in fourteen other languages have usually involved three volumes.[2]

Häring (1912–98) was the eleventh of twelve children in a devout Roman Catholic family.[3] He joined the Redemptorist religious community in 1934, studied theology at the Redemptorist theologate in Gars am Inn in Germany, and was ordained a priest in 1939. Despite the promise of his superiors that he could go to Brazil as a missionary, the theology faculty at Gars wanted him to be sent on for further study so that he could teach moral theology there.

At the beginning of the war, he was drafted into the German army as a medic (priests could not be assigned to fighting units) but was given a leave to teach moral theology for one semester at Gars. In light of his distaste for the manuals of moral theology and his familiarity with earlier attempts in German to produce a biblically inspired and Christ-centered moral theology, Häring even then began working on a newer approach to the discipline. During his five years in the German army, he carried out a vibrant, priestly work, often breaking official regulations to minister not only to German soldiers but also to civilians in France, Russia, and Poland. In a very moving book on that experience, Häring points out that it prepared him to work "to overcome a one-sided ethic of obedience and to teach a morality of personal responsibility and brotherly love with courageous obedience to one's own

sincere but ever searching conscience."[4] Such was the *Sitz im Leben* in which
Häring developed his moral theology.

After the war, Häring went to the University of Tübingen to work with
Professor Theodore Steinbuchel and in 1947 defended his dissertation "Das
Heillege und das Gute" (The holy and the good), which was published in
1950.[5] He resumed his teaching at the Redemptorist theologate at Gars and
began serious work on *The Law of Christ*. From 1950 to 1953, he taught
one semester in Rome at the Accademia Alfonsiana. Later he taught there
full-time as the Alfonsiana developed into a degree-granting institution for
the study of moral theology. His position in Rome until his retirement in
1986 gave him the opportunity to teach students from all over the world and
provided a platform that he used to become the most influential Catholic
moral theologian in the twentieth century. He retired to Gars and died there
in 1998.

The Law of Christ

In the very first content chapter of *The Law of Christ* dealing with "the essential concepts of moral theology," Häring insists that responsibility, not law or
commandment or salvation, is the focal center of Catholic moral teaching.[6]
The understanding of religion animates the Christian moral life and determines the centrality of responsibility. Here Häring bases the Christian moral
life on his understanding of the holy and the good developed in his doctoral
dissertation. Religion has the essential character of response to the loving
coming of the Holy One. For Christians, the I-Thou relationship and intimacy with God flows from a person who is the word of God. In Christ, the
word made flesh, God comes in loving gift to us, and we respond in Christ
to God's gift. Christian personalism is not to be considered individualistically.
Yes, God calls us personally by name, but in God's presence we also find our
neighbor and the way to fellowship and community. To be in Christ means
necessarily to be bound up with all those who have fellowship with Christ
and all that was created by God.

In this chapter, Häring also briefly examines the most significant of the
central moral concepts and key terms in light of this religious criterion
of responsibility. Commandment and love must be understood as religious
concepts. The commandments of God are words of divine love addressed
to us in the great commandment of love; the fulfillment of the command is
the response of obedient love. Such an approach differs from a manualistic
concept of law, which is based on the sovereign will of God and not on the
all-holy essence or nature of God, who is love.

The three theological virtues of faith, hope, and love must be seen in light of the response relationship with God. The virtue of religion is our response to the majesty of God our creator and father. The other moral virtues do not directly and immediately respond to God since they are directly concerned with the created order. Response assumes there is a person to whom the response is made. The believer, however, detects in the order of creation the loving work of the Lord and creator. The believer responds to God to the extent that one takes terrestrial tasks seriously and earnestly accepts created values. Self-perfection and personal salvation must also be seen in the light of responsibility. The moral-religious formation of a person takes place by slow degrees and continuous growth. Religion as fellowship with God and morality as responsibility for God necessarily involve the imitation of Christ.

Häring explicitly develops the centrality of responsibility in the moral life from the perspective of religion and theology at the very beginning of *The Law of Christ*. In my judgment, there is also an ethical basis for the centrality of responsibility—the approach of value ethics. Häring, however, does not develop this aspect in a systematic way at the beginning of his book, but throughout *The Law of Christ* there can be no doubt of the importance of value ethics and its grounding of the centrality of responsibility in the moral life and in moral theology.

The footnotes in *The Law of Christ* indicate Häring's acceptance of the value theory and value experience proposed by Max Scheler and Dietrich von Hildebrand (1: 120–35, 189–95). A profound difference exists between mere theoretical knowledge of the law that something must be done or avoided and the insight into the value as the basis of the obligation. The deepest knowledge of value arises from an intimate connaturality with the good. Authentic experience of values requires an inner presence and participation of a loving will (1:125).

All values are rooted in the basic value, which for the believer is the loving God. A perfect and comprehensive grasp of the basic value of God as the good would include full knowledge of all the other values. But such a complete and perfect grasp does not exist in this world. The specific types of value include the various virtues. Particular values involve the recognition of and response to value in a concrete situation. The perception and attractiveness of value depend on the depth of the subject who strives to know, love, and do the good. Since the supreme value is God, to respond to value is to respond to the value of God (1:124–30). Thus, the theory of value from an ethical perspective also serves as a basis for the centrality of responsibility in the Christian moral life and theology.

Contrast with the Manuals

The primary difference with the manuals is the focus. As exemplified in the work of John Ford, the manuals focused on preparing seminarians and priests to be able to know and judge in the confessional which acts are sinful and their degree of sinfulness. *The Law of Christ* does not neglect the discussion of which acts are sinful, but the focus is on the fullness of Christian moral life and not just on the minimum. The broader focus of Häring's method comes through in the subtitle of *The Law of Christ, Moral Theology for Priests and Laity*. The three volumes in the English translation testify to this broader focus.

The manuals almost completely neglected scripture, except for an occasional proof text—one text from scripture was used to support a position that had already been arrived at primarily by human reason. Häring's insistence on the importance of scripture fits perfectly with his recognition of religious ethics as involving God's coming to us and our response. Scripture is the word of God that comes to us and calls for our response. The title of the whole work is taken from Romans 8:2, which is quoted on the title page of the first volume: "For the law of the Spirit of the life in Christ Jesus has delivered me from the law of sin and death."

Unlike the manuals, Häring insisted on the theological character of moral theology. Christology is central for Häring. The first page in the foreword begins with this sentence: "The principle, the norm, the center, and the goal of Christian Moral Theology is Christ." In Christ, the Father has given us everything; in the love of God, through the love of Christ for us, God the Father invites our love in return in the imitation of Christ (1:vii). In keeping with a deeper understanding of the religious ethic as response to God's coming to us, Häring's Christology is a Christology from above. Christ is the word of God who comes to us as the God-man with the Father's love. Other Christologies begin with the human and historical Jesus, but Häring sees Jesus the Christ as the mediator bringing God to human beings and bringing us to God (2:xxi–xxxviii).

The manuals of moral theology usually concentrated a separate volume on the sacraments, but the treatment was almost totally canonical—what is necessary for the valid and licit administration and reception of the sacraments. *The Law of Christ*, even in special moral theology, does not have a treatise on all the sacraments as such, probably because of the canonical nature of the older approach. However, the discussion of marriage includes the sacrament of matrimony, and the discussion of conversion includes the sacrament of reconciliation (2:321–29, 1:387–481).

In volume 2's treatment of life in fellowship with God, however, Häring treats the sacraments in general under the development of the virtue of religion. For Häring, religion is a living dialogue between God and the human person. The sacraments are the most intimate and personal encounter with God. But the sacraments do not involve just a narrow I-Thou relationship with God. The sacraments are essentially a social reality. They form a real and objective bond uniting all the members of the mystical body of Christ. Their communal character and spiritual significance should be evident from the beauty and decorum of the celebration of the sacramental rite itself (2:139–72). In subsequent writings, Häring developed in great detail his understanding of the sacraments and their role in the Christian moral life.[7]

The manuals were criticized for separating moral theology from spiritual theology, but *The Law of Christ* brings the two together. In fact, spirituality permeates the entire three volumes. Long before Vatican II (1962–65), *The Law of Christ* insisted that every Christian, regardless of one's state in life, is called to perfection. The new law of grace, which is formulated in the command of love, demands that no one can cease striving for its perfect fulfillment (1:306). The early chapter on the essential concepts of moral theology has a section on the fundamental role of prayer. To pray is nothing less than to hearken reverently to the word of God and to attempt, however falteringly, to respond to it. Religion and religious morality call for the central importance of prayer in the Christian moral life (1:37–38). Under the virtue of religion in volume 2, prayer is the first special way of honoring God (2:245).

The manuals showed no influence of or interest in Protestant theology. From his doctoral studies, Häring showed a strong ecumenical interest. His doctoral dissertation discussed three prominent Protestant theologians: Friedrich Schleiermacher, Rudolf Otto, and Emil Brunner. These and other Protestant theologians are cited favorably in *The Law of Christ*, but Protestant thought by no means played a significant role in *The Law of Christ*. When Häring first taught in Rome from 1950 to 1953, one of his two original courses dealt with what Catholic moral theologians can learn from Protestant and Orthodox Christians.[8] *The Law of Christ*, however, written in the early 1950s, mirrored the Catholic approach of the times. For example, under no conditions may a Catholic be a bridesmaid or best man for a Catholic in a mixed wedding before a Protestant minister (2:517). Later in his life, especially during and after Vatican II, all recognized Häring's significant ecumenical interest.[9]

The manuals emphasized human nature and with it the immutable and unchanging reality of human nature. *The Law of Christ* in its first full discussion of the human person sees being in history as an integral part of being a person. Historicity is the polarity between being and becoming. The becoming comes about through the interaction of the inner potentialities of the person and the historical context of time and space (1:87–92). Häring here points the way toward a greater appreciation of historical consciousness replacing the immutability and unchangeability of the classicism that characterized pre–Vatican II Catholic theology. I have consistently maintained that this shift from classicism to historical consciousness constitutes one of the most important, if not the most important, changes in Vatican II theology in contrast to the pre–Vatican II structures.[10]

Emphasis on the Person

As noted, the manuals gave almost total attention to external acts, whereas Häring puts primary emphasis on the person. Even with regard to the external act, *The Law of Christ* insists that true moral value is personal. The inner disposition of the person is the heart of morality, but its most evident proof and effective safeguard is action. External acts flow from the heart of the person, but the external act also builds up the interior dispositions of the person. The Christian has the mission from Christ to cooperate responsibly in working for the reign of God in the world (1:191–94).

Three significant aspects in Häring's moral theology illustrate the priority of the person: the concept of conversion, the particular call of each person, and the understanding of sin. The call to conversion is the good news of Mark 1:15: Repent, for the kingdom of God is at hand. The call of the sinner to conversion involves a change of heart. Part 5 of the first volume spends almost one hundred pages on this concept of conversion. Conversion is the gift of God's grace but requires the response of the person. The primary emphasis in this section is on first conversion from sin, with the penitent's response spelled out in the three traditional dispositions and acts of contrition, confession, and satisfaction. This section, however, also recognizes the importance of a second or continual conversion. We are all in need of constant and continual conversion. The invitation to this more intimate conversion is an imperative coming from God's grace (1:387–481). In a long article published in 1961, Häring develops in much more depth the call for continual conversion and growth in the Christian life.[11]

Second, *The Law of Christ* insists on a Christian personalism with a recognition that persons have different gifts and situations and can have particular callings responding to the attitudes of the person and the historical situations in which she finds herself. The New Law is the Spirit knocking at the door of the individual person's heart. The grace of the Holy Spirit is not just the aid and means to fulfill the law. All this occurs in the larger context of the Spirit calling each one to perfection (1:257–63).

The Law of Christ discusses this personal call again in describing prudence. Prudence is not just the application of universal principles to particular situations. Prudence attempts to discern the particular will of God for me in each concrete situation. Häring here refers to the *kairos*. This is the opportune time in the purpose of God for this person in this situation (1:502–3).

Third, Häring's personalist approach also comes through in his consideration of sin in general and mortal sin in particular (1:350–64). His treatment here also shows how he often takes the material found in the manuals and interprets it in a more personalist way. *The Law of Christ* briefly summarizes the traditional teaching as found in the manuals. Mortal sin extinguishes the supernatural life of sanctifying grace in the soul. Venial sin affects the life of grace but does not destroy it. Three elements must be present in order to have a mortal sin: grave or serious matter, full advertence, and full consent of the will. For the manuals in their discussion of particular individual acts, the latter two are presumed, and all the emphasis is on the grave or serious matter.

Häring then goes on to explain that a very great difference exists between mortal sin and venial sin; in fact, venial sin is called sin only analogously. The manuals see the difference based on the fact that mortal sin involves grave or serious matter, while venial sin only light matter. But Häring rejects such a solution. For him, the objective aspect of the gravity of the matter is not the reason for the great difference between mortal and venial sin. The reality and nature of mortal sin stems from the fact that such a sin comes from the inner depth of an evil heart—a personalist criterion. For Häring, even a light objective matter can involve a mortal sin if the act comes from this deep inner attitude of heart. At best the older objective criterion of grave and light matter grounds a prudential criterion that light matter usually does not come from such a bad heart. Some twenty years later, Häring sees mortal sin in terms of a fundamental option that expresses and determines the self in one's basic existence. The fundamental option involves a deep self-determination.[12] Thus, this later understanding gives even greater significance to the personalistic understanding of mortal sin.

The Structure and Outline

The Law of Christ brought a whole new approach to moral theology. Häring covered all the material (except for the canonical) that was found in the manuals, but the older material dealing with sinful acts was now found in a much different and positive context and sometimes modified by the newer personalist approach. Volume 1 treats the same material as found in the manuals in their first volume of general moral theology, which deals with the approach that is true for all the different acts, while special moral theology concentrates on the particular acts—for example, acts against justice or acts against the first commandment. Thus, *The Law of Christ* considers law, sin, and the moral object of the act, but Häring's newer approach affects all of these. In discussing the moral object of the act, for example, *The Law of Christ* recognizes the traditional essentialist ethic based on the human essence or nature that we all share but also insists on an ethic of the singular. This individual ethic does not contradict the essentialist ethic but exists within the framework of the essentialist ethic (1:296). Throughout *The Law of Christ*, Häring accepts all the traditionally proposed moral norms found in the Catholic tradition. He does not disagree with any of these teachings. Recall that before Vatican II and *Humanae vitae* (1968), no Catholic moral theologian disagreed with any of the existing Church moral teachings as proposed by the hierarchical magisterium. However, as will be developed later, Häring himself played a major part in the work of Vatican II, later making it better known throughout the Catholic world; he also opposed the teaching of *Humanae vitae* condemning artificial contraception.

Most of the manuals developed special moral theology in light of sinful acts against the Ten Commandments or the virtues.[13] The two volumes of special moral theology in *The Law of Christ* discuss sinful acts but in the broader context of his Christological, personalistic ethic of responsibility in trying to respond ever more fully to the call of the Spirit and the needs of the neighbor in all aspects of Christian existence.

Evaluation

The Law of Christ was a monumental achievement. It was the most significant volume in moral theology in the twentieth century. *The Law of Christ* was truly a magnum opus—1,446 pages in the original German—and is impossible to analyze and evaluate adequately in a short space. I have analyzed it primarily through the lens of a comparison with the accepted manualistic approach to moral theology in order to show why it is such a significant work.

The Law of Christ has its shortcomings. Perhaps the major problem is the attempt to pour new wine into old wineskins. Häring follows the basic outline of the manuals of moral theology, since he attempts to also provide a text for seminarians preparing for ministry. The subtitle indicates his twofold intended audience to be priests and laity, but the work follows the older manualistic outline. If one started from scratch to write a moral theology for laity, one would not use the format of the manuals. In addition, Häring's approach is often eclectic, bringing together many different aspects but not always developing a unified whole. His approach is not rigorously scientific and academic. At times it is homiletic. Häring has also been criticized for being too optimistic. There is some truth in this criticism, but his is an optimism based on the mercy and forgiveness of God. Despite these and other shortcomings and problems, *The Law of Christ* stands as the most important work in moral theology in the twentieth century.

Vatican II and *Humanae Vitae*

The two Church events in the 1960s that greatly affected the Sitz im Leben of Catholic moral theology were Vatican II and Pope Paul VI's encyclical *Humanae vitae*. Häring was intimately connected with both.

The Law of Christ was truly a precursor of what Vatican II called for: a primary emphasis on scripture and theology in the life of the Church, a need for a living liturgical celebration that would nourish both moral theology and the moral life, a need to make moral theology truly theological, a call of all Christians to holiness, a recognition of the importance of the signs of the times, an openness to dialogue with the world, and a truly ecumenical approach.

Since Häring was teaching full time in Rome at the Accademia Alfonsiana from 1957 and was well known throughout the Catholic world as a progressive and reforming Catholic theologian calling for change in the life of the Church, it was only natural that he would play a significant role in the council. Häring worked tirelessly both in the broader context of the council and in preparing and working on the documents.[14] Since Häring was fluent in five languages, he frequently addressed in Rome different bishops' conferences from all over the world. The talk he gave before the council to French-speaking bishops was soon developed into a book published in 1963 in six languages, with the English title *The Johannine Council: Witness to Unity*.[15] Pope John XXIII expressed his appreciation of this book.[16] Häring frequently appeared on press panels to explain the workings of the council. He was a well-known and respected voice in Rome for change in the Church.

Häring also worked intensively on preparing some conciliar documents. He was appointed by Pope John to the preparatory commission before the council but expressed his dissatisfaction with the proposed documents, which were basically just repeating what had already been said. His main contribution was in the drafting of an earlier text of *Gaudium et spes* (The Church in the modern world).[17] He also worked on the subcommission on marriage.[18]

Häring was asked by the secretary of the commission for the document on priestly formation to draft something on theological studies. His draft was accepted almost word for word in the final document. Häring wrote that special care should be given to the perfecting of moral theology. Its scientific presentation should draw more fully on the teaching of scripture and should shed light on the exalted vocation of the faithful in Christ and their obligation to bring forth fruit in charity for the life of the world.[19] After Vatican II, Häring, who was truly a precursor of its work, became a strong advocate throughout the world for its reforms.

Häring was also heavily involved in the contraception debate before and after *Humanae vitae*. In the almost two thousand pages of the three-volume English-language *Law of Christ*, Häring devotes just five pages to submission to the magisterium in his discussion of duties flowing directly from faith. The obedience of faith that the Church demands is not the obedience of slaves but brings us into the beauty and depth of faith. This absolute assent of divine faith is owed to the infallible teaching of revealed truth by the Church. Beyond such an absolute assent to revealed truth, there is a reverential and filial adherence given in joyous freedom to the decisions of popes and bishops, but this is not necessarily an assent of faith. This is an important distinction, for there are various degrees of certitude involved here. Even though a teaching might not be infallible, there is a presumption of being correct about it. History, however, shows that certain decisions of papal congregations and commissions have subsequently been reversed. Häring's treatment was more nuanced than most others at that time.[20] This issue was to become much more prominent in the 1960s and subsequently.

Häring was appointed in 1964 to the papal commission studying marriage and family, shortly before John Ford. In his memoir, Häring remarks that he already had changed his position on contraception. He now believed that every marriage act must be an expression of marital love and a promotion of marital loyalty, but in no way must every marital act be directed to procreation. Häring, however, recognized at this time that the majority of the members of the commission did not favor changing the condemnation of artificial contraception in *Casti connubii* in 1930. The most significant meeting of the papal commission took place in 1965, but Häring did not attend, because he had a previous engagement to lecture with Protestants. In the meantime, after the commission submitted its report, Häring tried two or three times to speak with the pope but was not successful, even though he had given the spiritual retreat to the pope and the Vatican curia in 1964.[21] Recall that apparently through the intervention of Cardinal Alfredo Ottaviani, the conservative head of the Holy Office, John Ford visited with the pope on a number of occasions at this time.

Häring publicly disagreed with the reaffirmation of the condemnation of contraception for Catholic spouses in Paul VI's encyclical *Humanae vitae*. Häring disagreed with the teaching of *Humanae vitae* for a number of reasons. The position in the encyclical comes from a biological understanding of the

natural law. According to the encyclical, one cannot interfere with the biological act of conjugal relations. But the biological is only one aspect of the
human and must be subordinated to the good of the person and the good of
the marriage. In addition, the encyclical insists that "each and every marital
act must remain open to the transmission of life." Such an assertion, however,
is not true for every marital act. Sexual relationships when the wife is sterile
are not open to the transmission of life. Catholic teaching accepts the rhythm
method, by which couples choose to have relations precisely during the time
when the woman cannot conceive. Such acts, by the intention of the people
involved, are not open to the transmission of life.[22]

In addition, the encyclical claims that it is proposing what has been the
constant teaching of the Church. However, there had been some significant
developments in this Church teaching, and one must consider the tradition
in a more historically conscious manner. The encyclical *Casti connubii*, for
example, used the example in Genesis of Onan, who spilled his seed, as an argument against contraception. But in keeping with modern biblical scholarship, *Humanae vitae* no longer makes such an argument. Häring also addressed
the issue of papal teaching authority. As acknowledged when the encyclical
was released, the teaching is noninfallible. There have been many instances
of such noninfallible teachings in the past that were wrong and were later
changed. In addition, *Humanae vitae* involved a noncollegiate exercise of the
teaching authority. The pope paid attention only to a small group of close
advisers but failed to listen to the experience of many Catholic couples.[23]

Häring thus became not only the primary voice for the renewal of Catholic moral theology but also a leading figure in recognizing the possibility
of dissent from noninfallible papal teaching and the need to rethink the
Catholic teaching on contraception and sexuality.

Häring's Later Contributions to Moral Theology

To understand and appreciate Häring's contribution to moral theology, one
must, as pointed out, understand his Sitz im Leben. Häring was not primarily an academic; he was a churchperson and a minister of the Gospel.
Throughout his life, he retained a very strong pastoral concern. Although he
was not a chaplain in the German army in World War II, he exercised a vibrant pastoral ministry to soldiers and civilians, Catholics and non-Catholics,
including half a year as pastor in a Polish parish at the end of the war. While
teaching at Gars in the late 1940s and early 1950s and writing *The Law of
Christ*, he spent his holidays doing pastoral work with refugees.[24] Even before
Vatican II, Häring gave lectures, courses of studies, and retreats throughout
Europe. After Vatican II, he continued this pastoral activity, which involved

lectures, courses of study, and retreats dealing not only with moral theology but also with spirituality and Church reform in the light of Vatican II throughout Africa (seventeen countries) and Asia (ten countries).[25] The Redemptorist priest was indefatigable. The fact that he was fluent and even wrote in five languages made it possible for him to speak and to communicate to people all over the globe.

In addition to all this traveling and speaking, he wrote 117 books.[26] With his broad understanding of moral theology, Häring recognized the importance of sacraments, liturgy, spirituality, and prayer. Most of these books were not of a scholarly nature but came from his many other interests. Very few, if any, people have done as much in one lifetime as Bernard Häring. In addition, all recognized him as a deeply spiritual person. At one time he asked his superior to allow him to become a Trappist monk, but his superior rejected Häring's request on the grounds that he had too many other responsibilities for the good of the Church.[27]

In this context, moral theology was only one of his many interests and involvements. After Vatican II, Häring had neither the time nor the opportunity nor the vocation to continue to do groundbreaking work in moral theology. Despite all his other activities, however, Häring continued to make some contributions to moral theology, especially in four areas: medical and bioethics, moral theology (writing a new three-volume work), the issues of peace and nonviolence, and the legitimacy of dissent from authoritative Church teaching.

Medical Ethics

Catholic medical ethics in the pre–Vatican II period was primarily the work of casuists who applied principles to particular cases. These principles included the right to life, the right of use or stewardship, the principle of totality, the principles governing sexuality, the principles involved in cooperation and scandal, and the principle of double effect.[28] Even after Vatican II, casuists remained very prominent not only in Catholic bioethics but also in most other approaches. Developments in technology continually raised new issues, such as in vitro fertilization, cloning, and genetic modification.

For Häring, theology's contribution to medical ethics lies mainly in providing a holistic view of the human person. In *Medical Ethics*, he gives more importance to ethos than to principles. The ethos characterizes the professional culture of morally grounded persons, whereas principles are formulated for concrete issues.[29] In keeping with the approach of *The Law of Christ*, *Medical Ethics* gives primary importance to the broader aspects of the meaning of the realities of human life, human death, and human health while also considering specific issues such as contraception, sterilization, abortion, the prolongation of life, and euthanasia. In his excellent study of Häring's *Medical Ethics*, Ron Hamel points out that instead of the application of principles to cases, one finds theological and anthropological orientations, perspectives, dispositions, and values. Häring frequently refers to the decision-making process as "discernment" and not the analytic, rational, systematic approach of the casuists.[30]

In 1975, Häring published *Ethics of Manipulation* in English after spending a year of research at the Kennedy Institute of Ethics at Georgetown University. The book discusses manipulation in general and then considers behavioral manipulations, brain research, and genetics.[31] He describes his method in the title of chapter 2: "Criteria for Discerning the Meaning of Manipulation." He describes ten objective criteria, including such aspects as personhood, freedom, sin, and limits of a teleological approach. But objective criteria are not enough. The main purpose of the ethicist is to help people to acquire the virtues of critical discernment, but he does not elaborate on precisely what this discernment involves.

Free and Faithful in Christ

From 1978 to 1981, Häring published a new, comprehensive moral theology that he wrote in English over a four-year period. Its three volumes, totaling more than fifteen hundred pages, were entirely new and not just a new edition of *The Law of Christ*.[32] Such a work would be a lifetime achievement for most people, yet Häring wrote it in the context of his many other writings and his manifold other pastoral activities. This work was translated into seven languages, but it could never come close to the formidable impact of *The Law of Christ*. Häring himself mentioned some historical factors that had influenced him since the earlier work: Vatican II, ecumenism, and his exposure to the worlds of Africa and Asia.[33] In this chapter, it is impossible to give a complete treatment of *Free and Faithful in Christ*, but a short discussion will give the flavor of the work.

Häring emphasizes many of the same methodological approaches found in *The Law of Christ* but develops them in a somewhat different way, stressing his broad holistic vision; the leitmotif of responsibility; a strong Christological emphasis; a Christian personalism within a covenantal context that recognizes the historical, communal, and social dimensions of the person; and a lesser emphasis on the morality of moral acts and norms. By joining creative fidelity to freedom, the work avoids the extremes of a static essentialism or a one-sided existential situationism. His broad vision relates the moral life to other aspects of the Christian life, especially spirituality, liturgy, prayer, and the sacraments.

Free and Faithful in Christ also shares some of the same weaknesses found in *The Law of Christ*: a failure to develop a philosophical and in-depth grounding for the leitmotif of responsibility; the lack of integration of his value theory into other aspects of the moral person and the person's response to God and others, including the new emphasis found in this work on the fundamental option; a descending Christology that does not give enough importance to conflict, struggle, and power; and an eschatology that emphasizes the fullness of redemption in Christ and therefore seems too optimistic about the present possibilities in this world.

The two volumes of special moral theology deal with the specific areas of human existence, and here the breadth of Häring's work stands out. The range of the material covered is intimidating, and his insightful analyses are often striking. Volume 2 has the unifying theme of the truth by which Christ sets us free. In particular, this volume treats the liberating truth, a morality of beauty and glory, ethics of communication, and various aspects of the virtues of faith, hope and love, including a section on sexuality.[34] The unifying theme of volume 3 is "light to the world; salt for the earth."[35] The first part deals with bioethics, whereas the second, larger part deals with the healing of public life, including responsibility for the world, ecology, culture, socioeconomic life, political life, and peace. Here again he also deals, especially in volume 2, with the particular sins involved, but the emphasis is always on the much broader theological vision and the attitudes and dispositions of the person. In these two volumes of special moral theology, Häring shows his familiarity with a wide range of sources, not only in theology and scripture but also in sociology, psychology, political science, and economics. His knowledge of many languages also comes through in the extensive bibliography.

The comprehensive nature of *Free and Faithful* is most impressive, but the literary genre of a comprehensive treatment of the Christian moral life has its own inherent limitations. Such a treatment fits very well with the teaching of moral theology in seminaries and theologates but not in other contexts. Here I am speaking primarily in terms of the US scene. Many seminaries in the early 1980s were quite conservative and would not be that receptive to using Häring's work as a text. And by then the primary locus of moral theology had shifted from the seminary to the college and university, which were not that interested in such comprehensive works. In addition, the growing academic nature of moral theology brought a greater depth in its approach to particular problems. By its very nature, a comprehensive treatment of all aspects of moral theology could not match the depth of individual monographs on these subjects.

Peace

The most significant development in Häring's moral theology comes from the importance given to peace and nonviolence and the move away from the just war theory. *The Law of Christ* devotes eleven pages to "Preservation of Peace and the Morality of War." Here Häring deals explicitly with just war principles and applies them in keeping with the best of this tradition to recognize the serious limits in going to war (a last resort in a defensive war) and the limit of noncombatant immunity in waging war.[36] In 1970, he published *A Theology of Protest* in English, with subsequent translations into five European languages. Nonviolence is a courageous love-based approach, which is both an attitude (in keeping with Häring's emphasis on vision and attitudes) and a practical method of action. Here the emphasis is on nonviolence and not on peace.[37]

Free and Faithful in 1981 gives great prominence to peace by making it the last chapter in volume 3. Peace is our world's most needed gift of God and the most urgent task of all people. War is a curse and the most inhumane fact of history, which we need to eliminate. Peace research, peace education, and peace policies and structures are necessary to overcome the slavery of war.[38]

In 1986, Häring published *The Healing Power of Peace and Nonviolence*,[39] a book he considers his most important publication.[40] In developing his emphasis on peace, nonviolence, and peacemaking, Häring employs many of the approaches already mentioned but also adds new aspects. In this book, the emphasis again is on vision and attitude. Peace and nonviolence with their scriptural roots constitute the vision and basic attitude of the book. Häring, however, puts these in a new context as he tries to develop a systematic, therapeutic approach to peace and nonviolence. Hence the title *The Healing Power of Peace and Nonviolence*. The pathologies of violence and war can be overcome only by this healing power of peace and nonviolence. This therapeutic vision replaces the older consideration of war and peace in light of justice, which could use violence to remove the injustices that have been done and were continuing to exist. Christ the redeemer and liberator is the healer of the evils of violence.[41]

The Healing Power recognizes that more than vision and attitudes of healing peace and nonviolence are required. The healing power of peace and nonviolence must become incarnate in all human relationships. Using Erik

Erikson's life stages, the book shows that nonviolent commitment is fundamental for the healthy development of psychic and spiritual health.[42] The healing power of nonviolence must become pivotal in the political realm. We must work for a structured order of peace to be accepted by all nations. Meanwhile, every effort must be made by nations, superpowers, and great powers to realize that their threats and use of violence are an extremely dangerous pathological aberration that cries out for healing. Instead of self-destructive deterrence, the world needs a transarmament and civilian nonviolent defense with a goal of healing humankind of inclinations to and ideologies of violence. Häring insists on the need for training in small groups and strongly supports the approaches of Mahatma Gandhi and Martin Luther King Jr.[43] However, many readers might want more concrete strategies and approaches than those discussed by Häring.

On this issue, Häring again is open to the charge by some of being too optimistic. Perhaps he does not give enough importance to the fact that the fullness of redemption will come only at the end of time. Meanwhile, sin and evil will continue to exist in our world, but Christians definitely are called to struggle against the sinful structures of our human society. A close reading of *The Healing Power*, however, shows that Häring is not a total pacifist. On the road to peace, there is need for open-ended compromises that recognize that all are pilgrims and can take only one step at a time.[44] Häring insists that everything must be done to prevent the case of having to use violence as a last resort, but he never spells out the best possible open-ended compromises or strategy.[45]

At the very least, Häring has made the important contribution of calling on Christians to see peacemaking as an essential aspect of what it means to be a follower of Jesus. One has to begin with a vision and an attitude—a goal commandment—that hopefully will bear fruit in concrete strategies and structures.

Authoritative Teaching and Loving Criticism

By far the longest chapter in Häring's autobiography deals with his life in the Church. He describes his life in the Church both chronologically and also in the light of his various ministries. At the end of the chapter, he describes his experience of an inquisitor Church and his role as a loving critic of the Church. Only those who appreciate the goodness of the Church and have experienced it in their lives can offer loving criticism at its failures and shortcomings. A theologian in the Church has to be absolutely honest, sincere, and forthright.[46]

Anyone who knew Häring recognized both his love for the Church and his loving criticism. He often criticized the suffocating legalism in the Church and the careerism that motivated some people in the Vatican and throughout the Church. People in general and the press in particular always appreciated Häring because of his honesty and forthrightness. His strong and public dissent from *Humanae vitae* has already been mentioned. Even before *Humanae vitae*, Häring had some negative experiences with the Holy Office, the guardian of orthodoxy in the Papal Curia whose name was changed to the Congregation for the Doctrine of the Faith by Pope Paul VI.[47] As the foremost progressive Catholic moral theologian because of his voluminous writing, his teaching and lecturing throughout the world, and especially his permanent teaching in Rome, Häring, in the context of the post–Vatican II cloud, was bound to run into conflict with the Congregation for the Doctrine of the Faith. A major event was the doctrinal trial in connection with his book on medical ethics.

Häring in 1989 published the full documentation of this doctrinal trial. He received a letter from Cardinal Franjo Šeper, the head of the Congregation for the Doctrine of the Faith, dated December 16, 1975, chronicling the problems found in *Medical Ethics*. (Joseph Ratzinger only became the head of the Congregation for the Doctrine of the Faith in 1981.)[48] The primary problem was his dissent from noninfallible Church teaching. His last letter from Cardinal Šeper came on April 2, 1979. There had also been a meeting between Häring and the congregation in February 1979. The final letter did not say that the trial was over but expressed the confidence that Häring would adhere to the admonitions of the congregation to work together with the magisterium for a better and more precise understanding of the teaching presented by the Church.[49] In the course of his correspondence with the congregation, Häring pointed out the lack of justice in the whole process and the shoddy theological work done by his accusers, and he insisted on the many times in the past that the Holy Office had been in error, explaining in detail the legitimacy of dissent from noninfallible papal teaching. All these efforts were to no avail. During the trial, there also appeared articles in *L'Osservatore Romano*, the official Vatican newspaper, criticizing Häring's moral theology.[50] There could be no doubt that Häring was a lightning rod for the more conservative elements in the Church.

The most important reality during this trial was Häring's deteriorating health, which began with cancer of the throat. Three intricate operations produced a new set of vocal chords. During one of these operations, he experienced a heart attack that almost killed him. Unfortunately, the cancer returned. The larynx and part of the windpipe had to be removed. Häring had to learn to speak from the esophagus—at times a difficulty for people trying to hear him. All this was occurring during his doctrinal trial, and he was absent from Rome quite a bit of the time.[51] There is no doubt that Häring was deeply hurt by this whole process.

Häring's loving criticism of the Church came through in his honest and forthright positions. His correspondence with the congregation illustrates such an approach. Perhaps the best illustration was Häring's reaction to the 1993 encyclical of Pope John Paul II, *Veritatis splendor* (The Splendor of Truth), condemning many newer approaches in moral theology.[52] Writing from his retirement in Gars, Häring acknowledged that the document contains many beautiful points, but the real splendor is lost because the whole document is directed toward one goal—to endorse total assent and submission to all utterances of the pope: "Let us ask our pope: are you sure your confidence in your supreme human, professional and religious competence in matters of moral theology and particularly sexual ethics is justified? We should let the pope know that we are wounded by the many signs of his rooted distrust, and discouraged by the manifold structures of distrust that he has allowed to be established." This was truly a cri de coeur of an old man who had contributed so much to moral theology and the life of the Church in all parts of the globe. Häring, however, ends his article by recognizing the deeper Christian realities that should be present in all our relationships in the Church. We need to honor God's gracious forgiveness by forgiving each other for the harm we have inflicted on each other and the anger we may have harbored in our hearts.

In conclusion, no one had a greater influence than Bernard Häring in replacing the older manuals or textbooks of Catholic moral theology. His major work, *The Law of Christ*, however, is not a classic that will be read by future generations. His writings are generally transitional works responding to the contemporary signs of the times and the needs of the discipline of moral theology and the Church. But this is true of all works of moral theology that by their nature respond to their own Sitz im Leben. Häring, however, stands out as the most significant Catholic moral theologian in the twentieth century.

Notes

1. Bernard Häring, *Free and Faithful: My Life in the Catholic Church; An Autobiography* (Liguori, MO: Liguori, 1998), 18–22. This volume will be subsequently cited as *Autobiography*.

2. Bernhard Häring, *Das Gesetz Christi: Moraltheologie dargestellt für Priester und laien* (Freiburg im Br.: Erick Wewel, 1954). For the English translation, see Bernard Häring, *The Law of Christ*, 3 vols., trans. Edwin G. Kaiser (Westminster, MD: Newman, 1961–66).

3. The following bibliographical information comes from Häring, *Autobiography*.

4. Bernard Häring, *Embattled Witness: Memories of a Time of War* (New York: Seabury, 1976), vii.

5. Bernhard Häring, *Das Heilege und das Gute: Religion und Sittlichkeit in ihrem gegenseitigen Bezug* (Krailling vor München, 1950). For a complete bibliography of Häring's numerous writings and writings about him, see Adam Owczarski, "Bibliografia di Bernhard Häring," *Spicilegium Historicum Sacrae Congregationis SSmi Redemptoris* 56 (2008): 403–537. This bibliography is also available at http://www.alfonsiana .org/italian/istituto/risorse_scientifiche/bibliografia_haring_1108.pdf.

The books and the articles are listed chronologically. Subsequent references to translations of Häring's work will be taken from this bibliography. This complete bibliography lists 117 books by Häring and 1,141 articles.

6. Häring, *Law of Christ*, vol. 1, 38–53. Subsequent references to *The Law of Christ* will be given in the text with the volume number followed by the page number (e.g., 2:312).

7. See Kathleen A. Cahalan, *Formed in the Image of Christ: The Sacramental-Moral Theology of Bernard Häring* (Collegeville, MN: Liturgical, 2004).

8. Bernard Häring, *My Witness for the Church*, trans. Leonard Swidler (New York: Paulist, 1992), 28–34. See also Häring, *Autobiography*, 73–75.

9. E.g., James M. Gustafson, "Faith and Morality in the Secular Age," *Commonweal* 100 (April 12, 1974): 140. See also the many references to Häring in James M. Gustafson, *Protestant and Roman Catholic Ethics: Prospects for a Rapprochement* (Chicago: University of Chicago Press, 1978).

10. Charles E. Curran, *Contemporary Problems in Moral Theology* (Notre Dame, IN: Fides, 1970), 116–36.

11. Bernard Häring, "La conversion," in *Pastorale du péché*, ed. Ph. Delhaye et al. (Tournai, Belgium: Desclée, 1961), 65–146.

12. Bernard Häring, *Free and Faithful in Christ: Moral Theology for Clergy and Laity*, vol. 1, *General Moral Theology* (New York: Seabury, 1978), 400–410.

13. James F. Keenan, *A History of Catholic Moral Theology in the Twentieth Century: From Confessing Sins to Liberating Consciences* (New York: Continuum, 2010), 9–34. For Keenan's discussion of Häring, see 83–110.

14. Raphael Gallagher, "Häring at Vatican II," in *Bernhard Häring: A Happy Redemptorist*, ed. Martin McKeever (Rome: Editiones Academiae Alfonsionae, 2008), 73–91.

15. Bernard Häring, *The Johannine Council: Witness to Unity* (New York: Herder & Herder, 1963).

16. Häring, *My Witness*, 50.

17. Häring, *Autobiography*, 94–100.

18. Häring, *My Witness*, 65–69.

19. Brennan Hill, "Bernard Häring and the Second Vatican Council," *Horizons* 33 (2006): 92–93.

20. Häring, *Law of Christ*, vol. 2, 48–52.

21. Häring, *My Witness*, 73–80.

22. Bernard Häring, "The Inseparability of the Unitive-Procreative Functions of

the Marital Act," in *Contraception, Authority and Dissent*, ed. Charles E. Curran (New York: Herder & Herder, 1969), 176–92.

23. Bernard Häring, "The Encyclical Crisis," *Commonweal* 88 (September 6, 1968): 588–94.

24. Häring, *My Witness*, 28–29.

25. Häring, *Autobiography*, 162.

26. Owczarski, "Bibliografia," 420–63.

27. Häring, *Autobiography*, 131.

28. Charles E. Curran, *Transition and Tradition in Moral Theology* (Notre Dame, IN: University of Notre Dame Press, 1979), 191–95.

29. Bernard Häring, *Medical Ethics* (Notre Dame, IN: Fides, 1973), 11–16.

30. Ron P. Hamel, "On Bernard Häring: Constructing Medical-Ethics Theologically," in *Theological Voices in Medical Ethics*, ed. Allen Verhey and Stephen E. Lammers (Grand Rapids, MI: Eerdmans, 1993), 230–31.

31. Bernard Häring, *Ethics of Manipulation: Issues in Medicine, Behavioral Control and Genetics* (New York: Seabury, 1975), 44–84.

32. Bernard Häring, *Free and Faithful in Christ: Moral Theology for Clergy and Laity*, 3 vols. (New York: Seabury, 1978–81).

33. Häring, *Free and Faithful in Christ*, vol. 1, *General Moral Theology*, 1.

34. Häring, *Free and Faithful in Christ*, vol. 2, *The Truth Will Make You Free*.

35. Häring, *Free and Faithful in Christ*, vol. 3, *Light to the World and Salt for the Earth*.

36. Häring, *Law of Christ*, vol. 1, 126–33.

37. Bernard Häring, *A Theology of Protest* (New York: Farrar, Straus and Giroux, 1970).

38. Häring, *Free and Faithful*, vol. 3, 391–426.

39. Bernard Häring, *The Healing Power of Peace and Nonviolence* (Mahwah, NJ: Paulist, 1986).

40. Regina Wolfe, "A Way of Healing and Peace," *Tablet* (June 27, 1987): 9.

41. Brian V. Johnstone, "Abandoning the Just War Theory? The Development of B. Häring's Thought on Peace, 1954–1990," *Studia moralia* 33 (1995): 309. For an earlier study on the same subject, see Sean O'Riordan, "Bernard Häring's Theology of Nonviolence," in *Sean O'Riordan: A Theologian of Development; Selected Essays*, ed. Raphael Gallagher and Sean Cannon (Rome: EDACALF, 1998), 365–83.

42. Häring, *Healing Power*, 68–74.

43. Ibid., 81–115.

44. Ibid., 86.

45. Ibid., 61.

46. Häring, *Autobiography*, 169–76.

47. Häring, *My Witness*, 111–16.

48. Ibid., 115–88.

49. Ibid., 184.

50. Ibid., 155–72.

51. Ibid., 215–17. See also Häring, *Autobiography*, 171–72.

52. Bernard Häring, "A Distrust That Wounds," *Tablet* 247 (October 23, 1993): 1378–79.

3

Josef Fuchs

Josef Fuchs was born on July 5, 1912, in Bergisch Gladbach, Germany. After studies at the Gregorian University, he was ordained a priest for the diocese of Cologne but then joined the Society of Jesus, still with the intention of becoming a parish priest. He received a doctorate in sacred theology from the Jesuit theologate at Falkenberg, the Netherlands, with a dissertation on ecclesiology. After four years as a parish priest, he was assigned to teach moral theology and did some studies to prepare himself for teaching at a Jesuit theologate in Germany. He went to the Gregorian University in Rome in 1954, where he taught for almost thirty years. After retiring from active teaching, he remained at the Gregorian until in ill health he returned to Germany, where he died in 2005.[1]

Josef Fuchs's *Sitz im Leben* strongly influenced his approach to moral theology. Like John Ford, Fuchs was a Jesuit theologian; he taught moral theology at the Pontifical Gregorian University in Rome for almost thirty years. In this capacity, he taught seminary students from all over the globe. In addition, he worked with many doctoral students who later became prominent Catholic moral theologians. Fuchs enjoyed a worldwide reputation, and he was also well known in the United States. Many of his writings were translated into English; he frequently came to give lectures and attend conferences in this country and spent time at the Kennedy Institute for Ethics at Georgetown University.

Fuchs saw his vocation exclusively in the Catholic academic and theological world. Unlike Häring, he was not a popular champion of broad reform in the Church after Vatican II, nor did he ordinarily give lectures, talks, or retreats to groups that were not academic.

The two most significant events affecting moral theologians of Fuchs and Häring's vintage (they were both born in 1912) were the Second Vatican Council (1962–65) and Pope Paul VI's 1968 encyclical *Humanae vitae* renewing the condemnation of artificial contraception for spouses. *Humanae vitae* was a pivotal event in his academic life. As will be treated in detail below, during the course of his work on the papal commission studying the issues of marriage including contraception, Fuchs changed his position on the morality of artificial contraception. In his discussions on *Humanae vitae*, he never made public statements or comments but confined himself to his work on the commission and subsequent scholarly writings.

Early Writings and Positions

His earliest writings were his doctoral dissertation on the threefold division of power in the Church: order or ministry, jurisdiction or governance, and teaching.[2] In the later 1940s, he wrote on the sexual ethics of Thomas Aquinas.[3] In the early 1950s, he published on situation ethics, defending the absolute norms taught in the Catholic tradition, criticizing the approach of situationists based either on an existentialist philosophy or a notion of Christian love that allowed of exceptions but also recognizing specific moral calls and obligations for individual Christians in their own historical and cultural situations.[4]

In 1955, just after joining the faculty at the Gregorian University, he published in German what was later translated and published in English in 1965 as *Natural Law: A Theological Investigation*.[5] This was the last monograph he ever wrote. In the late 1950s and early 1960s, he published his notes for students in his different courses at the Gregorian University, and these volumes were also made available for sale by the Gregorian University Press. For our purposes, the two most important were the volumes on general moral theology and sexual ethics, which will be discussed below. After *Humanae vitae*, he continued to publish but in the form of scholarly articles and essays developing further the concepts that came into discussion after *Humanae vitae*, especially absolute moral norms and the natural law.[6]

In his writings before *Humanae vitae*, Fuchs clearly shows his opposition to the manualistic approach to moral theology. The early chapters of his textbook on general moral theology emphasize that the purpose of moral theology is not simply the determination of negative moral norms but the moral growth of the human person. To change human beings into children of God is the principal end of the work of Jesus. Christian morality is a personal, theological, and Christological morality. Fuchs supports the absolute and universal moral norms found in the Catholic tradition but also recognizes the individual call of God based on personal characteristics of the individual person and the circumstances of one's existence. The emphasis here is on the human person and not human nature. The very fact that in his general moral theology Fuchs cites Bernard Häring more than any other author well indicates the approach he takes to moral theology.[7] His 1955 book on the natural law was precisely a theological investigation that integrated the natural law into the whole history of salvation. Most significant here is his attempt to overcome the separation between the natural order and the supernatural order.

As mentioned, the most significant change in Fuchs's moral teaching centered on the issue of contraception, which is closely related to the concepts of the natural law, the role of the papal teaching office, and conscience. In the third edition (1963) of his textbook on sexuality for his students, Fuchs explains his position on sexuality and contraception. The criterion for sexual actuation, or use, is the nature of the human sexual faculty and its act. The primary end of sexuality is the procreation of offspring, and the secondary end that is subordinate to the primary end is the intimate love union of husband and wife as found in the sexual matrimonial embrace.[8] Contraception goes against the primary end, which requires an act that by its nature is apt for the procreation of offspring, and it goes against the secondary end by interfering with the total giving of the spouses to each other in the sexual act. Fuchs also insists on the authoritative teaching of Popes Pius XI and XII condemning artificial contraception.[9]

Fuchs's dramatic change on contraception came about during his membership on the Pontifical Commission on Population, Family, and Birth.[10] Pope John XXIII established this commission with only seven members and no theologians in 1963 to prepare for an upcoming international meeting on population. Pope Paul VI expanded the membership a number of times, and it gradually took on the focus of dealing with artificial contraception. In 1964, he appointed seven new members, five of whom were moral theologians including Häring and Fuchs. At the second meeting in spring 1964, Fuchs opposed Häring's and Canon Pierre de Locht's proposal to raise the basic moral issues because he strongly supported the existing teaching. His position based on his writing had been well known to all. The third meeting in 1964 did not break any new ground, but afterward Pope Paul VI expanded the committee to fifty-eight members, including John Ford and three married couples.

The fourth meeting in 1965 discussed explicitly the reformability of the teaching condemning artificial contraception. Many were surprised when Fuchs stated the teaching is reformable but that he thought it was still valid. The fifth and final session took place over a longer period in April and May 1965. Here Fuchs expressly changed his mind on the morality of artificial contraception. He played a major role in drafting two documents from the commission: the final report of the commission itself (often inaccurately called the "Majority Report") and a paper refuting another paper written primarily by John Ford. Fuchs was apparently deeply impressed by the testimony of the lay couples, especially the Crowleys, who had been the founders of the Catholic Family Movement in the United States, and the Potvins from Canada.

The final report gave the reasons for the position accepting the morality of artificial contraception for spouses under certain conditions. The natural law is not just the physical or biological aspect of human nature. To interfere with the biological or physical aspect of the sexual conjugal act is a physical evil that can be justified for the good of the person and the love relationship of the spouses. It is natural for human beings to exercise human control over what is given in physical nature. With regard to the noninfallible papal teaching on artificial contraception, the document points out that such papal teaching in the past has been mistaken. There also have been significant changes in the teaching with regard to procreation even in the twentieth century, as exemplified by the acceptance of rhythm and the unwillingness to continue speaking about procreation as the primary end of marriage. In addition, there are many new circumstances and developments that affect the teaching.[11]

Rahner's Influence

The main focus of Fuchs's writings after *Humanae vitae* was on the issues raised originally in the controversy over contraception, and that continued to be a major preoccupation of Catholic moral theologians in the subsequent decades. Another factor influencing the Gregorian University professor's work was the influence of Karl Rahner, which had been present even before *Humanae vitae*. Rahner's influence shows itself, especially on two particular issues: fundamental option and the material content of behavioral norms of morality.

Fundamental Option

Others have spoken of the role of fundamental option in moral theology but did not develop it on the basis of Rahner's transcendental approach.[12] In light of Rahner's theological eminence and prestige, however, the theory of fundamental option often became identified with his approach.

The manuals of moral theology recognized only one type of freedom: freedom of choice. Thus, for example, one is free to study, to play, to listen to music, or to go to the theater. Fuchs, following Rahner, recognizes and distinguishes two types of freedom: basic freedom and freedom of choice.

This distinction emphasizes the primacy of the person and not the primacy of the act.[13] Basic freedom involves the self-determination of the person. It is ultimately the question of the moral goodness or badness of the person. This basic self-commitment is the gift or refusal of the self in love to God in light of God's loving grace. God's grace is accepted or refused in the very depth and center of the person. Following the well-founded theory that the grace of God is offered also to those who do not explicitly know or recognize Christ, the grace of God is also offered to the non-Christian in the depth and center of her person. This basic orientation constitutes the reality of salvation—offered by God's love and accepted in grace by the person.

This basic self-commitment is never complete or perfect in this world. This distinguishes the fundamental option or basic orientation from the final option at the time of death. This also explains why one can change one's fundamental option in this world. This orientation occurs not on the level of the categorical (the particular acts that are done) but on the level of the transcendental.

The person's awareness of the basic or transcendental freedom and the freedom on the level of categorical acts is quite different. On the categorical level, one is aware of the act as an object and can be reflexively conscious of the act. But on the transcendental level, the person is involved as a subject related to God who is also a subject. Here it is a question of the subject who is not an object, and one thus cannot have reflex awareness of oneself as a subject. The person is present to oneself in a transcendental, unreflexive, and athematic awareness. Since the fundamental option involves a free act, it is conscious but not in the same way that we are conscious of an object such as our categorical acts. There can be no objective reflection on the self as subject.

What is the relationship between the fundamental option and particular categorical acts? In reality, there is no separate act of basic orientation. This fundamental option is always involved with particular categorical acts. Particular acts of free choice may express and derive from the basic freedom involving the opening of the self to the absolute, but particular acts also often do not come from the depths of the person's self-disposition. This explains the reality of venial sin in a person in the state of grace or the act of forgiveness by one who has refused the fundamental option in response to God's love. The categorical acts may occasion the intensification or diminution of the fundamental option. Total lack of concern for venial sin will diminish or even endanger the basic fundamental commitment to God. Likewise, through better and more frequent right categorical acts, the sinner is disposed to be open to accepting the grace of God in the depths of the sinner's own person.

Since the option of self-determination occurs and is known only in a transcendental and unreflexive manner, we cannot be certain of what our fundamental option is. This position coheres with the teaching of the Council of Trent that no one can ever have certain knowledge of one's state of grace. According to Aquinas, we can come to a knowledge of the state of our soul by conjecture. Aquinas gives some signs that can serve as the basis for such conjecture. Thus, on the basis of the preponderance of right categorical acts, one can arrive at a conjecture about the state of one's soul. It is impossible to have absolute certitude in this matter.

Corresponding to the distinction between the person and acts, the transcendental and the categorical, is the important distinction between moral goodness and the rightness of behavior. Goodness refers to the moral goodness of the person; rightness refers to the behavior or categorical act. The question of personal moral goodness involves morality in the proper sense of the term "morality." The rightness of behavior does not directly involve morality in this proper sense. Rightness in behavior shares by analogy in the moral goodness of the person and is therefore also by analogy called moral. Likewise, the issue of salvation is directly connected to the moral goodness of the person and not to the rightness of a particular act.

Fuchs points out without any further development an important pastoral aspect. The fundamental option tends to orient a person in a perduring way. One can never judge the person's fundamental orientation based solely on one particular categorical act. In light of the fundamental option, it is impossible for one to continually and frequently change from mortal sin to the love of God or vice versa. Fuchs himself claims that the theory does not aim to deal with practical questions. Rather it focuses on a more thorough understanding of the theological and anthropological depths of the human person as the subject of moral action. The preoccupation with the distinction between mortal and venial sins misses the point.[14]

In the United States, Timothy O'Connell, in the first moral theology textbook for seminarians written after Vatican II, drew out the ramifications of Fuchs's approach for what is a mortal sin. Mortal sin is not precisely the doing of any particular categorical act. It is the act of self-disposition occurring *through* and *in* the categorical act. As a result, it follows that mortal sin is a comparatively rare phenomenon in the Christian life. We lack any clear reflex knowledge of the fundamental option. The distinction between mortal and venial sin comes from the reality that venial sin does not engage our transcendental freedom at its core level. It does not involve a fundamental option. The act itself is somewhat peripheral. The threefold criteria for mortal sin in the manuals had disastrous consequences not only in our understanding of mortal sin but also in the understanding of venial sin.

(Chapter 1 on John Ford described the manualistic approach to mortal and venial sin.) In this understanding, the difference between mortal and venial sin was the gravity of the matter or the lightness of the matter. Grave matter involved grave or mortal sin, and light matter involved venial sin. The difference between mortal and venial sin in reality is much more radical since it is a question of whether it involves the core of one's being with a transcendental act of loving God. Venial sin is not simply a lighter version of mortal sin. Thanks to O'Connell's book, Fuchs's theory of fundamental option and its practical implications for the understanding of sin became quite well known in the United States.[15]

There has been much discussion in the moral theology literature about the Rahnerian fundamental option theory.[16] Those who have expressed disagreement see especially too great a difference or even separation between the person and the act, the transcendental and the categorical, goodness and rightness, and salvation and categorical acts.

Pope John Paul II in his 1993 encyclical *Veritatis splendor* addressed the issue of the fundamental option. He recognized the importance of a fundamental choice that qualifies the moral life and engages freedom on a radical level before God. The pope, however, objected to some authors (no names are mentioned) in whose writings the distinction between the transcendental and the categorical becomes the separation between the two levels. Moral good refers only to the transcendental level, and as a consequence the properly moral assessment is reserved to the fundamental option prescinding from the choice of particular actions. To separate the fundamental option from concrete behavior contradicts the substantial integrity of the human person. This separation of fundamental option from deliberate choices of particular acts denies the Catholic teaching on mortal sin.[17]

Fuchs responded to the encyclical in an article in which he refers to "the Pope's theological advisers" or "papal consultors" and often not to the pope himself. Fuchs denies the separation between the transcendental and the categorical. Precisely because the fundamental option and particular moral choices are on different levels, the theory of fundamental option stresses their mutual relationship and interpenetration. Even individual actions that are peripheral—that is, not rooted in the fundamental option—can nevertheless bring a person to the point of making an opposite fundamental option. According to Fuchs, the critical assessment of fundamental option indicates that the pope's advisers are not familiar with the thought-world of Rahner and those moral theologians who have embraced and developed the Rahnerian approach to fundamental option. The encyclical claims that the separation of fundamental option from particular disordered choices, which would not engage the fundamental option, is a denial of the Catholic teaching on mortal sin. Fuchs maintains that the fundamental option develops a better understanding of mortal sin.[18] In my judgment, the difference between the encyclical and Fuchs comes down to the fact that the encyclical holds on to the concept of objective mortal sins that, however, might not be subjectively culpable.

Is There a Distinctively Christian Morality?

The second area where Fuchs employs the distinction between the transcendental and the categorical levels is what he describes as the question "Is there a distinctively Christian morality?" He answers the question by appealing to the distinction between the transcendental and the categorical levels and the different ways in which we are conscious of each.[19] The specific and decisively Christian morality is not to be sought first of all in the particularity of the categorical actions. It is only on the transcendental level that the person makes the fundamental Christian choice to accept God's love in Christ and to respond to it as one who believes, loves, and assumes responsibility for life in this world in imitation of Christ. Fuchs refers to this decision or commitment as Christian intentionality. The Christian intentionality involving the fundamental option is a full perduring decision (remember that the person cannot be reflexively conscious of it since it is athematic).

What is the relationship between the Christian intentionality and the categorical acts? Again, he insists that there is no separate transcendental act apart from our categorical actions. The athematic, nonreflexive consciousness is deeper and richer than the thematic, reflexive consciousness. The self-realization of the person before the absolute constitutes the more precise element of Christian morality. But again, the self-realization takes place through and manifests itself in the realization of particular individual categorical acts. While pervading the categorical content, Christian intentionality does not determine its content. Categorical material acts derive their content from the *humanum*—a morality of genuine human existence.

What is the nature of this *humanum*? God's will is nothing more than the divine desire that the human person exist and live. The human person discovers herself and her world and sees herself as a genuinely human but spiritual being. It is up to the human person to discover the kind of life that is proper for one who is responsible to the absolute and oriented toward fellow human beings. The will of God is not some extrinsic command coming from God conceived as another being. The will of God is that the human person oneself discovers what is genuinely human conduct.

This approach differs from what began to appear in Catholic moral theology in the 1930s that started with what is proper to the Christian and contrasted the Christian way of living with the human. But what about the Sermon on the Mount, the twofold love commandment, and the love of enemies? Are these not distinctively Christian? As a matter of fact, non-Christians and atheists have also advocated love of enemies as well as the need for renunciation and self-denial. The "fallen" human person is also called to overcome egoism and love one's neighbor, even the enemy. Because of sin, however, this person might not recognize the law of the cross and the need for renunciation.[20]

What is the relationship of the distinctively Christian element to the concrete categorical conduct of Christians? It is absolutely clear that the fundamental option as the response to God's grace does not determine the material content of the categorical. But there is some lack of clear development about the exact role the properly Christian has in the categorical order. In an early discussion, Fuchs clearly states that the "meaning of the *christianum* for our concrete living is to be found in its motivating power."[21] Later, Fuchs sees the transcendent element—the *christianum*—as striving to find the rightness of behavior in this world and as much as it is found to realize it. Personal moral goodness has intentionality. It has the negative role of not being closed in on oneself in egoism and the positive role of being open to truly human behavior in this world.[22] Moral goodness requires a serious endeavor to attain true insight into human behavior.[23]

In my judgment, Fuchs would be better to speak not of the distinctiveness but rather the uniqueness of the concrete moral behavior in the world. Thus, for him there is no unique Christian moral content in inner worldly categorical behavior. Something can be distinctive without necessarily being unique. There is no doubt that the twofold commandment of love, the love of enemies, the Sermon on the Mount, and the law of the cross are distinctively Christian, but for Fuchs they are not unique to the Christian in their moral content.

The question that Fuchs raises here—is there a distinctively Christian morality?—is closely related to two other questions that will only be mentioned. The first question concerns the soteriological import of the categorical dimension of morality—in other words, of our particular moral actions in the world. The Catholic tradition before Vatican II, including the early Fuchs, tended to see these acts as constitutive of one's relationship to God. Our good acts, especially insofar as they make the person good, determine our relationship to God. The transcendental-categorical distinction, however, indicates that categorical actions are no longer directly linked to one's relationship to God and salvation. But the totality of the categorical actions can give us conjecture or probability about our relationship to God. Fuchs also does recognize that the moral goodness of the person and the material rightness of the action should coincide.²⁴ Those opposed to Fuchs's position again see too great a separation between one's salvation and one's particular behavior in this world.²⁵

The second question concerns the discussion between proponents of an autonomous ethics and the proponents of an ethic of faith that took place beginning in the late 1960s, especially in Germany. For autonomous ethics, moral norms or human morality or the morality of categorical actions are not derived from faith. Faith provides a new horizon of meaning. The ethics-of-faith school insists that faith purifies, deepens, and goes beyond human reason with regard to the material content. To avoid some of the misunderstandings of the autonomous school, Fuchs insists on the theonomy of autonomous morality. The Creator has entrusted to humanity the mission to determine through the understanding of the human what is the morally right thing to do in this world.²⁶

Issues First Raised in the Contraception Discussion

These two issues of fundamental option and no distinctive moral content for Christian morality were important developments in Fuchs's understanding of moral theology. Most of his focus, however, after 1970 was on issues raised in the debate and subsequent discussions over *Humanae vitae* and the considerations raised in this debate: What is natural law? Are there norms that are always obliging and without exception? What is the role of the hierarchical magisterium or teaching authority of the Church? What is the role of conscience? The two issues already treated related to Rahnerian anthropology are also quite relevant to these other questions.

After *Humanae vitae*, Fuchs never wrote a systematic moral theology or even a systematic monograph. He wrote at least seventy essays from 1968 to 1988, but in general even these essays were not systematic treatments of a particular issue. In his own words, "I usually read what people are writing on a particular topic. If I think otherwise, then I write."²⁷ Thus, by his own admission his essays, which were often republished in his books, were especially responses to the writings of others. Hence it is somewhat difficult to put these comments together in a more systematic and synthetic whole.

The Natural Law

In his understanding of the natural law, the first issue concerns his objection to the understanding of the natural law that undergirded the teaching of *Humanae vitae* opposing artificial contraception and served as the criterion for the moral theology of the hierarchical magisterium on many other issues of sexuality. As already mentioned, the report of what was popularly called the papal birth control commission, of which Fuchs was a primary author, pointed out some of the problems with the natural law theory used to support the conclusions of the encyclical with regard to artificial contraception.

Fuchs criticizes the approach to the natural law found in Thomas Aquinas's writings for identifying the natural law with the physical and biological aspects of human nature and not with human reason. Aquinas unfortunately accepted Ulpian's definition of the natural law as that which is common to human beings and all the animals. There is a tension, however, and even contradiction in Thomas, who at times understands the natural law as human reason as, for example, when discussing polygamy and monogamy. But at times in light of Ulpian, he understands the natural law as based on human nature, which makes the natural sexual union of husband and wife morally normative. This fact has put a burden on the natural law argumentation "up to the present day."[28]

Fuchs sees the problem with this natural law theory as involving the naturalistic fallacy addressed in philosophy by David Hume and G. E. Moore. One cannot deduce moral conclusions from the static realities that exist. You cannot go from the "is" to the "ought." One cannot deduce a particular ethical obligation from the givenness of human sexuality. The question of how we should use what is given in nature in a human and rational way is exclusively an ethical question that must be solved by human reason. It is a question of interpreting and evaluating the relevance of nature for human reality as a whole.[29] Another problem with the emphasis on the givenness of human nature is that the approach is too static. Fuchs underscores the role of historicity. The inner worldly realities in which the person acts are historical and changing. The person who interprets and evaluates these realities in the decision-making process is also changing and developing over time.[30]

In agreement with Aquinas, Fuchs insists that the natural law is an internal law. The natural law for Fuchs is not a law "formulated or capable of formulation" or a summary of such laws.[31] The natural law is the possibility given to the person's practical reason of understanding and judging ethical behavior—what he calls the rightness of behavior in this world. This judgment concerns the moral rightness of categorical behavior, not the goodness of the person. What we human persons attempt to judge and formulate remains always a fallible attempt. At most we can have moral certitude.[32]

How does the person make this judgment? The answer is by means of a hermeneutical reading of the total concrete reality. The more difficult question is how this hermeneutical reading is done. The person who is rational, prudent, and historical makes the moral judgment about the concrete historical reality. What is to be interpreted, evaluated, and judged is the ensemble of the various realities that constitute a concrete human act. This hermeneutical reading by the person has its own history in the history of the personal subjects who have made similar evaluations over time. Thus, there is a continuity with past judgments, but there can also be present historical realities that are new, and the subject oneself can have become somewhat different from past experiences. The interpreting and evaluating reason must examine the entire human significance and values of concrete actions. This judgment is not a quantitative mathematical evaluation but a qualitative evaluation of the elements and values involved in the concrete situation. As a matter of common sense, humanity has always believed and shown itself to be capable of such a judgment. This is what we try to do all the time, since it is the only way to make an ethical judgment. Fuchs calls this approach teleological. It is obviously inductive and not deductive. Now we must act the same way in those few areas where the Catholic tradition has mistakenly employed the naturalistic fallacy of reading moral norms in the givenness of nature. The problem with this approach of the naturalistic fallacy is that it isolates only one aspect of the act and fails to consider the concrete act in its totality.[33] Unfortunately, Fuchs does not develop in any greater detail what is involved in such an evaluation. The reader is left wondering more precisely how this evaluation is made.

Our author is, however, somewhat ambivalent and maybe even confusing about the use of the term "natural law." He also maintains there is good reason to avoid the term, which can easily be misunderstood today. One could use the terms "recta ratio" or "human self-understanding," but the name is not the most important thing. In the United States, some people prefer the term "proportionality" as another name for the natural law. Without ever discussing the theory of proportionalism in any depth or detail, he finds some possible problems with the term itself.[34]

Individuals, societies, cultures, and the Church have all proposed norms for human existence. Experience shows that persons generally live comfortably with these given norms of moral rightness. These norms, however, are essentially human judgments made in particular historical circumstances by persons with their own mind-sets. As a result, doubt can arise about their validity today. Also, these norms may have been formulated inadequately by not taking account of all the aspects of the concrete act. They may have been based on the naturalistic fallacy. When grave doubts about these norms arise, we must make a serious hermeneutical reading of the norms in question. Aquinas himself required a hermeneutical reading of concrete moral norms and not merely an unconditional application of the norm. He maintains that concrete norms, unlike general principles, are true in most cases, but they could be wrong. Many contemporary ethicists speak of prima facie norms. On first sight they oblige, but there might be serious reasons why they do not oblige in this case. In this theory, there is a presumption in favor of such norms, but the presumption always falls to the truth.[35]

In the Aristotelian-Thomistic tradition, *epikeia* refers to the correction of a particular human law in light of the natural law precisely because of the limitations of human law that cannot cover all possible situations. For Aquinas, epikeia is a virtue concerned with justice in such cases. Some today want to employ the concept of epikeia to the natural law in those cases in which the given norm does not hold. One can use epikeia in this case provided one recognizes that epikeia would then be used analogously.[36]

Absolute Norms

Fuchs addressed on a number of occasions the question of the absolute and absolute norms in moral theology. Moral theology could not exist without the absolute. The person essentially has an experience of an *absolutum*, an experience of nonarbitrariness. The primal experience of the person as an ethical being is formulated in the principle "Do good and avoid evil." From this absolute, there proceed other absolutes in the plural, but they are very formal and not material—for example, be concerned for others or be merciful. In keeping with his distinction between goodness and rightness, right conduct is concerned with the nonabsolute realities of the contingent human world that change in history. The human person must interpret and evaluate these changing contingent moral actions. In this realm of behavioral norms, there can be no universally binding norms.[37]

In the recent past, the Catholic tradition has insisted on such absolute and universally binding norms, especially in the areas of true speech, sexuality, and aspects of medical ethics, but in these areas such universally binding norms were based on the naturalistic fallacy. Recall that the early Fuchs in his treatment of sexual ethics used just such an approach. The criterion for the rightness of human sexual act is recta ratio—right human reason and not the givenness of nature. Ethical moral reflection in this manner is always associated with moral experience and the evaluation of this experience and not with a priori metaphysical reasons. But this experience cannot be the solipsistic experience of the self-enclosed individual. The moral consciousness is shaped by manifold experiences and affected especially by the communities to which one belongs. Within the Christian community, faith and the Holy Spirit play a role in this moral experience, but still the discernment process is always a work of human right reason.[38]

Fuchs here, like many others, accepts a distinction between moral and premoral evil. Killing is a premoral evil. Killing as such does not describe a human act since it says nothing about the human purpose or intention. Killing for the sake of self-defense can be a right act. Killing for avarice is a wrong act. The problem arises if one intends good effects (Fuchs in keeping with his own theory should speak of rightness and not goodness here), but this necessarily involves also effecting evil. The evil can be justified if there is a proportionate cause justifying it. The evil in a premoral sense effected by a human agent must not be intended as such and must be justified in terms of the totality of the action by proportionate reasons.[39]

Fuchs, however, never develops in any detail exactly how this teleology works, although many other Catholic moral theologians at the time attempted to do so. Fuchs also does not enter into any casuistry to determine when and how these particular actions (e.g., masturbation and contraception) can be right behavior. One looks in vain for more specific understanding of how Fuchs's theory develops and also for its application in a casuistry considering the individual issues.

Fuchs frequently recognizes a role for norms of moral behavior, which he calls a pedagogical role. They can be helpful for the Christian in daily life, but they can never claim an absolute certitude or universality. They can even be wrong. He has frequently appealed to Aquinas's statement that behavioral norms oblige in most cases but can be different in some cases. They do not always and necessarily point to true objectivity.[40]

In addition to these behavioral norms that are not universal, there are some other types of norms that are universal. Formal norms such as to be just, charitable, or merciful are always obliging, but they have no material content as such. Also, some universal norms are basically tautological. Murder is always wrong, but murder is unjust killing. Certain behavioral moral norms in which the conditions are spelled out can also be universally binding, thus harming a child not for the child's own good is always wrong. But for Fuchs, behavioral norms are not absolutely certain and can be understood as prima facie—obliging at first sight but always subject to further moral reflection and evaluation in the light of experience.[41]

There is no doubt that Fuchs is much clearer and more detailed in what he is opposing than what he is proposing positively. With regard to the method of the manuals of moral theology and even the approach found in some magisterial documents, especially in the area of sexuality, Fuchs clearly disagrees. The extent of his disagreement can be shown from how he differs from the way in which these other sources often dealt with the following concepts of intrinsically evil, Christian morality, eternal law, and the will of God:

- *Intrinsically evil:* The more recent moral theology manuals, including some papal documents, have insisted that some behavioral norms are intrinsically evil—for example, contraception, masturbation, and homosexual acts. Fuchs disagrees with this appraisal because of their acceptance of the naturalistic fallacy. Concrete behavioral norms have to be established teleologically, based on moral experience, and even then they cannot claim absolute certitude and universality precisely because the human person as subject and the concrete historical conditions are mutable and subject to change.[42]
- *Christian or Catholic morality:* The impression is often given that Church teaching proposes a Christian and Catholic morality or moral norms. Here again Fuchs insists that concrete behavioral norms are determined by recta ratio and are truly human. Faith, revelation, and Church teaching do not propose any unique Christian morality with regard to these concrete behavioral norms that are required of all people. These norms are based on what is truly human in accord with creation and right reason.[43]
- *Eternal law:* Even Vatican II insisted that human beings participate in the eternal law by which God orders, directs, and guides the universe in the ways of human society. The eternal or divine law is objective and universal. This can readily be misunderstood as if one begins from a material participation in eternal law and proceeds to true moral knowledge. The reality, however, is in the opposite direction. In one's autonomous knowledge of moral truth—which, with regard to concrete behavioral norms, will allow only moral certitude—one acquires a certain participation in the eternal law. By definition, the eternal law itself contains everything, including the changeable and the unchangeable.[44]
- *The will of God:* With respect to concrete behavioral norms of inner-worldly existence, this is not some extrinsic command coming from God conceived as another being. The will of God is that the human person oneself discovers what is truly human conduct. When, on the basis of human reason and experience, we believe we have good human reasons for such norms, then they should be followed as the will of God. However, even then they might be wrong.[45]

Teaching of the Magisterium

A very important question in the post–*Humanae vitae* discussion concerned the role and function of what I (but not Fuchs) call the "hierarchical magisterium," or teaching office, especially of the pope. Fuchs usually refers just to "the magisterium."[46] His position flows directly from his understanding of the natural law and especially the rightness of categorical moral behavior in the world. The question of specific behavioral categorical norms is not a question of faith or revelation. Recta ratio or human experience provides the answers in these issues. Fuchs here, too, builds on his previous understanding that there is no distinctive (in my word, "unique") material content to Christian morality. It is basically truly human conduct determined by right reason: "The Church's search for the truth of ethical norms takes place along the path of human knowledge."[47] It is basically the people who must make judgments, which for its part the Church's magisterium watches over, reflecting on them and ultimately making a statement.[48] The magisterium can and must provide well-reasoned and well-motivated solutions to moral questions of this type. The magisterium ought to propose its specific moral teachings, however, with more cautious formulations and without referring with too much certitude to "Christian tradition," the "will of God," and "Christian" moral law.[49]

Yes, the magisterium has the assistance of the Holy Spirit in this work, but one cannot appeal to the Holy Spirit to guarantee the truth of these teachings. In fact, some teachings of the magisterium in the past have been shown to be wrong. Remember, we are dealing with contingent historical realities. The believer, however, can be helped by these norms proposed by the magisterium, but there is only a presumption that they are correct. At times, dissent from such teaching can be acceptable.[50]

Fuchs devoted one essay to an often-heard comment by some, calling it "The Faithful Must Not Be Unsettled." Within the essay, in a stronger way than is his usual custom, he turns the title around, directing its meaning to "some members of the magisterium." There have been abuses of authority by the magisterium that are capable of upsetting the faithful in the Church.[51]

Conscience

Three significant factors strongly influenced Josef Fuchs's understanding of conscience. First was his experience on the so-called papal birth control commission. His change on the issue of contraception resulted in a radical change that affected his whole approach to moral theology as brought out in the previous pages, but a primary factor in his change on artificial contraception for spouses came from his listening to the experience of married people. It was their personal experience that brought him to recognize that universal behavioral norms and papal teaching could both be wrong.

Second, after the commission he developed his teaching on norms and on papal teaching. He insisted that specific behavioral norms are not universally applicable (*ut in pluribus*). These behavioral norms can be of help to the conscience of the individual, but they oblige only as prima facie criterion—they might be wrong. For the same reason, plus the fact that norms of moral behavior proposed by the Church's magisterium are not matters of faith but are justified on the basis of human reason and experience (recta ratio), these teachings could be erroneous.

The third factor influencing Fuchs's approach to conscience comes from his turn to the person as subject. For Fuchs, the primary moral reality is the free, historical, human person. This is the anthropological understanding that is incorporated into his understanding of the fundamental option. In a nutshell, the moral person in striving for goodness (for Christians this is the realm of salvation) and for moral rightness in one's concrete behavioral decisions is more fundamental than so-called objective norms or even magisterial teaching. For these three reasons, conscience is the most important reality in the Christian moral life.

Fuchs explicitly considers conscience in the light of the anthropology recognizing the two levels of human freedom—the core freedom on the transcendental level and the freedom of particular decisions on the categorical level. Conscience, as it has been used in the Catholic tradition, refers to the judgment about the morality of particular categorical actions. What explains the binding force of conscience in making particular moral decisions? The basic freedom, the fundamental option with regard to personal goodness, strives to realize itself in free, particular concrete actions, thus explaining where the obligation to follow conscience comes from.[52]

How should we understand how one goes about the process of answering the question "What ought I to do?" that refers to categorical human acts? The model that was predominant in the pre–Vatican II moral theology and is still held by many today speaks of the subjective application of objective norms to the situation. Although Fuchs does not mention it, this understanding comes from the manuals of moral theology that referred to law as the objective norm of morality and conscience as the subjective norm. The model that Fuchs supports comes from his emphasis on the primacy of the free, historical, human person. The person's efforts should be directed primarily toward an objective moral understanding of the "I" in this concrete particular historical situation calling for decision and action. The fundamental option calls for the person to strive to find what is the right or correct decision, which, however, is always the work of recta ratio. Yes, conscience can and does make wrong choices about what is right or wrong. At best, conscience can only arrive at a moral certitude, but objective moral norms might also be wrong. In this light, Fuchs strenuously objects to referring to conscience as the subjective aspect and the law or norm as objective.

In reality, both can and have been wrong. Calling the conscience subjective and the norms objective distorts the true reality. The process in which the person strives to express goodness in concrete acts that are known through evaluating and interpreting concrete realities is truly objective.[53]

The Gregorian University professor saw Vatican II as ambivalent about this issue of subjective conscience versus the objective norm. On repeated occasions, the council affirmed that conscience with respect to categorical behavior must proceed not arbitrarily but conscientiously, carefully, and objectively. The council also stated that we share in the law written in our hearts or in the divine law by means of our conscience. But we also find statements to the effect that the person in making her judgments should conform to the divine law. The council was thus somewhat ambivalent on this issue.[54]

The fear of subjectivism lurks behind those who see the norm as objective and conscience as subjective. Adherents of conscience as also objective likewise do not want to embrace subjectivism. The personal conscience is not a decision arbitrarily made by a selfish individual. The person herself is striving to express her goodness in these categorical actions, and the person is not alone. She profits from the experience of other individuals, cultures, and societies in trying to discern and do a morally correct categorical act. The Christian is also helped by her faith and her church community, including the magisterium, but the ultimate decision rests with her final judgment.[55] Once again Fuchs does not spell out in great detail how one makes the judgment of conscience. In light of the primary importance of conscience, all persons should develop their responsibility to make correct decisions.[56]

Fuchs's primary and overwhelming interest was in issues confronting fundamental moral theology, especially those that came to the fore in the discussion following *Humanae vitae*. He very occasionally wrote on bioethics and spent some time at the Kennedy Institute of Ethics at Georgetown University. His writings in bioethics tend to the more theoretical aspects, but there are a few discussions of particular issues.[57] The best example of his dealing with a particular issue is the beginning of human personal life, or what the Catholic tradition called ensoulment.[58] On the basis of his interpretation and evaluation of the realities involved, Fuchs concludes that in the early development of a fetus, the process has not yet reached the status of personal human existence. This theoretical position was quite common in the Catholic tradition before the nineteenth century and has not been rejected in the present. In practice, Catholic teaching embraces the tutiorist approach: One must always take the safer course in dealing with human life. He concludes his discussion, as is often his wont, with a question: Is it not possible that in certain circumstances the protection of other urgent, important, and certain values justify the taking of what is only probably human personal life? A casuist would spell out in detail what these values are and would never end with just a question. Thus, even here Fuchs shows that his approach is probing and not primarily casuistic.

Conclusion

As mentioned, many factors in his Sitz im Leben influenced Josef Fuchs's moral theology: the controversies over contraception and the natural law, his interest in fundamental moral theology and not in casuistry or social ethics, his preference to raise questions and not give answers, his essays mostly in response to what others had written, and his teaching seminarians and doctoral students at the most prestigious Catholic university in Rome—the Gregorian University run by the Jesuits. One important aspect has not been mentioned. In the post–*Humanae vitae* era, many progressive Catholic moral theologians have been investigated and even condemned by the Vatican. Fuchs was very conscious that he had to be careful in what he said and wrote and where he said it and wrote it. He said to me many times and also in print that he never said all he believed but he never said or wrote something that he did not believe.[59] Fuchs once commented that American moral theologians are very emphatic in their judgments. He preferred to raise questions.[60] Bernard Hoose, an English moral theologian who studied under Fuchs, dedicated his book on proportionality to "Der Fuchs"—the fox.[61]

As to be expected and as a necessary aspect of the academic discipline of moral theology, Fuchs has been criticized in a number of areas. Has he separated too much the transcendental and the categorical? For one who emphasized the importance of human experience, why is it that many people do not seem to have experienced even athematically the fundamental-option theory that he has proposed? By concentrating on the person, has he downplayed the importance of the social, the political, and the economic? Does his theory sufficiently embrace the Vatican II and liberationist emphasis that action on behalf of justice in the transformation of the world is a constitutive dimension of the preaching of the Gospel and the mission of the Church? Fuchs himself would be the first one to admit that he never developed a total systematic moral theology, and even in writing about particular questions he often did not approach them from a systematic perspective.

All must recognize, however, his outstanding contributions. Teaching at the most prestigious university in Rome, he was a primary leader in the revisionist approach to moral theology, opposing the teaching not only of the manuals of moral theology but occasionally of the hierarchical magisterium. He broke new ground in moral theology with his distinction between moral goodness and rightness. Fuchs was a champion of conscience.[62] Even though he did not write systematically, he consistently applied this theory to many of the most controversial areas in fundamental moral theology. While doing all this in his writing, his teaching influenced seminarians from all over the world, and he trained many doctoral students who have themselves become significant moral theologians.

Notes

1. Timothy E. O'Connell, "Josef Fuchs," *New Catholic Encyclopedia*, 2nd. ed., vol. 6 (Detroit: Gale, 2003), 18–19.

2. Fuchs's dissertation in German does not seem to be available. Much later, a summary was published by Yves Congar: Josef Fuchs, "Origines d'une trilogie ec-clésiologique à l'époque rationaliste de la théologie," *Revue des sciences philosophiques et théologiques* 53 (1969): 185–211. For the complete bibliography, see Franz Josef Busch, ed., "Bibliographie Josef Fuchs, 1940–1996," in *Für eine menschliche Moral: Grundfragen der theologischen Ethik* (Freiburg, Switzerland: Herder, 1997), 219–64.

3. Josef Fuchs, *Die Sexualethik des heiligen Thomas von Aquin* (Köln: Bachem, 1949).

4. Josef Fuchs, *Situation und Entscheidung: Grundfragen christlicher Situationsethik* (Frankfurt: Knecht, 1952).

5. Josef Fuchs, *Natural Law: A Theological Evaluation* (New York: Sheed & Ward, 1965).

6. For a well-done study of Fuchs's moral theology, which I have relied on in this chapter, see Mark Graham, *Josef Fuchs on Natural Law* (Washington, DC: Georgetown University Press, 2002). For a very helpful overview, see James F. Keenan, "Josef Fuchs and the Question of Objectivity in Roman Catholic Ethical Reasoning," *Religious Studies Review* 8, no. 3 (1998): 253–58.

7. Josephus Fuchs, *Theologia moralis generalis: Pars prima* (Rome: Editrice Univer-sitá Gregoriana, 1966).

8. Josephus Fuchs, *De Castitate et ordine sexuali*, 3rd. ed. (Rome: Editrice Univer-sitá Gregoriana, 1963), 39–43.

9. Ibid., 78–80.

10. Graham, *Josef Fuchs on Natural Law*, 87–95.

11. "On Responsible Parenthood: The Final Report," in *The Birth Control Debate*, ed. Robert G. Hoyt (Kansas City, MO: National Catholic Reporter, 1968), 79–111.

12. Brian V. Johnstone, "Fundamental Option," in *The New Dictionary of Theol-ogy*, ed. Joseph A. Komonchak, Mary Collins, and Dermot Lane (Wilmington, DE: Michael Glazier, 1987), 407–8.

13. The following paragraphs in the text summarize the approach found in a number of places in Fuchs's writings. See especially Josef Fuchs, *Human Values and Christian Morality* (Dublin: Gill & Macmillan, 1970), 92–111; Josef Fuchs, *Christian Morality: The Word Became Flesh* (Dublin: Gill & Macmillan, 1987), 19–61, 105–17.

14. Josef Fuchs, "Good Acts and Good Persons," *Tablet* (November 6, 1993): 8–9.

15. Timothy E. O'Connell, *Principles for a Catholic Morality* (New York: Seabury, 1978), 70–82.

16. For pros and cons on Fuchs's notion of the fundamental option, see *Philosophy and Theology* 10 (1997): 113–241. For overviews of the discussion, see James F. Keenan, *A History of Catholic Moral Theology in the Twentieth Century* (New York: Continuum, 2010), 186–88; and Darlene Fozard Weaver, "Intimacy with God and Self-Revelation in the World: The Fundamental Option and Categorical Activity," in *New Wine, New Wineskins*, ed. William C. Mattison III (Lanham, MD: Rowman & Littlefield, 2005), 143–63.

17. Pope John Paul II, "*Veritatis splendor*," nos. 65–70, in *The Encyclicals of John Paul II*, ed. J. Michael Miller (Huntington, IN: Our Sunday Visitor, 2011), 626–30.

18. Fuchs, "Good Acts and Good Persons," *Tablet* (November 6, 1993): 8–9.

19. Josef Fuchs, *Personal Responsibility and Christian Morality* (Washington, DC: Georgetown University Press, 1983), 55–58.

20. Ibid., 58–63.

21. Ibid., 63.

22. Josef Fuchs, *Christian Ethics in a Secular Arena* (Washington, DC: Georgetown University Press, 1984), 51.

23. Josef Fuchs, *Christian Morality: The Word Becomes Flesh* (Washington, DC: Georgetown University Press, 1987).

24. Fuchs, *Christian Ethics*, 52–53.

25. Mark E. Graham, "Rethinking Morality's Relationship to Salvation: Josef Fuchs, SJ, on Moral Goodness," *Theological Studies* 64 (2003): 750–72.

26. Fuchs, *Personal Responsibility*, 98. For an overview of this discussion, see Keenan, *History of Catholic Moral Theology*, 178–83.

27. James F. Keenan, "Champion of Conscience," *America*, April 4, 2005, 6.

28. Josef Fuchs, "Natural Law," in *The New Dictionary of Catholic Social Thought*, ed. Judith A. Dwyer (Collegeville, MN: Liturgical, 1994), 670.

29. Josef Fuchs, *Moral Demands and Personal Obligations* (Washington, DC: Georgetown University Press, 1994), 32–34.

30. Ibid., 91–93.

31. Fuchs, "Natural Law," 671.

32. Fuchs, *Moral Demands*, 41–44.

33. Ibid., 41–44, 96–104.

34. Ibid., 44–48.

35. Ibid., 105–7.

36. Fuchs, *Personal Responsibility*, 185–99.

37. Fuchs, *Moral Demands*, 162.

38. Fuchs, *Personal Responsibility*, 142–46.

39. Ibid., 136–39.

40. Fuchs, *Moral Demands*, 145–47.

41. Fuchs, *Personal Responsibility*, 142–44.

42. Fuchs, *Christian Ethics*, 71–90.

43. Fuchs, *Personal Responsibility*, 201–3.

44. Ibid., 208–10.

45. Ibid., 203–6.

46. Fuchs, *Moral Demands*, 138–50.

47. Ibid., 195.

48. Ibid., 194.

49. Fuchs, *Personal Responsibility*, 208.

50. Fuchs, *Moral Demands*, 194–96.

51. Ibid., 196.

52. Fuchs, *Personal Responsibility*, 218–19.

53. Ibid., 220–25.

54. Josef Fuchs, "A Harmonization of the Conciliar Statements on Christian Moral Theology," in *Vatican II: Assessment and Perspectives*, vol. 2, ed. René Latourelle (New York: Paulist, 1989), 496–97.

55. Fuchs, *Personal Responsibility*, 225.

56. Fuchs, *Christian Morality*, 118–33; Fuchs, *Moral Demands*, 52–62, 153–71.

57. E.g., Fuchs, *Christian Ethics*, 91–99; Fuchs, *Christian Morality*, 189–210.

58. Fuchs, *Moral Demands*, 74–87.

59. Ibid., 149.

60. Keenan, "Champion of Conscience," 6.

61. Bernard Hoose, *Proportionalism: The American Debate and Its European Roots* (Washington, DC: Georgetown University Press, 1987), dedication page.

62. Keenan, "Champion of Conscience," 6.

4

Richard A. McCormick

Richard A. McCormick (1922–2000) entered the Society of Jesus in 1940, studied theology at the Jesuit theologate in West Baden, Indiana, received a doctorate in sacred theology from the Gregorian University in Rome in 1957, and began teaching at West Baden in 1957. Father McCormick became the Rose Kennedy Professor of Ethics at the Kennedy Institute at Georgetown University in 1974 and in 1988 became a chaired professor at the University of Notre Dame. He died in February 2000 after suffering a severe stroke a few months earlier.[1] His trajectory well illustrates the journey of Catholic moral theology in the United States. Until the middle 1970s, moral theology found its home in seminaries and theologates, with the focus of training seminarians to hear confessions, but in the middle and late 1970s the primary home of Catholic moral theology began to move to colleges and universities. With this move, more people became professional moral theologians with academic doctorates, and the academic aspect of the discipline became much more prominent.

Birth Control

McCormick's *Sitz im Leben* shared with those already discussed the importance of Vatican II and of the debate in Catholic theology in the 1960s over contraception and the reaction to Pope Paul VI's 1968 encyclical *Humanae vitae* reiterating the condemnation of artificial contraception for spouses. McCormick himself recognized "the profound effect" *Humanae vitae* had on Catholic theologians and the dramatic change it brought about in his own approach. He described the theology that he learned and that he taught for some years "as all too often one-sidedly confession-oriented, magisterium dominated, canon law-related, sin-centered, and seminary-controlled."[2]

The first articles questioning the hierarchical Church teaching on contraception only appeared in late 1963 and early 1964.[3] On June 23, 1964, Pope Paul VI told a group of cardinals of the existence of the commission originally established by Pope John XXIII to study the issues of marriage and sexuality but pointed out that the norms of Pius XII remained binding. Paul VI spoke of this commission and its work again on June 24, 1965, and October 29, 1966. Recall from the discussions of John C. Ford and Josef Fuchs that, at the fourth session of Vatican II in the fall of 1965, the pope himself had proposed some additions to the document on the Church in the modern world to condemn artificial contraception, but these documents were then significantly modified. McCormick and most other commentators agreed that the council did not condemn contraception in the light of the existing commission. In April 1966, the *National Catholic Reporter* published the documents from the commission, including the final report, which argued in favor of changing the teaching. In July 1968, Pope Paul's encyclical *Humanae vitae* condemned artificial contraception. McCormick addressed the issue of contraception in the 1960s in light of this background.

From 1961 to 1966 in articles and reviews, he defended the teaching of the hierarchical magisterium condemning artificial contraception. In 1965, he began writing the recurring articles "Notes on Moral Theology" in the journal *Theological Studies*, and there he responded to the discussions that were taking place in the periodical theological literature.[4] In 1965, McCormick supported the existing teaching and disagreed with those who proposed arguments against contraception. However, he also considered Pope Paul's address to the cardinals of June 23, 1964, and responded to the important practical question of what pastors and confessors should do about people practicing artificial contraception. The pope in this address authoritatively repeats the existing norms. But in light of the study by the commission, the continuing debate, the practical urgency of the question, and the papal promise to speak authoritatively on the issue, if the pope fails to speak out on the subject, McCormick reasoned, one can conclude only there is practical doubt on the issue. Thus, priests and confessors could indicate this to the people.[5]

In the "Notes" covering January to June 1966, McCormick points out that in the June 1964 papal statement the pope has maintained that the arguments against the present teaching are not persuasive. But McCormick admits that these arguments could become persuasive even before the pope said so. McCormick, however, cannot bring himself to say that the arguments against the present teaching are persuasive and convincing.[6]

McCormick's "Notes" covering the literature from January to June 1967 treat of the published report of the commission favoring a change in the teaching (then called "the majority report" of the commission) and the comments of Pope Paul on October 29, 1966. After discussing the majority report, he concludes only that the reasons found in this report "could lead one to believe" that the arguments proposed in the majority report should be regarded as intrinsically the more probable opinion. But he does not say that he himself makes such a conclusion. He then goes on to address the practical matter of pastoral practice. He concludes that the matter of contraception is now in a state of practical doubt. This is important for the pastoral actions of priests and confessors.[7]

The "Notes" reviewing the moral theology literature from January to June 1968 discuss the position of Jesuit fathers John Ford and John Lynch, who taught at the Jesuit theologate in Woodstock, Maryland, disagreeing with McCormick's earlier position that there is now practical doubt in the Church on the issue of contraception. The crux of the issue is the differing positions on the relationship of the magisterium to theological investigation. McCormick adds that this relationship is one of the most important theological problems of the day.[8]

McCormick then extended the 1968 "Notes" beyond the June 1968 time frame to include the encyclical *Humanae vitae*, which was issued in July 1968. His discussion of *Humanae vitae* differs from his usual approach insofar as it does not involve a literature search and a discussion with other theologians but gives his own reaction to *Humanae vitae* in three sections: the analysis and criticism of the argument, the teaching authority aspect, and pastoral matters.[9] His major criticism of the reasoning of *Humanae vitae* is the problem of physicalism—the identification of the human moral aspect with the physical, biological, or natural structure of the sexual or marital act. Instead, he calls for a personalist criterion for determining the morality of contraception and quotes *Gaudium et spes* of Vatican II that the moral criterion is the nature of the person and the person's acts. The moral object of the act is more than the physical aspect of the act. (This was the primary problem expressed by the many Catholics who disagreed with the conclusion of the encyclical.) McCormick does not claim that the teaching is erroneous, only that it is subject to solid and probable doubt.

McCormick's discussion here gives more space to the teaching authority issue. This is a noninfallible teaching to which Catholics owe *obsequium religiosum*—religious docility of intellect and will. There is a presumption in favor of such teaching, but such teaching has been wrong in the past. McCormick is very cautious here. The first question for a theologian to ask is if there are other arguments to defend the authoritative teaching. Perhaps also the document should be read as expressing the ideal, but he rejects such an approach. In all these discussions, the theologian has to be very conscious of his own limitations. If many theologians and others concur in the conclusion, then the presumption cedes to the truth. However, theologians should not become a private magisterium opposed to the authoritative magisterium. His reflective and cautious approach developed here helps to explain why he did not make any public statements immediately after the encyclical appeared.

The third section deals with pastoral practice. Bishops and bishops' conferences should not speak out on the matter without personal reflection and consultation. It would be a mistake for a bishop to insist on assent from his priests to this teaching. However, the priest's first obligation is to distinguish between his personal opinion and the authoritative teaching. In confessional practice, when asked he must state the authoritative teaching, but he should not deny absolution to married people who have conscientiously decided that contraception is morally acceptable for them.

The issues raised by *Humanae vitae* continued to be addressed for some time by McCormick and all Catholic moral theologians, as already illustrated in the discussion of Fuchs. McCormick points out that the issues include the identification of the human moral act with the physical aspect or natural process of the act, intrinsic evil, the existence of absolute moral norms, the magisterium and dissent, and the role of the theologian.[10] In my judgment, the primary ethical issue here is the identification of the human or moral reality with the physical structure of the act or natural processes. This has been the crux of many questions of sexuality because the present teaching insists that all sexual acts be open to procreation and expressive of love. Thus, contraception, sterilization, masturbation, and homosexual acts are always wrong. This also explains the opposition of the hierarchical magisterium to artificial insemination even with the husband's semen and in vitro fertilization. The Catholic condemnation of divorce is based on the fact that divorce breaks the indissoluble bond of marriage, which results from the matrimonial consent of the persons in a valid marriage. The metaphysical bond is quite analogous to a physical reality. If the ultimate criterion was the personal commitment of the persons, one could more easily accept that marriages can break down. The Catholic tradition in other areas (e.g., religious life) recognizes that such commitments can cease to exist. The Catholic tradition developed a theory of double effect to explain what should happen when an action produces both good and bad effects. The third condition of the principle of double effect is that the good effect is not caused by the evil effect. In other words, causing the evil as a means to achieve the good is always wrong. This criterion of the physical causality of the act explains the hierarchical teaching that one cannot abort the fetus to save the life of the mother. In these areas, McCormick and many other so-called revisionist Catholic moral theologians have distinguished between physical or nonmoral evil and moral evil. As will be discussed later, McCormick developed his theory of proportionalism to deal with these issues. On all these issues, the authoritative, noninfallible hierarchical teaching is also involved.

McCormick's Casuistry

Before considering Richard McCormick's approach to issues in moral theology after *Humanae vitae*, it is important to first discuss his method. He never wrote a systematic moral theology; he followed the method and approach of casuistry. The casuist is concerned by definition with cases that call for solutions. The Catholic tradition in general and the Jesuit tradition in particular have a long history of being concerned with the morality of particular actions. The purpose of the manuals of moral theology was to train confessors for their role in the sacrament of penance. They employed casuistry as their method.[11] McCormick follows in that casuistic tradition while very much charting new directions.

McCormick was formed in the tradition of the manuals with their emphasis on casuistry. He wrote his doctoral dissertation at the Gregorian University in 1957 for Edwin Healy, SJ, a casuist who wrote a significant casuistic book on medical ethics. McCormick, whose father was the first Catholic to be president of the American Medical Association, wrote his doctoral dissertation on "The Removal of a Fetus Probably Dead to Save the Life of the Mother." Later on, he was very conscious of the limitations of the manuals, but he expressed his appreciation for the fact that he started teaching moral theology at a time when he had to teach from the manuals. He read six or seven manuals for every single presentation of every subject and thus got to know the manuals very thoroughly. Although he recognized the manuals' limitations, McCormick found much wisdom in the way the manuals went about their casuistry and their qualification of moral obligation. They were very careful.[12]

As pointed out in chapter 1, John Ford began publishing what became "Notes on Moral Theology" in 1941, the second year after the American Jesuits founded *Theological Studies*. From the very beginning, this genre consisted of a review of the periodical literature in English and many European languages in moral theology. The first "Notes" also included canon law. The focus of the "Notes" was especially to help the priest in his roles as counselor and confessor. The "Notes" dealt primarily with the quandaries and dilemmas that can arise for moral theologians and confessors. Ford and Gerald Kelly wrote the "Notes" until 1954. After that time, other Jesuits took up the task.[13] Richard McCormick started writing the "Notes" in 1965 when they appeared twice a year, sharing the role each year with other Jesuit theologians. In 1977, McCormick became the sole contributor to the "Notes," which were then published on a yearly basis. He continued writing the "Notes" until 1984.[14] The earlier discussion of McCormick's contribution to the "Notes" from 1965 with regard to contraception confirms the casuist method he employed. Mention has already been made about the difference between himself and Ford over whether there was a practical doubt about the teaching on contraception after 1965. There is an ironic element here: the founder of the "Notes" and the Jesuit who would succeed him as the outstanding Jesuit moral theologian in the United States both using their skills as casuists to make their opposing arguments.

As noted, McCormick moved in 1974 to the Kennedy Institute at Georgetown, specializing in bioethics there for twelve years. Bioethics at the time was primarily concerned with quandary ethics, especially in light of the many new technological developments that were taking place. In this context, philosophical bioethics discussed the merits of the two different methodologies of teleology and deontology. The Jesuit scholar participated in this debate and also learned from it. André Hellegers, the director of the Kennedy Institute, described McCormick's approach as responding to problems and putting out fires.[15]

McCormick and the "Notes" fit together like hand in glove. Writing the "Notes" gave him the opportunity to use and develop his talents as a casuist, and his work made the "Notes" a most significant source in the ongoing development of Catholic moral theology. In his writings, McCormick did more than just survey what had been written about moral theology in the periodical literature in English and the major European languages. He perceptively analyzed and thoughtfully criticized what was found in the literature. In the process, he both taught and learned from other moral theologians. In keeping with the Vatican II approach, he made the "Notes" a truly ecumenical encounter. The dialogue carried out in the "Notes" was unique and contributed greatly to the development of moral theology.

The casuistic approach, with its analytic and critical analysis of the literature dealing with particular issues, actually became the primary way in which McCormick thought and wrote over the years. A later section will treat his approach to proportionalism, for which he is probably best known. He did not think out and propose this theory in a systematic way, as most theologians and philosophers would do. He developed his theory over time by analyzing, criticizing, and commenting on the writings of others with regard to the specific issues themselves and the way in which they could all hang together consistently in a theory. He developed his theory not from the top down but from the bottom up in a dialogue with other writers dealing with the same problem.

McCormick was a casuist par excellence. His incisive and penetrating intellect went to the heart of the particular problem or issue, quickly bypassing the more peripheral aspects. He dissected complex moral issues with the skill of a brain surgeon. He brought to the "Notes" an ideal temperament for a moral theologian. He was judicious, objective, fair, calm, and a well-balanced analyst and critic. He exemplified the virtuous middle by his need to be convinced by reasonable arguments balanced by his willingness to change and accept new positions once he was convinced. His skills plus his fluency in reading the literature in all modern European languages made him a leading moral theologian in the whole Catholic world. James M. Gustafson, the eminent Protestant ethicist, claimed that in the "Notes" McCormick left us "a model of scholarly comprehensiveness and precision to emulate" to such an extent that McCormick's "identification with 'Notes' will remain as long as moral theology in North America is given attention."[16] McCormick truly lived up to his own goals for the future authors of the "Notes": firmness in what is certain, freedom in what is doubtful, charity in all, and with clarity in what is obscure.

The "Notes," like any other genre, also had its limitations. The subject matter was limited to particular issues and quandary ethics, with the emphasis on whether acts were right or wrong. McCormick and the "Notes" did not deal with broader methodological and systematic approaches to the whole discipline of moral theology. The person, the virtues, and the positive actions of the Christian person called to live out the Gospel received comparatively little attention. Social issues, except for some quandary ethics such as war and capital punishment, receded into the background. The cultural ethos and broader societal perspectives were generally not touched. In addition, the "Notes" themselves dealt only with the periodical literature and therefore did not deal with the many monographs that were then being published that went more deeply into questions of a methodological, theological, and systematic nature.

At the end of the "Notes" in 1984 dealing with the periodical literature of 1983, McCormick announced that he would no longer be writing the "Notes" and was passing the baton on to the next generation of moral theologians.[17] The 1985 "Notes" announced a new format in which a number of moralists would write on different aspects, but McCormick led off the "Notes" that year.[18] The 1985 "Notes" stated that it would deal with the literature from the last year, but within a few years this was no longer the case. The "Notes" consisted of individual authors dealing with three or four topics in some depth, but the authors did not limit these discussions to what had been published in the past year. The literary genre of the "Notes" had changed, and McCormick's casuistic approach no longer characterized them.

What explains the change? Three factors influenced this change and perhaps even influenced McCormick's decision to retire from his writing the "Notes." First, the moral theology literature was growing by leaps and bounds. No one could attempt to review all the periodical literature from the previous year. In a sense, before 1980 most of the literature in Catholic moral theology after Vatican II was in periodicals and not in monographs, but around this time many more monographs were published. In addition, the number of periodicals in all languages also increased dramatically.

Second, not only the quantity of writing grew, but the focus of moral theology was changing. Well into the 1970s, priests teaching in seminaries and theologates did most of the writing in moral theology. But in the 1980s, the home of moral theology shifted from seminaries and theologates to colleges and universities. In this new setting the professors of moral theology had to meet the academic standards of scholarly publishing. Consequently, there was much more scholarly writing in this discipline. In the 1980s, there was no doubt that the focus of the discipline shifted from the pastoral to the academic.

Third, at the same time, dramatic changes occurred in the role and importance of confession in the life of the Church and its members. The number of confessions decreased every year. In the process, the number of parish priests subscribing to *Theological Studies* decreased. In light of these three factors, the literary genre of the "Notes" changed.

McCormick himself, however, continued to employ his exemplary casuistic approach in other areas. He used the genre of the essay to deal with dilemmas and other topics facing moral theology and the life of the Church. He published three volumes of these essays: *How Brave a New World? Dilemmas in Bioethics* in 1981, *The Critical Calling: Reflections on Moral Dilemmas since Vatican II* in 1989, and *Corrective Vision: Explorations in Moral Theology* in 1994.[19] In these essays, he continued his approach of dealing primarily with dilemmas and developing his thought in dialogue with the writings and comments of others—the same approach he had used in the "Notes." These essays are usually less scholarly than the "Notes." He was, for example, a frequent contributor to *America*, the Jesuit journal of opinion in this country. The same characteristics that made the "Notes" so significant also came through in the essays he wrote: an ability to zero in on the central points, a penetrating analytic mind, a charitable but critical approach, a spritely writing style, and a clear and succinct phrasing of his thought to the extent that he never seemed to use more words than was necessary to make his point.

In 1984, he published his only true monograph, *Health and Medicine in the Catholic Tradition*, which was part of a project funded by the Lutheran General Health Care System to show how the different religious faiths look at health care.[20] The perceptive reader will recognize in this volume the same basic approach described above.

Core Aspects of the Natural Law

McCormick used his casuistic method with his own twist of developing his thought on the issues raised by *Humanae vitae* by dialoguing with other moral theologians writing in English and in the major European languages. A more synthetic approach would have begun with the theoretical foundations of the moral life, which serve as the basis for casuistry, but McCormick did not write systematically. He briefly alluded to, but did not develop in any depth, the more theoretical aspects that served as a basis for his casuistry.

McCormick was trained in the Catholic natural law tradition and throughout his career held on to what might be called the core understanding of the natural law, although he definitely challenged some of the characteristics of the natural law found in the manuals of moral theology. This section will develop his core aspects of the natural law.

The two core aspects of Thomistic natural law that McCormick accepted are the fact that morality for life in this world is based on human reason and that the basic human goods based on the inclinations of the person bring about human flourishing that serves as the basis for moral reasoning.

McCormick followed the Catholic natural law tradition in insisting that human reason reflecting on our humanity can arrive at moral wisdom and knowledge to determine how all human beings (Catholics and all others) should live in this world. McCormick's writings in the 1970s illustrate his use of human reason to discern what is morally right or wrong.[21] However, Vatican II had insisted that the split between faith and daily life is one of the most serious problems of our age.[22] Catholic theologians in Europe and the United States began discussing what was the proper role of faith and theology in ethics.[23] Protestant ethicists in the United States also addressed the issue of the theological contribution to ethics.[24] In light of these ongoing discussions, McCormick also addressed these issues. In accord with his own approach as developed especially in his writing of the "Notes," he dealt with what other authors said on the subject. He described his own approach as "reason informed by faith." Faith in Christian ethics does not add any material content that is in principle foreign or strange to human experience. Christian insights are confirmatory and not originating.[25] Faith informs reason because the reasoner has been transformed, and such transformation involves a view of persons and their meaning, Christian motivation, and a style of performing moral tasks. But the conclusions are in principle available to human reason and insight.[26]

While maintaining that faith and theology do not give any new moral content, McCormick referred to what he called essential ethics—those norms that are regarded as applicable to all persons, wherein one's behavior is but an instance of the general, essential moral norm, such as the rightness or wrongness of killing actions, of contracts or promises, and of all those actions whose demands are rooted in the dignity of the human person. This essential ethic is different from an existential ethic, which refers to a decision made by an individual about what that individual should do (e.g., not working in a particular industry). Such decisions very well can be based on one's faith.[27] In this context, he also frequently invoked the Vatican II understanding of the autonomy of earthly affairs, which provided powerful support for his position. According to Vatican II, the autonomy of earthly affairs means that created things and societies themselves enjoy their own laws and values, which must be gradually deciphered, put to use, and regulated by human beings.[28] One of his longest discussions of this issue of reason and faith is his essay "Theology in the Public Forum," which reflects among other things on his own role as a member of boards and committees providing norms for public policy. He concludes his essay by saying, "For me, that realism means that my moral convictions are inherently intelligible. But it also means the willingness to acknowledge at some point that others may not think so."[29]

A second concept of the Thomistic tradition accepted by McCormick concerns the metaphysical understanding of basic human inclinations and goods as the foundation of moral reasoning. What are the goods or values that we should seek—the values that define true human well-being and flourishing? We can answer the question of what are the basic goods by examining the basic inclinations that are present in human beings before any acculturation. The human person is called to act on and thus achieve one's well-being on the basis of these tendencies. Our author never develops in detail what these inclinations are but lists some of these tendencies—the tendency to preserve life, the tendency to mate and raise children, the tendency to explore and raise questions, the tendency to human friendship, the tendency to use intelligence in guiding action, the tendency to develop skills and exercise them in play and the arts. In these inclinations, our intelligence spontaneously and without reflection grasps the possibility to which they point and prescribes them. These inclinations tell us what it means for human beings to flourish and achieve their well-being and can serve as the moral principles and values that we are called to pursue.[30]

Differences with Traditional Natural Law

McCormick's approach differed, however, from the approach of the manuals of moral theology by its insistence on the person as the criterion for determining the morality of action, a historically conscious approach rather than the classicist approach of the manuals, and the recognition of the importance of prediscursive reasoning.

In his first treatment of *Humanae vitae*, he recognized how important the role of the person is for the discussion of contraception and sexuality. The moral criterion applied in *Humanae vitae* is the physical and biological structure of the act based on the nature of the sexual power or faculty. The sexual faculty has a twofold end or finality: procreation and love union. Every sexual act, therefore, must be open to procreation and expressive of love union. One cannot interfere with the physical sexual act. But contemporary theology insists that the best criterion for the meaning of human action is the person. Here McCormick cites *Gaudium et spes*, no. 51, that the moral criterion must be determined by objective standards based on the nature of the person and his or her acts.[31]

In subsequent writings, he often goes back to this criterion proposed in *Gaudium et spes*, but in 1980 he points out an interesting development in the wording of *Gaudium et spes* found in a study by Marcellino Zalba. An earlier draft of *Gaudium et spes* proposed an even broader criterion: "objective criteria based on the very dignity of the human person." The final text made the criterion "the nature of the human person and his acts." However, McCormick and the many theologians disagreeing with *Humanae vitae* see in the final text the emphasis on the person as opposed to the physical or biological structure of the act based on the nature and purpose of the sexual faculty.[32] McCormick later in 1982, without referring to the earlier draft mentioned by Zalba, cites the official commentary on *Gaudium et spes* as indicating that the criterion of the person applies to all moral actions and describes the moral criterion as "the human person integrally and adequately considered."[33] He then frequently insists on this criterion.

The question naturally arises: What is the meaning of the criterion of the human person integrally and adequately considered? Here he appeals to the definition or description proposed by Louis Janssens from the University of Louvain, who was one of the earliest Catholic theologians to call for change in the teaching on contraception. In the context of the "Notes," McCormick does not seem to develop in any depth his own understanding of the human person integrally and adequately considered but relies on the approach of Janssens. McCormick maintains that Janssens's insistence on the person integrally and adequately considered as a normative criterion is absolutely correct, and his elaboration of what that means is very helpful. Janssens lists and discusses eight essential aspects of the human person. The human person is (1) a subject (normally called to act according to conscience, in freedom and in a responsible way); (2) a subject in corporeality; (3) a corporeal subject that is part of the material world; (4) essentially directed toward other persons (only in relation to a Thou do we become I); (5) ordered by human nature to live in social groups with structures and institutions worthy of persons; (6) called to know and worship God; (7) a historical being with successive life stages and continuing new possibilities; and (8) utterly original but fundamentally equal with all other persons.[34]

McCormick explicitly recognizes that because of our limitations (in my judgment, perhaps the realities of finitude and some sinfulness should also be added to the description of the person), our actions are characterized by ambiguity. Sometimes simultaneously actions can be both detrimental and beneficial to the human person, such as an amputation to save one's life. The key for Janssens and other moralists is when there is a proportionate reason to perform an activity in a morally responsible manner that spontaneously results in values and disvalues. Here McCormick recognizes that his basic understanding of the human person leads by its very nature to the question of proportionate reasoning.[35]

A person integrally and adequately considered as the criterion of what is morally right serves as the basis for the fundamental distinction made by McCormick between moral and nonmoral evil. *Humanae vitae* insisted that contraception is a moral evil. McCormick and the many Catholic moral theologians who disagreed with *Humanae vitae* accused it of physicalism or biologism. The encyclical identifies the human moral act with the physical structure of the sexual act. Contraception is a physical or nonmoral evil. Thus, for example, killing is a nonmoral evil, whereas murder is the moral evil. False speech is a nonmoral evil, whereas lying is a moral evil. This distinction grounds the moral criterion that one can never intend a nonmoral evil, but one may do a nonmoral evil as a means if there is a proportionate reason. McCormick and others point out that the Catholic tradition ordinarily does not identify moral evil with nonmoral or physical evil except in the area of sexuality, which describes the moral act in terms of the physical structure of the act. Whereas McCormick distinguishes between nonmoral and moral evil, others use different terminology such as premoral, physical, or ontic evil.[36]

A second difference from the manuals of moral theology involves the shift from classicism to historical consciousness. McCormick recognized that it is commonplace to say that what happened in moral theology after Vatican II was the abandonment of a classical consciousness for a new historical consciousness. For the American Jesuit, historical consciousness means taking our culture seriously as soil for the signs of the times and as a framer of our self-awareness. This calls for a fresh look at some of our formulations and approaches, since what was appropriate at one time might no longer be appropriate in new historical circumstances.[37]

In my judgment, McCormick points out three significant ramifications of this historical consciousness that affect his understanding of method in moral theology. First, after Vatican II, McCormick insists that whether our actions or policies are supportive or detrimental to human persons cannot be deduced from general precepts as before Vatican II. A more inductive methodology is required.[38] A second ramification closely associated with a more inductive method is the importance of experience for moral reflection. After Vatican II, we have become more aware than ever that experience and reflection are indispensable sources of moral knowledge. In the pre–Vatican II manuals, Catholic theology formed and shaped experience but was hardly ever shaped by experience. Today we realize that experience is truly a *locus theologicus*—a source for moral learning.[39] Third, clearly and closely connected with the roles of induction and experience, is the tentativeness of moral formulations. This is an aspect of historical consciousness that is upsetting to many people. Our formulations are the product of limited persons, with limited insight, and with imperfect philosophical and linguistic tools. We cannot claim the same certitude that we often claimed in the past.[40] Thus, historical consciousness and its significant ramifications greatly changed his approach to moral theology after Vatican II.

The third difference between McCormick and the manuals of moral theology concerns his recognition of the importance of prediscursive reasoning in addition to discursive reasoning, but again he never develops in a systematic way what he means by prediscursive reasoning.[41] In his response to Bruno Schüller in *Doing Evil to Achieve Good: Moral Choice in Conflict Situations* (coedited with Paul Ramsey), he describes his own position by saying that an act is wrong because its very description when carefully made (and not without some intuitive elements) entails an attack on the value it seeks to serve, but there is no developed understanding of these intuitive elements.[42] McCormick agrees with Franz Böckle that there can be no mysterious ethical norms that are simply impervious to human insight. Human insight, however, must be understood in its broadest sense. There are factors at work in moral convictions that are reasonable but not always reducible to the clear and distinct ideas that the term "human reason" can mistakenly suggest. The term "human reasoning" is defined most aptly by negation: Reasonable means not ultimately mysterious.[43]

In two different places McCormick agrees with points made by Daniel

Maguire about the role of moral feeling and creative imagination in moral inquiry. McCormick recognizes emotion to function in our value judgments in a way that is sometimes beyond reduction to reasoning processes or analytic arguments.[44] McCormick himself admits that the discussion on moral norms and their grounding in Catholic moral theology in the decade before 1982 can lead to a one-dimensional perspective on moral reasoning. Again, based on Maguire, McCormick wants to highlight the expansive and deepening role of affect in moral knowledge.[45] Although McCormick does not develop in any detail this understanding of prediscursive, intuitive, and affective ways of moral knowing, I will show later that it has a definite influence in developing his theory of proportionalism.

Proportionalism

Richard McCormick is best known for his theory of proportionalism. But if he is primarily a casuist, how is he best known for this theory? He developed the theory to explain consistently and coherently his positions on a number of specific issues that were debated in moral theology after *Humanae vitae*.

In 1965, Peter Knauer, SJ, published in French his seminal essay on the principle of double effect. This began a long and widely participated in debate about moral norms that, in one way or another, involved the vast majority of Catholic moral theologians in Europe and the United States.[46] McCormick was unique in that he analyzed and criticized the writings of most of these other moral theologians and developed his own position in and through his discussion of others. He did this work in the "Notes" in *Theological Studies*, in his 1973 Père Marquette Lecture at Marquette University published as *Ambiguity in Moral Choice*, and in *Doing Evil to Achieve Good*.[47] The latter book begins with McCormick's 1973 Marquette lecture, followed by essays commenting on McCormick's lecture by Baruch Brody and William Frankena, well-known American philosophers; Paul Ramsey, a leading Protestant ethicist in the United States; and Bruno Schüller, a German Jesuit professor of moral theology at the German university of Münster who had a great influence on McCormick's thinking. McCormick himself wrote the final essay, "A Commentary on the Commentaries." Notice how in this volume McCormick follows his method of analyzing the positions of others and developing his own position in light of his criticism of others.

When we look back on McCormick's development of his theory, three major points stand out. First, he disagreed with the traditional Catholic position still taught by the hierarchical magisterium that such acts as contraception and sterilization are morally evil. These are not moral evils, he believed, but premoral evils that can be justified for a proportionate reason. The only intrinsically evil acts are those that involve moral evil, such as murder. He also disagreed with the principle of double effect, according to which evil that is directly caused is always wrong. Second, in the end he also wanted to avoid the approach of strict consequentialism, which claims that an evalu- ation of all the consequences determines whether an act is right or wrong. In the course of his own development, McCormick had made statements that definitely had a utilitarian or consequentialist ring, with reference es- pecially to the case of targeting noncombatants in order to prevent the loss of more life in a longer war. McCormick opposed such killings because the consequences in the long run would undermine the good involved.[48] In this context, McCormick talked about virtually exceptionless norms. The weighing of all the moral values made noncombatant immunity a virtually exceptionless moral rule.[49]

In his concluding remarks in *Doing Evil to Achieve Good*, McCormick explicitly admits he has changed his mind about long-term effects as the criterion in the case of directly killing noncombatants. He now proposes a different reason why such killing is wrong. An action such as killing is mor- ally wrong when it turns against a basic good, which involves an attitude of approving the evil. This occurs when the evil (nonmoral) is intended as an end or when it is caused without necessity. When the killing is the only way imaginable to prevent greater loss of life, then it is morally acceptable, but there must be a necessary connection between the evil done and the good that is sought. Thus, McCormick justifies an abortion (killing of the fetus) if this is the only means to save the mother's life. Such a case is very rare, but traditional Catholic teaching has deemed such a killing wrong. The same criterion of necessity serves as the basis for saying that the direct killing of noncombatants is morally wrong; there is no necessary connection be- tween directly killing noncombatants and saving more lives in the long run. Targeting noncombatants is a form of extortion that constitutes an implicit denial of human freedom. Such an action thus undermines human freedom. Freedom, however, is an example of a basic good in the *ordo bonorum* (order of goods) that is associated with the good of life. The direct targeting of non- combatants to save more lives in the long run undermines the value of hu- man freedom. Undermining the associated good of freedom in the defense of life undermines life itself.[50]

The American Jesuit thus distinguishes his position from consequential- ism. Consequentialism maintains an act is wrong because of the bad conse- quences it will have in both the short and long runs. For McCormick, an act is wrong because its very description when carefully made (including intuitive elements) entails an attack on the value it seeks to conserve.[51] Mc- Cormick has recognized the fact that terms such as deontology, teleology, utilitarianism, and consequentialism are often understood in different ways, but he refers to his own position of proportionalism as moderate teleology and is opposed to consequentialism.[52]

Third, in the development of his position, McCormick was always personally convinced that the direct targeting of noncombatants is wrong. He never explains how he arrived at this position, but here the role of intuition and prediscursive reasoning obviously played a significant role. In other words, the theory of proportionalism did not prove that such targeting was wrong. In fact, the theory was adjusted and changed to fit in with his position opposing direct targeting.

McCormick explicitly recognized that one of his major problems in this whole discussion was the issue of targeting noncombatants.[53] In *Ambiguity in Moral Choice*, he then opposed Schüller's contention that it makes no difference whether the evil (the killing of noncombatants) is directly targeted as a means or targeted only as an indirect effect. McCormick does see a moral difference in the way in which noncombatant death is done, but even the prohibition of direct targeting of noncombatants is still proved teleologically, based on the foreseeable and suspected consequences in the broadest sense.[54] As mentioned above, when he later rejects the apparently strict consequentialist approach of *Ambiguity*, he still wants to condemn such targeting of noncombatants as wrong, but he introduces a new element in his theory: Such targeting is wrong because it undermines the good of life by undermining the associated good of liberty. In *Ambiguity*, he called the norm against such killing virtually exceptionless, but now it seems he should explicitly acknowledge that such direct targeting is always wrong because it always undermines the associated good of freedom.[55]

In this short discussion it is impossible to touch the depth and breadth of all the issues involved in this very complicated discussion of proportionalism. This section has tried to explain accurately the general approach without going into all the details. McCormick himself recognized the tentative nature of his own position and that the discussion would continue as it should.[56]

Other Issues

This section will briefly discuss the more significant issues in bioethics and in Catholic moral teaching that McCormick addressed in his writings. Our author frequently discussed, especially in light of many celebrated legal cases, the issue of to treat or not to treat, with regard to both infants and adults, in light of the traditional understanding that we only have to use ordinary means to preserve life.[57]

The foundation of his position is that biological life is a basic but relative value and is not absolute. Here he quotes Pope Pius XII to show that prolonging biological life could render the higher, more important good too difficult. The higher good reflected in the call of the Gospel to love God and neighbor in this case comes down to the criterion of relational potential, but he proposes a very basic level of such relationality. For adults, attention should be paid to excessive hardship for the patient and a poor prognosis. McCormick recognizes these criteria as merely helping the prudential judgment that is required in all such situations. The criterion for the termination of treatment is the "best interests" of the patient and not just a medical indications policy. McCormick recognizes that his approach definitely involves quality-of-life considerations. One can see here the emphasis on the person and not just on the physical or medical aspect of the person. Conscious patients and the family, if possible for unconscious patients, should make the decision to terminate treatments on the basis of the best interests of the patient.[58] McCormick also addressed the specific issue of terminating artificial nutrition and hydration. While recognizing the great symbolic value of feeding, he still maintains that it can be in the best interest of some patients (e.g., because such means are futile) to withdraw such artificial nutrition and hydration.[59]

McCormick opposed physician-assisted suicide and euthanasia. He recognized that the traditional Catholic distinction between direct and indirect is not absolute. He admitted that the rational arguments against euthanasia are not totally convincing. He appealed to intuition, prudence, and vision to support his opposition. In addition, he also proposed an argument derived from positive law: A law can be based on a common and universal danger, such as no fires in the midst of a drought. McCormick also maintained, in light of the short- and long-term consequences coming from allowing such interventions, that there is a virtually exceptionless norm against euthanasia.[60] As noted above, elsewhere he abandoned this apparent consequentialist approach.

With regard to abortion, as already mentioned, McCormick viewed it as justified only if necessary to save the life of the mother.[61] He held that phenomena in the preimplantation stage of the embryo (e.g., possible twinning or recombination and the appearance of the primary organizer) raise doubts about the beginning of human life from the time of fertilization. However, he gave very great value to nascent life in the preimplantation stage, but it is not the same as the protection due to human life after implantation in the uterus (about fourteen days into the pregnancy). Because the pre-embryo has intrinsic potential and because of the many uncertainties in the whole issue, McCormick concluded there are good grounds for saying the pre-embryo should be treated as a person. This is a prima facie obligation only, albeit a strong one.[62] In other words, one would need a very strong reason to go against this prima facie obligation.

On the two issues of the indissolubility of marriage and homosexual relationships, he opted for a nuanced pastoral practice but not a change in the Church's teaching as such. The contemporary problem of divorce does not call for a change in the Church's teaching. This response must remain essentially at the pastoral level. Indissolubility is a moral ought that requires spouses not to allow their marriage to die and to resuscitate it if it has fallen apart. He puts heavy emphasis on the social character of marriage in order to uphold the good of marriage as a social institution. He proposes the following pastoral solution. The Church should not tolerate second marriages but should deal with the issue pastorally. The decision to marry after the death of a first marriage is essentially related to individual strengths and needs, and therefore such freedom should be left to the individual's decision before God.[63]

On the issue of homosexual relations, McCormick insists on the Church's conviction that the sexual expression of interspousal love offers us the best chance of overall growth as loving human persons made in God's image if it exists within a covenantal, permanent, and exclusive relationship of husband and wife. For the same reason, he opposes AID (artificial insemination from a donor), whereas he accepts AIH (artificial insemination with the husband's semen).[64] For the irreversible homosexual person not called to celibacy, he proposes a pastoral approximation of doing the best one can to achieve the normative. The Church should respect the judgment made by such persons before God.[65]

McCormick frequently (e.g., abortion, indissolubility, and homosexual relationships) invoked a distinction between the doctrinal (or the objective) and the pastoral (or subjective). One sees here the influence of his role in the "Notes" of writing for both theologians and pastors dealing with individual persons, especially in the sacrament of penance. Some Catholic theologians have objected to McCormick's use of this distinction.[66] There is some merit in this distinction in general, but there is the danger that one can use the distinction to have it both ways—the teaching is correct but the nuanced pastoral practice is acceptable. The emphasis on experience in Catholic moral theology indicates that the experiences of people and pastoral practices very often are the way that leads to a change in Church teaching. I think this is true with regard to indissolubility and homosexual relationships. In Mc-Cormick's approach to these two questions, I see another influence at work. On the basis of prediscursive and intuitive reasoning, he came to accept the official hierarchical teaching on these two issues and wanted to hold on to such teachings while providing on the pastoral level for persons who were not able to achieve these norms.

The Magisterium and Moral Teaching

A primary issue in the discussions over *Humanae vitae* in 1968 was the role of the hierarchical magisterium, or teaching office, in the Catholic Church and the possibility and legitimacy of dissent from noninfallible teaching. The issue of such dissent was a most contentious issue within the Church.[67] Just as *Humanae vitae* occasioned a change in McCormick's approach to moral theology, it also changed his understanding of the role of the Church, the magisterium, and the legitimacy of dissent from authoritative noninfallible Church teachings. The older juridical model of the Church and teaching authority required submission and obedience from all. Theologians had the role to explain and defend this teaching. McCormick points out three problems with such an approach: The teaching function also involves a learning function for the magisterium, the total teaching function of the Church is broader than the hierarchical teaching office, and the judgmental aspect of the magisterium should be only one part of its teaching function.[68]

McCormick strongly defends such dissent from noninfallible teachings. These teachings are remote from the core of faith, heavily dependent on reason, and involve complex and specific issues in which one cannot claim unchangeable certitude. History has shown that such teachings have changed over time.[69] According to Vatican II's Constitution on the Church, no. 25, the proper response to such teaching is *obsequium religiosum*. There has been much discussion about the meaning of this term. McCormick understands it as "a docile personal attempt to assimilate and appropriate the teaching—a process that can end in failure or dissent."[70] The classical theological formulation states that there is a presumption in favor of such teaching of the magisterium. Presumptions, however, are not all of the same weight. Official teachings enjoy this presumption to the extent that they have tapped the available sources of human understanding. When they short-circuit this process, the presumption is definitely weakened.[71]

The search for truth, especially moral truth, involves a developing process in the Church. The unwillingness of the Church to accept public dissent by theologians would stifle theology's critical role and the process of searching for the truth and thus have detrimental effects on the life of the Church itself. The US bishops, in their 1968 response to *Humanae vitae*, implicitly recognized this need for such dissent. They said theological dissent from noninfallible teaching is acceptable under three conditions: when the reasons are serious and well founded, when the teaching authority of the Church is not impugned, and when no scandal is given.[72] Moral formulations by their very nature call for change and involve a developmental process that McCormick calls the teaching-learning function of the Church. We would not have had the Vatican II teaching on religious liberty if John Courtney Murray had not conducted a long, uphill, dissenting critique of existing Church teachings. Such criticism and dissent have been in the past and can be in the present the work of the Holy Spirit. Dissent in the Church under proper conditions thus is not a liability for the life of the Church but a necessary and loyal service in the quest for truth.[73]

McCormick's later writings on Church teaching and authority come from the 1980s and later in the midst of what he called "the chill factor" brought about by Vatican disciplinary action and even the apparent denial of the legitimacy of dissent. His writings reflect this historical condition.[74] McCormick's teaching-learning process in the Church has three important components: the hierarchical teaching office, the role of the faithful, and the critical role of theologians. This constitutes what he and so many others describe as the *sensus fidelium*.[75] There will always be a tension in this search for truth in the Church. At times, tensions can be unnecessarily exaggerated and exacerbated. But the pilgrim people of God will always experience the tension of trying to do the truth in love.[76]

This chapter has shown why Richard A. McCormick was a leading figure in moral theology, not only in the United States but throughout the world. The majority of Catholic moral theologians who chronologically followed McCormick depended very heavily on him in their disagreement with some controversial Catholic moral teachings. In light of McCormick's leadership, they frequently appealed to proportionalism to explain their positions.

By the end of the twentieth century, however, proportionalism was no longer a major topic in moral theology. What happened? Recall that even McCormick himself frequently nuanced and developed his own understanding as he attempted to disagree with the problem of physicalism in official Catholic teaching and a purely consequentialist approach. His own work here was truly a work in progress. Proportionalism as a theory was quite limited because it dealt with only a comparatively small part of the broad reality of Catholic moral theology and even continued the focus of the manuals on determining which acts were right or wrong. Moral theology obviously must consider much more than just acts. As this volume indicates, many different approaches dealing with the whole of moral theology have come to the fore since McCormick's days. The controversial issues treated by McCormick are still discussed today but often without mention of proportionalism.[77]

In light of his Sitz im Leben, McCormick was the right person at the right time. His many intellectual skills made the "Notes" the most significant readings in moral theology at the time. All moral theologians today should strive to learn from McCormick the ability to perceptively analyze and thoughtfully criticize the work of others. His contributions to bioethics continue to be most relevant many years later.

Notes

1. Paulinus Ikechukwu Odozor, *Richard A. McCormick and the Renewal of Moral Theology* (Notre Dame, IN: University of Notre Dame Press, 1995), 1–3.

2. Richard A. McCormick, *Corrective Vision: Explorations in Moral Theology* (Kansas City, MO: Sheed & Ward, 1994), 47.

3. For the best exposition of this history, see Robert Blair Kaiser, *The Politics of Sin and Religion: A Case Study in the Development of Doctrine, 1962–1984* (Kansas City, MO: Leaven, 1985). See also William H. Shannon, *The Lively Debate: Response to Humanae Vitae* (New York: Sheed & Ward, 1970).

4. Richard A. McCormick, *Notes on Moral Theology, 1965–1980* (Washington, DC: University Press of America, 1981), 113–14. This volume contains the "Notes on Moral Theology" written by McCormick in *Theological Studies*. Future references to this volume will be "*Notes 1*." The second volume deals with the later period: Richard A. McCormick, *Notes on Moral Theology, 1981–1984* (Lanham, MD: University Press of America, 1984). Future references to this volume will be "*Notes 2*." These volumes make it very easy to access McCormick's writings that originally appeared in *Theological Studies*.

5. McCormick, *Notes* 1, 38–52.

6. Ibid., 114–16.

7. Ibid., 164–68.

8. Ibid., 208–14.

9. Ibid., 266–71.

10. McCormick, *Corrective Vision*, 44–45.

11. James F. Keenan, *A History of Catholic Moral Theology in the Twentieth Century: From Confessing Sins to Liberating Consciences* (New York: Continuum, 2010), 1–34.

12. Odozor, *McCormick*, 8–24.

13. John C. Ford and Gerald Kelly, *Contemporary Moral Theology*, vol. 1, *Questions in Fundamental Moral Theology* (Westminster, MD: Newman, 1958), v–vi.

14. Charles E. Curran, *Catholic Moral Theology in the United States: A History* (Washington, DC: Georgetown University Press, 2008), 95–96.

15. Odozor, *McCormick*, 23.

16. James M. Gustafson, "The Focus and Its Limitations: Perceptions on Catholic Moral Theology," in *Moral Theology: Challenges for the Future: Essays in Honor of Richard A. McCormick*, ed. Charles E. Curran (New York: Paulist, 1990), 189.

17. McCormick, *Notes* 2, 365.

18. Richard A. McCormick, "Notes on Moral Theology 1984," *Theological Studies* 46 (1985): 56.

19. Richard A. McCormick, *How Brave a New World? Dilemmas in Bioethics* (Garden City, NY: Doubleday, 1981); Richard A. McCormick, *The Critical Calling: Reflections on Moral Dilemmas since Vatican II* (Washington, DC: Georgetown University Press, 1989); McCormick, *Corrective Vision*.

20. Richard A. McCormick, *Health and Medicine in the Catholic Tradition: Tradition in Transition* (New York: Crossroad, 1984).

21. Odozor, *McCormick*, 26–28.

22. "Pastoral Constitution on the Church in the Modern World," no. 43, in *Documents of Vatican II*, ed. Walter J. Abbott (New York: Guild, 1966), 243.

23. Charles E. Curran and Richard A. McCormick, eds., *Readings in Moral Theology No. 2: The Distinctiveness of Christian Ethics* (New York: Paulist, 1980).

24. E.g., James M. Gustafson, *Can Ethics Be Christian? An Inquiry* (Chicago: University of Chicago Press, 1975); and James M. Gustafson, *The Contributions of Theology to Medical Ethics* (Milwaukee: University of Marquette Press, 1975).

25. McCormick, *Health and Medicine*, 59–60.

26. Richard A. McCormick, "Does Religious Faith Add to Ethical Perception?," in Curran and McCormick, *Readings in Moral Theology No. 2*, 170.

27. Ibid., 157–58.

28. McCormick, *Critical Calling*, 197.

29. Ibid., 207.

30. McCormick, *How Brave a New World?*, 4–5.

31. McCormick, *Notes* 1, 219.

32. Ibid., 306–7.

33. McCormick, *Notes* 2, 49.

34. Ibid., 49–51. See also McCormick, *Critical Calling*, 14–16.

35. McCormick, *Notes* 2, 50.

36. McCormick, *How Brave a New World?*, 209–59.

37. McCormick, *Critical Calling*, 9.

38. McCormick, *Corrective Vision*, 35.

39. Ibid., 19–20.

40. McCormick, *Critical Calling*, 16–17.

41. James B. Tubbs, *Christian Theology and Medical Ethics: Four Different Approaches* (Dordrecht, Netherlands: Kluwer, 1996), 35, 45.

42. Richard A. McCormick and Paul Ramsey, eds., *Doing Evil to Achieve Good: Moral Choice in Conflict Situations* (Chicago: Loyola University Press, 1978), 261.

43. McCormick, *Critical Calling*, 196–97.

44. McCormick, *Notes* 1, 543–44.

45. McCormick, *Notes* 2, 122.

46. Bernard Hoose, *Proportionalism: The American Debate and Its European Roots* (Washington, DC: Georgetown University Press, 1987).

47. Richard A. McCormick, *Ambiguity in Moral Choice: The 1973 Père Marquette Theology Lecture* (Milwaukee: University of Marquette Press, 1973); McCormick and Ramsey, *Doing Evil to Achieve Good*.

48. McCormick, *Ambiguity*, 93.

49. Ibid., 90.

50. McCormick and Ramsey, *Doing Evil*, 236.

51. Ibid., 261.

52. Tubbs, *Christian Theology*, 19–28.

53. McCormick and Ramsey, *Doing Evil*, 259.

54. McCormick, *Ambiguity*, 59–60.

55. James J. Walter, "The Foundation and Formulation of Norms," in Curran, *Moral Theology*, 143.

56. McCormick and Ramsey, *Doing Evil*, 265. For more in-depth discussions of McCormick's proportionalism, including criticism of it, see Lisa Sowle Cahill, "Teleology, Utilitarianism, and Christian Ethics," *Theological Studies* 42 (1981): 601–29; Tubbs, *Christian Theology*, 13–53; and Walter, "Foundation and Formulation," in Curran, *Moral Theology*, 125–54.

57. For an in-depth discussion of McCormick's approach to treating or not treating, see Lisa Sowle Cahill, "Richard A. McCormick's 'To Save or Let Die: The Dilemma of Modern Medicine,'" in *The Story of Bioethics: From Seminal Works to Contemporary Explorations*, ed. Jennifer K. Walter and Eran P. Klein (Washington, DC: Georgetown University Press, 2003), 131–48. For a helpful bibliography of McCormick's writings on this issue, see Richard C. Sparks, *To Treat or Not to Treat? Bioethics and the Handicapped Newborn* (New York: Paulist, 1988), 213–14.

58. McCormick, *How Brave a New World?*, 339–51. The original article is Richard A. McCormick, "To Save or Let Die," *Journal of the American Medical Association* 229 (1974): 172–76, also published in *America* 131 (July 7, 1974): 6–10.

59. McCormick, *Critical Calling*, 379–87.

60. Cahill, "To Save or Let Die," 140–43; Richard A. McCormick, "Physician Assisted Suicide: Flight from Compassion," *Christian Century* 108 (December 4, 1991): 1132–34.

61. McCormick, *Corrective Vision*, 192–93.

62. McCormick, *How Brave a New World?*, 194; McCormick, *Corrective Vision*, 187; McCormick, "Ethics of Reproductive Technology: AFS Recommendations: Dissent," *Health Progress* 68 (March 1987): 33–37.

63. McCormick, *Notes* 1, 554–61; McCormick, *Critical Calling*, 233–53. For an analysis and criticism of his approach, see Margaret A. Farley, "Divorce, Remarriage, and Pastoral Practice," in Curran, *Moral Theology*, 213–39.

64. McCormick, *Critical Calling*, 333–43.

65. Ibid., 308–9. For an analysis and criticism of his approach, see Lisa Sowle Cahill, "Human Sexuality," in Curran, *Moral Theology*, 193–212.

66. John Mahoney, "McCormick on Medical Ethics," *The Month* (December 1981): 412; William P. George, "Moral Statement and Pastoral Adaptations: A Problematic Distinction in McCormick's Theological Ethics," *Annual of the Society of Christian Ethics* (1992): 135–56.

67. See, e.g., Charles E. Curran and Richard A. McCormick, eds., *Readings in Moral Theology No. 3: The Magisterium and Morality* (New York: Paulist, 1982) and *Readings in Moral Theology No. 6: Dissent in the Church* (New York: Paulist 1988).

68. McCormick, *Critical Calling*, 20.

69. McCormick, *Corrective Vision*, 115.

70. McCormick, *Critical Calling*, 20.

71. McCormick, *Corrective Vision*, 73.

72. Ibid., 114–65.

73. McCormick, *Critical Calling*, 25–46.

74. Ibid., 71–74.

75. McCormick, *Corrective Vision*, 69–99.

76. For my analysis and criticism of McCormick's approach to Church teaching authority, see Charles E. Curran, "The Teaching Function of the Church in Morality," in Curran, *Moral Theology*, 153–78.

77. Aline Kalbian, "Where Have All the Proportionalists Gone?," *Journal of Religious Ethics* 30 (2002): 3–22; James F. Keenan, *A History of Catholic Moral Theology in the Twentieth Century: From Confessing Sins to Liberating Consciences* (New York: Continuum, 2010), 158.

5

Germain G. Grisez

Germain Grisez (1929–2018) shares the same *Sitz im Leben* as the other authors already discussed: the experience of Vatican II and the debate over contraception with a focus on the encyclical *Humanae vitae*. In addition to the issue of contraception, *Humanae vitae* occasioned discussion about the natural law, absolute moral norms, and the teaching authority of the hierarchical magisterium. Grisez's viewpoint, however, was unique because he was a layman. In the beginning he approached these issues from the perspective of philosophy and not theology, disagreed with the accepted natural law approach, but staunchly defended the sexual teaching of the hierarchical magisterium.

Grisez, the youngest of nine children in a Roman Catholic family, graduated from John Carroll University, received an MA in philosophy from the Dominican College of St. Thomas Aquinas in River Forrest, Illinois, and then a PhD in philosophy from the University of Chicago, where he worked in the area of logic, not ethics.[1] In 1957 he started teaching philosophy at Georgetown University and two years later moved into the area of ethics, with an interest in the natural law. In spring 1964, in the midst of Catholic discussion about contraception and especially in discussion with his Georgetown colleague Louis A. Dupré, he wrote a book manuscript that was published in January 1965 as *Contraception and the Natural Law*.

Grisez's Book on Contraception

In this first book, Grisez shows himself to be an original and creative thinker. He strongly disagrees with the traditional manualistic approach to the natural law and the generally accepted Catholic arguments against contraception. He proposes a quite original concept of the natural law, which he then employs to strongly defend the position that artificial contraception for spouses is morally wrong. In the process, he begins the intellectual journey that preoccupies him for his whole intellectual life.[2]

Rejection of Conventional Natural Law Arguments against Contraception

The conventional argument against contraception based on conventional natural law theory can be stated in the following syllogism. Major: To prevent any human act from attaining its natural end is intrinsically immoral. Minor: Contraception prevents sexual intercourse from attaining its natural end. Conclusion: Therefore, contraception is immoral. The problem according to Grisez is that the natural end does not mean the same thing in the major premise and in the minor premise. To prevent one act from attaining the natural end of the function to which it belongs is intrinsically immoral only if the "natural end" refers to a good that one is morally required to seek. Contraception clearly prevents sexual intercourse from attaining the end proper to it as a biological, teleological process, but this does not prove that we are morally obligated to attain this end. The natural or biological teleology of the sexual faculty is not necessarily an end or good that one is morally required to seek (19–24). Grisez is thus in some basic agreement here with the later positions of Josef Fuchs, Richard A. McCormick, and many others who disagree with the Catholic position on contraception because of its biologism or physicalism.

Grisez thus opposes the perverted faculty argument, which was generally understood to be based on the natural teleology of the faculty or power of human sexuality. The argument maintains that the sexual faculty has the twofold finality of procreation and love union. Therefore, every marital act must be open to procreation and expressive of love. The analogy is often made with the Roman vomitorium. This repulsive practice is wrong because it frustrates the natural function of nutrition based on the purpose of the faculty of eating. But there exist many good reasons to vomit, such as even avoiding moderate discomfort. We have no moral obligation to seek the moral end of our faculties or powers such as nutrition or sexuality (27–32).

He also disagrees with the phenomenological argument against contraception that had recently been proposed by the French Jesuit Stanislas de Lestapis. Human sexual intercourse is an outward and objective expression of the total mutual self-giving love of husband and wife. Withholding one's generative power through contraception goes against this total self-gift in the sexual embrace. But the argument seems to proceed on the basic presupposition that contraception is morally wrong. Others have pointed out that no one act can be expected to show the total self-giving of the spouses in marital love (37–42). Grisez in this chapter goes very deeply into the inadequacies of these arguments. As a skilled logician, he develops many different possibilities here, thus making it somewhat difficult to summarize his arguments in a short space.

Grisez rejects what he calls the natural law theory originating with Francisco Suárez, which is usually found in Catholic textbooks and is commonly regarded as the only traditional explanation accepted by Catholic philosophers. This approach insists on the objectivity of moral norms based on human nature and the awareness of the fundamental moral imperative to act in conformity with nature. Grisez rejects this theory for a number of reasons. Part of the problem is that if nature is considered as an object of theoretical knowledge, the argument that we as creatures must act in accord with human nature suffers from the problem of going from the "is" to the "ought." The reality of what a human person is does not settle what the person can and ought to be. If human nature is understood as an object of moral knowledge, then nature refers both to the teleological biology of the sexual act and the morally obligatory good. The conventional natural law theory rests on this equivocation. Also, note that the conventional natural law theory insists on the negative—you cannot do what is opposed to nature. This theory thus emphasizes what is prohibited and contributes to the legalistic and negative approach of the manuals of philosophy and theology in their failure to develop the pursuit of the good. The conventional natural law theory separates moral motivation from moral goodness and thus forgets the importance of intention in considering the objectivity of moral actions (46–53).

A Different Approach to the Natural Law and Contraception

Our philosopher developed his theory of the natural law on the basis of the later works of Thomas Aquinas but proposed the theory on its own intrinsic merits and not as a historical study of Aquinas (60–72). Practical reason played the primary role. Theoretical reason involves "is-thinking"; practical reason involves "ought-thinking." Ought, however, does not refer exclusively to strict moral obligation, because practical reason controls the entire domain of free human action by creating its structures from within. Practical reason considers what is to be done, whether the ought refers to the minimal good of strict obligation or to the more adequate good, which is usually possible and always good to do. Every deliberate act must be either good or evil, because deliberation is the work of practical reason. Practical reason proceeds from principles, which practical reason itself forms as its own starting point. These principles are not derived from some natural facts as in the conventional theory of the natural law.

What are these principles of practical reason, and how does practical reason form them? Human action must have some intelligent object toward which it can be directed. One cannot act deliberately without orientation. The objective of practical reason requires some form of intelligible good. Consequently, the first prescription of practical reason is that good should be pursued and actions that are not helpful in achieving the good should be avoided. But this general norm excludes no particular good or value accessible to humans. It is open to every value and says nothing about the subordinate goods; it includes every good that humans can attain. This general norm is not something imposed from without; it comes from the necessity of reason itself because one must do something good if one is to act intelligently. What are the subordinate goods that humans should seek? The answer can be found only by examining all of human beings' basic tendencies or inclinations that humans are endowed with prior to any acculturation or choosing of their own. The answer can be settled only by empirical inquiry. Fortunately, psychologists and anthropologists have come to remarkable consensus about these basic inclinations or tendencies.

Here it is necessary to cite how Grisez summarizes these fundamental human inclinations: the tendency to preserve life, especially by food-seeking and by self-defensive behavior; the tendency to mate and to raise children; the tendency to seek certain experiences that are enjoyed for their own sake; the tendency to develop skills and to exercise them in play and the fine arts; the tendency to explore and to question; the tendency to seek out the company of human beings and to try to gain their approval; the tendency to try to establish good relationships with unknown higher powers; and the tendency to use intelligence in guiding actions (64).

These inclinations as psychic facts are not themselves principles of practical reason. How do we form the principles of practical reason? We form naturally and without reflection the basic principles of practical reasoning. We recognize in these inclinations the possibilities to which they point. In light of the general norm to direct action in pursuit of the good, intelligence prescribes every one of these objects of natural inclination. All of these basic principles are affirmative. They are open to every possible human good. Here situationists choose the approach that produces the most good even if one acts against a basic human good.

But how do these seemingly open-ended positive practical principles exclude moral evil? The principles demand only that the human possibilities they establish should be maintained. What the basic principles of practical reason exclude is any action against one of these basic goods in order to maximize others and in accord with reason call us to hold fast to all the primary principles of practical intelligence and never go against any one of them. Practical reason requires that all these goods be maintained in their irreducible position but that one never can go against a particular basic human good in order to maximize others.

The condemnation of artificial contraception as intrinsically evil is based on the natural law theory just outlined (76–103). To show that contraception is intrinsically immoral, one needs only to show it is a direct violation of one of the basic principles or basic goods. The principle or good violated by contraception is that procreation is such a basic human good, and human beings should not directly go against such a basic human good. Contraception is a directly willed intervention of any positive kind to prevent the realization of the procreative good that otherwise might follow from an act of sexual intercourse. The method of contraception is irrelevant. The malice of contraception is not the violation of the general obligation to cause conception. The malice is in the will's direct violation of the procreative good as a value in itself that one can never directly go against. The malice is in the intention, not in the external act itself, but the intention gives formal unity to the external act. The procreative good is a basic human good that one cannot directly go against in order to promote human life and health. (The problem with the Grisez approach, according to those who disagree with him, is precisely the recognition of the procreative good as a basic human good that one can never directly go against.) Grisez develops his position by responding to objections against it and explaining what is a directly willed positive act.

Grisez, like everyone defending the hierarchical magisterium teaching on contraception, needed to show the difference between contraception and the use of the infertile periods, which when he wrote was called the rhythm method but is now a more sophisticated reality called natural family planning. The Catholic philosopher dismissed as inadequate an argument based on the difference between an action and an omission. The malice of contraception is the directly intended and willed going against the procreative good. One using the rhythm method does not directly will and intend to go against the procreative good. Yes, the rhythm method does involve the non-realization of the procreative good, but it does not involve an intended and directly willed act against the procreative good. Rhythm does not involve the choice of conception avoidance as a means.

Two important distinctions are helpful in understanding the difference between contraception and rhythm. First, there is a difference between a condition without which one would not be willing to act (the use of the infertile periods) and the precise reason for one's act. For example, a physician willing to administer a certain treatment only in desperate cases need not directly will the desperateness of the case. The intention of the one having sexual intercourse in the infertile period is some other good such as the love aspect of the act or the psychological value of intercourse. The second distinction is between wishing and intending. They are not the same thing. The one having intercourse in the infertile period certainly wishes to avoid the procreative good but is not directly opposed to this good. Grisez recognizes that at least in the abstract and in theory, it might be possible for someone to intend to use rhythm to go directly against the procreative good, but in reality this does not often occur. In rhythm, conception avoidance is willed indirectly and not willed directly as in contraception. Rhythm wants to avoid procreation, but it does not involve the direct will and intention to go against the procreative good (158–67).

In this book, Grisez also mentions in addition to the conventional natural law approach and his own theory the theory of situationism. He understands situationism as a trend rather than as a specific philosophy or cohesive movement. The classical utilitarianism of Jeremy Bentham, dialectical materialism, and the ethic of ambiguity exemplify situationist thinking. What is characteristic in this approach is the flexibility in judging the morality of concrete actions. Outward behavior can never be put in a definite moral category. Contraception is almost always generally approved by situationists. Procreation is only a bodily good that is in competition with many other material goods that can easily justify the use of contraception. Grisez's primary theoretical problem with utilitarianism concerns the matter of moral choice. One cannot determine which acts have better consequences. Even if you could know it, there would be no free choice in that matter, for one would logically have to follow the position that has the better consequences. The moral rightness or wrongness of moral acts cannot be based on a calculation of consequences (53–60).

Subsequent Developments

Before writing *Contraception and the Natural Law*, Grisez realized that there were few Catholic philosophers interested in defending the Church's teaching on contraception.[3] The book put him into the forefront of those defending the teaching even though he employed a different approach to the natural law. *Our Sunday Visitor*, a conservative Catholic weekly, wanted Grisez to put together a four-article summary. Grisez, through the advice of a friend, contacted Russell Shaw, a journalist then working for Catholic News Service. Shaw produced a summary in the form of an interview that was later published also as a pamphlet. Shaw continued to work with Grisez and ultimately helped him in writing three other books.[4]

Grisez had asked John Ford to read the manuscript of *Contraception and the Natural Law* before it was published. Later Ford wrote a very favorable review.[5] Grisez helped Ford from the spring of 1965 to early July 1966 while

Ford was a member of the so-called birth control commission, including the final month working with Ford in Rome. Grisez made public in 2011 many of the documents and other information he had received from Ford about Ford's work with the commission, his private meetings with Pope Paul VI, and his working with Cardinal Alfredo Ottaviani, the powerful head of the Holy Office, to refute the report of the commission written by its general secretary, Henri de Riedmatten.[6]

With regard to the work of the commission, on April 28, 1966, Riedmatten recorded the vote for the members of the theological commission as fifteen in favor of change and four opposed, including Ford. But the pope had changed the nature of the committee by making the group of bishops the members; the former members were merely experts. To help these new members, it was agreed to provide them with papers representing both sides. These were the two papers leaked to the press as the so-called majority and minority reports. Ford himself basically wrote the minority report.

The bishop members of the commission met in Rome from June 20 to June 25. Ford stayed in Rome for this meeting, and Grisez joined him on June 8. They worked to try to influence the bishops on the commission but realized that the prospects were not that bright since a strong majority of the bishop members seemed to favor change. A final document from the bishop members supporting change was sent to the pope (the *Rapport Final*). At the request of Cardinal Ottaviani, Ford and Grisez put together documents they called "Materials Prepared by Ford and Grisez at the Request of Cardinal Ottaviani" for Ottaviani to use to convince the pope not to change the teaching.

After *Humanae vitae* was published in July 1968, Grisez again entered the Church fray. At the request of Cardinal Patrick O'Boyle of Washington, DC, he was given a leave of absence from Georgetown University in 1968–69 to work full time for O'Boyle, who was dealing with dissent on the issue by professors at the Catholic University of America, the pontifical university of which he was chancellor, and especially with a good number of Washington priests who in practice said they would follow the theological statement from the professors at Catholic University. After that, Grisez continued to give some help to the cardinal in the next few years.[7] Thus, from both the academic and Church perspectives, Grisez was heavily involved in the issue of contraception that strongly influenced his own future academic development.

Characteristics of Later Writings

Three characteristics distinguish Grisez's writings after *Humanae vitae*. First, although Grisez had been trained in philosophy and wrote as a philosopher through the very late 1970s, he decided then to write from the viewpoint of moral theology. He was quite disgusted with the direction of moral theology in this country and abroad and felt someone had to do something about it, so he became a moral theologian. With funding from some bishops, the Knights of Columbus, and the De Rance Foundation, he became the Flynn Professor of Christian Ethics at Mount St. Mary's Seminary in Emmitsburg, Maryland, so he could teach seminarians and produce a textbook and other writings from the perspective of moral theology and not just philosophy.[8] From 1983 to 1997, he published three volumes of a systematic moral theology under the general title *The Way of the Lord Jesus*.[9]

Second, Grisez frequently had help from others and often coauthored books. The bibliography on Grisez's website indicates fifteen books, most of which are coauthored. For example, *Christian Moral Principles*, the first volume of *The Way of the Lord Jesus*, lists Grisez as author with the help of Joseph M. Boyle Jr., John A. Geinzer, Jeannette Grisez, Robert G. Kennedy, Patrick Lee, William E. May, and Russell Shaw.[10] His most frequent collaborator was Boyle, who was the most gifted philosophy student he ever taught. Boyle spent the equivalent of a full year working on the three volumes of *The Way of the Lord Jesus*.[11] The response to the authors contributing to the Festschrift for Grisez published in 1998 is coauthored by Grisez and Boyle.[12] Many scholars speak of the Grisez-Finnis theory, but it is more accurate to call it the Grisez-Boyle theory.

Third, Grisez was obviously very well disciplined, and he published prodigiously. In his philosophical writings, he published on abortion, the responsibilities of freedom, philosophy of religion, free choice, and euthanasia. The major theological contribution is *The Way of the Lord Jesus*, which comes close to three thousand pages. *Living a Christian Life*, the second volume, deals with what might be called special moral theology considering the various areas of the Christian life. The third volume, *Difficult Moral Questions*, comes close to over nine hundred pages. He planned to publish a fourth volume, *Clerical and Consecrated Life and Service*, which he conceived as a systematic professional ethic for Church leaders, but was unable to bring it to fruition. However, chapter 1 and unrevised chapters 2 and 3, as well as notes for chapters 4 through 8, are available on his website. His other theological writings include books on nuclear deterrence, the teaching of *Humanae vitae*, and personal vocation.[13] His very extensive writing makes it very difficult for one trying to report on his work in a comparatively short number of pages.

A word should be said about the length and style of the three volumes of *The Way of the Lord Jesus*. The work was intended as a textbook for seminarians, and he used it at Mount St. Mary's Seminary, but the great length of the book made it very difficult to use as a text. I doubt that many people have read the three volumes. His coauthor and friend Russell Shaw frequently heard criticisms that this work "is too much for seminarians (as well as for many other people, of course); too long, too complex, too comprehensive, too carefully reasoned and closely argued, too innovative. Grisez continues to pursue his project in his own way."[14] However, Grisez and Shaw wrote a shorter, more readable version of volume 1, *Fulfillment in Christ: A Summary of Christian Moral Principles*.[15]

The Way of the Lord Jesus on Contraception and the Natural Law

This section will discuss Grisez's later approach to the issues first considered in his 1965 book on contraception. The first issue is contraception itself. His discussions in *Living a Christian Life*, volume 2 of *The Way of the Lord Jesus*, briefly summarize the argument. Contraception is always contralife, involving the choice to impede a new human life. But one cannot go against the basic good of human life. Consequently, contraception is always wrong.[16]

Note the primary development. The earlier approach maintained that contraception goes against the good of procreation, but now it goes against the good of life itself. His understanding of contraception is similar to his earlier approach. Contraception is understood not on the basis of the objective or external act but by the intention of the will. It is a matter of choice made by the will either as a means or as an end. It is not a sexual act but a contralife act. Many would object that contraception goes against a possible life but not a real life as in the case of murder. Thus, it is not contralife. Grisez disagrees because, in general, human acts bear on possible rather than actual goods. Choices concern only what is within human power. Homicide does not destroy the victim's past life but only prevents the victim from having a future life. The homicidal will, like the contraceptive will, is only against life that would be, not against life that is. He grants that the prospective life prevented by successful contraception is not continuous with anyone's actual life, but the intention is still contralife.[17]

Grisez consistently applies his understanding, even in the face of much opposition. Many Catholic thinkers and others maintain that an unmarried couple having sexual intercourse should use contraception rather than risk a pregnancy. Contraception, however, is always a contralife evil and in this case involves an added evil to the nonmarital sexual relations.[18]

Grisez accepts what is called today natural family planning because in choosing to have marital relations in the infertile time, the couple's intention cannot be to impede the beginning of a new life, because the infertility is due to natural conditions and not their intentions. But he admits that those practicing natural family planning could have a contraceptive intention just as those who use a contraceptive.[19] Throughout his discussion, one sees that Grisez's understanding of contraception as an act of the will or intention differs from the approach of many others who give primary importance to the external act of contraception itself.[20]

Especially in *Christian Moral Principles*, Grisez systematically develops his natural law theory (often called "the new natural law theory" or "the basic goods theory"), which he first sketched in the book on contraception. Grisez recognizes that the first principle of morality proposed by Aquinas— good is to be done and bad is to be avoided—is not entirely satisfactory. The first principle of morality should provide a criterion for distinguishing which alternatives of choice are morally good and which are morally bad. The first principle of morality is "In voluntarily acting for human goods and avoiding what is opposed to them, one ought to choose and otherwise will those and only those possibilities whose willing is compatible with the will toward integral human fulfillment."[21] This is the first principle of practical reasoning. How is the first principle to be specified?

The primary specifications of the first principle of morality are intermediary principles standing between the first principle and the specific norms that direct choices. These principles are called modes of responsibility, and Grisez proposes eight. The first mode of responsibility, for example, maintains that one should not be deterred by felt inertia from acting for intelligible goods.[22] The eighth mode of responsibility, which is most significant for Grisez's approach to absolute negative moral norms and his opposition to proportionalism, maintains that one should not be moved by a stronger desire for one instance of an intelligible good to act for it by choosing to destroy, damage, or impede some other instance of an intelligible good.[23]

What are these basic human goods? The basic human goods are not deduced from any first principle or derived from our understanding of human nature. Grisez proposes eight self-evident basic goods and summarizes them in this way. Four are existential goods: integration, practical reasonableness or authenticity, friendship and justice, and religion or holiness. Three are substantive goods: life and bodily well-being, knowledge of truth and appreciation of beauty, and skill for performance and play. The eighth good is the complex good of marriage and family. The permanent union of a man and woman, which normally enfolds a parental and family life, is both substantive and reflexive. Taken together, these eight goods tell us what human persons are capable of being, not only as individuals but in community.[24]

Specific moral norms come about by considering proposed human choices and the basic human goods in light of the will toward integral human fulfillment. Note here the heavily positive aspect of the basic approach of Grisez in pursuing integral human fulfillment, but there are also some negative moral absolutes. Most moral norms (e.g., promise keeping) are not absolute but admit of exceptions. Some specific moral norms, however, are absolute. These absolute moral norms are not determined by the external act but by the free choice against one of the eight modes of responsibility. Recall the argument that contraception involves a contralife intention.[25]

In the contraception book, Grisez claimed that his theory was founded on the later work of Thomas Aquinas, but he was proposing it as his own theory and not as a historical study of Aquinas.[26] Ralph McInerny maintained that Grisez was not a Thomist and disagreed with him from a Thomistic perspective on three points: the excessive distinction of value from fact, the claim that the first principle of practical reason is premoral, and the denial of any objective hierarchy among basic values.[27] Later Grisez and John Finnis responded to McInerny's criticism but recognized in the process that they did disagree with Aquinas on some aspects.[28]

The Gospel and the Law of Love

Much of what Grisez says about the natural law in *Christian Moral Principles* comes from a philosophical perspective. But his aim in this volume is to write a truly Catholic moral theology. He insists that moral theology must be renewed in the light of Vatican II, which called for three aspects in particular: a more Christocentric approach, a scripturally nourished approach, and the nobility of the Christian calling to bring forth fruit in charity for the life of the world.[29] As indicated earlier, his other concern in writing a moral theology was to overcome the crisis in post–Vatican II moral theology in this country and abroad. He is quite sharp and unnuanced in his criticism of the majority of post–Vatican II Catholic moral theology: Christian moral seriousness "is eliminated or greatly reduced by the new moral theology in its movement toward secular humanism. . . . Much effort is spent trying to lessen the obligations of Christian life. . . . Doing as one pleases is then called 'following one's conscience.'"[30] (Even after writing his magnum opus, he recognized that the Church was in crisis and the outlook was bleak. A true renewal of moral theology was not happening. His own writing had not been accepted that much.[31])

In addition to the natural law, *Christian Moral Principles* recognizes a significant role for the law of the Gospel. By the act of faith, the Catholic Christian accepts God's offer of friendship extended in Jesus, receives the gift of divine life, and undertakes to cooperate with Jesus's redemptive act. This act of faith is both a free human act and entirely God's free gift to us. It is the fundamental option of basic choice, which directs all that the Christian should do. All Christians have a vocation to live out their faith. Whatever commitments are made, such as marriage or the profession one follows, is an expression of the basic commitment of faith and baptism.[32]

The divine love abiding in our hearts calls us to love God and neighbor. Just as God's gift of grace transforms the human person, so love transforms the first principle of morality into a more definite norm. "One ought to will those and only those possibilities which contribute to the integral human fulfillment being realized in the fulfillment of all things in Jesus."[33] Christian love is the new nature of the baptized.[34]

Christian love also transforms the modes of responsibility. Based on the first beatitude—blessed are the poor in spirit—the first Christian mode of responsibility is "to expect and accept all good, including the fruits of one's work, as God's gift." The fifth mode of responsibility, corresponding to the fifth beatitude, is "to be merciful according to the universal and perfect measure of mercy, which God has revealed in Jesus."[35]

Christian moral norms are generated from the Christian modes of responsibility. The Christian moral life is in conformity with Christ's life.[36] Christians are called to love others as Jesus loved them. Christian love is the principle of the Christian life. How does the principle of love relate to natural law morality? Grisez explains the paradox that the New Testament contains distinctive moral teaching but that there is no room for specifically Christian moral norms. Grace does not change human nature into something else. It makes integral human fulfillment a possibility and a hope for the Christian. Thanks to Jesus's redemptive love and grace, integral human fulfillment is no longer simply an ideal but a realistic hope. Specifically Christian moral norms propose options for choice, which either would not appeal to people apart from faith or would not appeal to them as realistic possibilities apart from faith and hope—or both.[37] Even without faith, some upright people can and do arrive at some Christian norms, such as revenge is foolish or it is better to suffer injury than to do it. But even such people do not fully understand that the human condition is fallen and now redeemed.[38]

In *Christian Moral Principles*, Grisez devotes five chapters to prayer and the sacraments of baptism, confirmation, penance, and Eucharist, specifically from the perspective of moral theology. They are relevant to the Christian moral life because that way of life is fundamentally a communal, interpersonal relationship with the Trinity.[39]

Versus Proportionalism

In the early contraception book, Grisez disagrees strongly with the situationist approach, but in *Christian Moral Principles* he refutes proportionalism. Grisez sees a close relationship between proportionalism and consequentialism;

sometimes, however, he refers to restricted proportionalism. In fact, he puts McCormick into the category of restricted proportionalism but still strongly disagrees with him.[40] The primary problem is that proportionalism directly goes against basic human goods. In addition, these basic goods are incommensurable. How can you commensurate justice and truth? A related argument maintains that proportionalism acts as if moral situations have fixed boundaries, but they do not. You cannot really deal with all the possible paths and aspects of the moral situation, which extends in so many different directions.[41]

In response, McCormick points out that proportionalist reasoning has long been accepted in the Catholic tradition—one can go to war for a proportionate reason. The fourth principle of the double effect justifies an indirect evil if there is a proportionate reason. In a discussion about nuclear deterrence, McCormick points out that every episcopal and theological document he consulted in this time frame on this issue involves the type of weighing and balancing that Grisez excludes in principle. Even nonproportionalists have to weigh the alternatives in deciding if national self-defense justifies going to war with the aggressor.[42] In dialoguing with Fuchs and McCormick, Grisez concludes that proportionalism claims to be a reasonable method of moral judgment but ends up in intuitionism, unable to formulate any rational grounds for the exceptions they propose to traditional moral norms.[43] McCormick recognizes that "to say that proportionalism is a matter of political prudence and sometimes imprecise is not to say that it is irrational or arbitrary."[44]

Another argument claims that proportionalism leaves no real place for moral choice. Once one knows what choice produces the most good, the person has to follow that judgment.[45] Proportionalists respond that due to human finitude and sinfulness, the person could be attracted to and choose what does not result in the most good.[46]

As is to be expected, proportionalists and the new natural law theorists exemplified by Grisez have not been able to convince each other about which position is correct.[47] The heated debate between Grisez on the one hand and Catholic revisionist moral theologians such as Fuchs and McCormick on the other has very significant consequences for the practical questions of the existence of absolute moral norms. McCormick and Fuchs have disagreed with some of the absolute norms proposed by hierarchical teaching. Recall that, at least at one time, McCormick accepted some norms as being virtually exceptionless. Grisez appeals to the seventh and eighth modes of responsibility ("One should not be moved by hostility to freely accept or choose the destruction, damaging, or impeding of any intelligible good," and "One should not be moved by a stronger desire for one instance of an intelligible good to act for it by choosing to destroy, damage, or impede some other instance of an intelligible good, whether that same one or another") to defend absolute norms, including all those taught by the hierarchical magisterium.[48]

In the area of sexuality, Grisez appeals to the basic good, which he developed in *Fulfillment in Christ* but not in *Christian Moral Principles*. The permanent union of man and woman, which normally unfolds into parenthood and family life, is the eighth basic good. As a substantive good, it fulfills the natural capacities of man and woman to complement each other, have children, and bring them up. As a reflexive good, it includes the free choices by which the couple commits themselves to their marital responsibilities.[49]

Masturbation, premarital sex, and homosexual acts are always gravely wrong because they violate the good of marriage, each in its own special way. Masturbation violates the body's capacity for self-giving. Premarital sex achieves only the illusion of true marital communion. Homosexual acts use the body in a self-defeating way.[50] (Those who disagree with Grisez deny that marriage understood in this way is a basic human good that one can never directly go against.)

The Magisterium

In *Christian Moral Principles*, Grisez, writing as a theologian, addresses the response to authoritative Church teachings—the magisterium. In a significant 1978 article in *Theological Studies*, Grisez and John Ford maintain that the teaching of *Humanae vitae* is infallible by reason of the ordinary magisterium—the bishops' united witness in matters of faith and morals in their day-to-day teaching.[51]

All agree that infallibility is a gift to the whole Church. A common understanding distinguishes between the extraordinary infallible magisterium in solemn definitions made by the pope (ex cathedra teachings), the definitive teachings of an ecumenical council, and the ordinary magisterium of all the bishops in union with the pope in their "ordinary" teaching. Common teaching in the Church sees the object of infallibility as directly revealed truths or truths that have a necessary connection with revealed truth. The latter has been called the secondary object of infallibility. There is some dispute, however, about the exact meaning of a necessary connection with revealed truth, with the issue of natural law morality being most prominent.[52]

Vatican II understood the infallible exercise of the ordinary magisterium to occur when the bishops, dispersed throughout the world in communion with one another and in union with the pope, authoritatively teach on a matter of faith and morals with one judgment as something to be held definitively.[53] According to Grisez, "definitively" means the teaching is proposed as something certain—not probable or optional, and something that bishops are obliged to teach and Catholics are obliged to accept.[54]

According to Ford and Grisez, historical evidence shows that the Catholic bishops dispersed throughout the world agreed in one judgment on the morality of contraception—a judgment that remained substantially the same and was universally proposed until 1962. This universal and authoritative teaching was proposed to be held definitively. All recognized that this teaching was certain. Obeying this teaching was absolutely necessary to achieve salvation and avoid mortal sin. The magisterium permitted no differing opinions on the morality of contraception. The teaching was strongly reiterated, even when in the twentieth century other Christians no longer accepted it.[55]

In keeping with Vatican II, Grisez understood the religious assent of will to be the proper response to noninfallible teaching. According to Grisez, however, there are limits to the obligation of religious assent. There are times when an individual is unable to assent to such a teaching—for example, if a higher source drawn from faith itself makes it clear beyond reasonable doubt that some authoritative teaching is mistaken.[56]

Grisez thus recognized nonassent to such teaching as a possibility but strongly rejected the "radical dissent" that has characterized much of recent Catholic moral theology.[57] Radical dissent has introduced a new theory of the magisterium. Some even go so far as to see such dissent as a reformulation and development of doctrine. Radical dissenters have changed the very understanding of the Catholic Church. The very last line of *Fulfillment in Christ* expresses Grisez's anguish about what is happening in the Church. The dissenters are intelligent people who have tried to lighten the burdens of faith by allowing people to act contrary to the constant and very firm teaching of the Church without giving up hope of heaven. "Lightening, indeed. But at a great price."[58]

Much of Grisez's anguish came from the logic of his own position. The so-called radical dissenters (in addition to Fuchs and McCormick, Grisez also referred especially to me and Avery Dulles) insist they are disagreeing with noninfallible Church teachings. But for Grisez these are infallible teachings. His understanding of infallible moral teaching, developed in his article with Ford on contraception, logically applies to most of the other moral teachings challenged by dissenters in the Church today. Grisez himself was very willing to admit this: "Be that as it may, having been proposed with one voice by Catholic bishops as a requirement for eternal salvation, the whole body of common Catholic moral teaching concerning acts which constitute grave matter meets the requirements articulated by Vatican II for teaching proposed infallibly by the ordinary magisterium."[59] According to

Grisez, the moral issues currently disputed in Catholic circles—abortion, contraception, adultery, remarriage after divorce of persons who were sacramentally married, masturbation, premarital sex, homosexual behavior, and so on—are not noninfallible teachings that require religious assent. "Bishops for centuries have universally taught the norms on matters like these. The question of withholding religious assent only arises with regard to matters where that kind of consensus is lacking."[60]

What about Grisez's position on infallibility? First, it is a most extreme position in maintaining that the controverted moral issues in contemporary Catholic moral theology have been taught infallibly. No other Catholic theologian has made such an assertion. In one sense, it well illustrates Grisez's commitment to logical consistency. Once he based the infallibility of contraception on the certain teaching of all the bishops in union with the pope on something they were obliged to teach and the faithful obliged to obey, he logically had to see the other specific moral teachings as having been taught infallibly. Second, in my judgment, his conclusion came from a failure to recognize that the criterion that something is to be held definitively is much more restricted than the criterion that something is proposed as certain. These are two very different realities. The failure to recognize the all-important difference between teaching something as certain and teaching something to be held definitively lies at the heart of his position. This important distinction also recognizes the distinction between authoritative teaching and infallible teaching.

Third, with many others I maintain that moral teachings based on the natural law are not necessarily connected with revealed truth and hence cannot be taught infallibly.[61] In 1970, William Levada's doctoral dissertation at the Gregorian University defended this position.[62] Levada later served as prefect of the Congregation for the Doctrine of the Faith from 2005 to 2012. Grisez himself attempted in his writings to respond to these and other criticisms.[63]

Overview of Grisez's Moral Theology

Grisez's first two volumes developing his moral theology comprise almost two thousand pages. As the title of volume 1 indicates, the primary emphasis is on Christian moral principles. But Grisez insisted that his approach is in no way legalistic. The primary concern is with free choice in pursuit of the true and the good and the principles that should guide free choice. He mentions virtue and character, but they do not constitute the heart of his approach. The first part of this volume develops the theory we have already discussed. Then there is a long section on sin going from chapter 13 to chapter 18. Chapter 19 begins the discussion of fulfillment in Christ and the relationship to human fulfillment, with emphasis on the role of redemption through Jesus and God's redemptive work in the lives of Christians. Christian love is the principle of Christian life. He then treats extensively the roles of prayer and the seven different sacraments culminating in the hope of everlasting life. The final two chapters (35 and 36) deal with the truth of Christ living in the Church through the magisterium, which has been discussed earlier in this chapter.

Volume 2, *Living a Christian Life*, traces specific moral responsibilities of the baptized. Note that the title refers to *a* Christian *life* and not *the* Christian *moral life*. Grisez emphasizes the importance of the personal vocation of each person with one's distinctive gifts and opportunities. The author sees this approach as differing from the legalism of the manuals of moral theology and also secular humanism. Our author is quite negative about secular culture today. The volume begins with the role of faith, hope, charity, and repentance. In all the areas of a Christian life, one seeks moral truth through the proper moral judgment. The areas considered include interpersonal relationships, life, health, marriage, sexuality, work, property, political life, and citizenship. Grisez explores all these areas in the light of scripture, tradition, Vatican II, and the teachings of the magisterium.

Volume 3, *Difficult Moral Questions*, considers two hundred cases that laypeople might face. Here Grisez proposes his own casuistry but strongly opposes any reliance on probable opinions that characterized pre–Vatican II books on cases of conscience. In this book, Grisez applies moral principles and norms proposed by the Church to these cases. Question nine, for example, deals with the responsibilities of the professional suffering from burnout. If the professional can meet the minimum standards of the profession, one can continue on the job, but otherwise one must give up the profession. In response to question twenty-three, Grisez maintains that a mother must love her gay son but cannot condone his homosexual relationship. Grisez originally planned a fourth volume on the professional ethics of clerics and religious but was unable to finish this volume. Some of the work done for the volume is available on his website.[64]

Other Issues

Grisez treated at great length in separate monographs the issues of abortion, euthanasia, and nuclear deterrence. He began a study of abortion in 1965 and published his very comprehensive 559-page monograph in 1970.[65] The book contains great detail about the biological, sociological, medical, legal, religious, and ethical aspects of abortion. With regard to the ethical, he staunchly defends the beginning of human life from conception. Grisez maintains that any directly intended attack against innocent human life in general and the fetus in particular is always wrong. The traditional principle of the double effect, however, is too restrictive in demanding that in the order of physical causality, the evil aspect of the act (the abortion) cannot precede the good effect (saving the life of the mother). The initiation of an indivisible process through one's own causality renders all that is involved in that process equally immediate. Thus, if the abortion and the saving of the mother's life occur in the same moral act without the intervention of another act, the abortion is not direct. Here he is applying his understanding of direct killing, which he also illustrates by dealing with the issues of self-defense, capital punishment, and nuclear deterrence. He rejects capital punishment because the good effect (preventing the criminal from further crimes or deterring others from such crimes) is not achieved in the moral act of the execution itself but in other subsequent human acts. Note that his practical differences with the traditional Catholic approach are very few and limited to the context of the life of the fetus and the life of the mother.[66] In an important 1970 article, he developed in greater detail his understanding of direct killing.[67]

In his 1993 *Living a Christian Life*, he again treats the issue of abortion and proposes a somewhat different line of argument for the personhood of the unborn. Grisez also spells out in greater detail the four conditions that must be simultaneously verified to accept the baby's death to save the mother: (1) Some pathologies threaten the lives of both, (2) it is not safe to wait, or waiting will surely result in the death of both, (3) there is no way to save the child, and (4) an operation that can save the mother's life will result in the child's death. The example he gives here was relevant in past times and might even be present where modern medical treatment is still unavailable today: If the four conditions are met in the delivery of a baby whose head is too large, the death of the baby by craniotomy could be accepted as a side effect. Note again how very rare such a case would be. However, if this judgment is in conflict with the Church's teaching, he would follow the teaching.[68]

As early as 1970, Grisez dealt with the issue of nuclear deterrence, which was a significant issue for decades in American public policy. His very radical position logically followed from his ethical theory. One can never intend to or directly attack innocent persons. The United States' deterrence strategy involves the threat to destroy without discrimination nonmilitary targets, which is often called countercity warfare. This threat is effective only if there is a willingness and serious intent to do such an act in response to an enemy nuclear attack. Such an intent is morally wrong. He logically calls for unilateral renunciation of such a threat with nuclear weapons no matter what the consequences. Grisez recognizes that the nuclear threat to attack counterforce targets (as opposed to countercity nuclear weapons) does not involve such an immoral intention. However, he seriously doubts that such a deterrent would be effective.[69] A 1987 book coauthored with John Finnis and Joseph M. Boyle Jr. develops this same thesis in great depth and detail, spelling out the ethical theory and its application to nuclear deterrence.[70]

In 1982, Grisez published a most influential article that caused the bishops in the United States to change their position on deterrence in their pastoral letter on peace, which was ultimately published in 1983. Earlier drafts of the pastoral letter had accepted, with some conditions, nuclear deterrence involving countercity nuclear deterrence. In his 1982 article, Grisez points out that in the Catholic tradition, one cannot intend what one cannot do. To justify the moral evil of an immoral intention by the good effect of such deterrence is consequentialism. If the bishops accept such a position, they logically would have to agree with revisionist Catholic moral theologians on many other issues such as contraception, sterilization, and abortion.[71]

In the third draft and the final version, the bishops changed their approach and accepted Grisez's position. Countercity nuclear deterrence is immoral. But the bishops did not want to call for total unilateral nuclear disarmament. They accepted counterforce nuclear deterrence but worked out a quite complex argument to justify it. The pastoral letter condemned countercity or counterpopulation nuclear weapons and the first use of counterforce nuclear weapons, but they did not absolutely condemn the use of retaliatory or second-strike counterforce nuclear weapons. This position allowed them to logically accept some counterforce nuclear deterrence. (Many would agree with Grisez's position that such deterrence would not be effective.) The argument in the pastoral letter was so intricate and complex that many bishops themselves did not understand it. In the final discussion of the document, the bishops actually passed an amendment opposing any use of nuclear weapons whatsoever. Only after the explanation that no absolute condemnation of retaliatory, second-strike counterforce nuclear weapons was the basis for accepting some nuclear deterrence did they reverse themselves and continue not to absolutely condemn such retaliatory second-strike counterforce nuclear weapons.[72]

In 1979, Germain Grisez and Joseph M. Boyle Jr. published a five-hundred-page monograph on euthanasia. The authors discussed the jurisprudential aspect of the question in light of the relationship between liberty and justice. The book strongly opposes active euthanasia and deals with the moral responsibilities of all those who might be connected with doing euthanasia. The ethical treatment follows the trajectory of Grisez's previous works. The book proposes the theory of the basic human goods, using Grisez's understanding of direct killing of the innocent, and includes as well a brief discussion of killing in self-defense, war, and capital punishment. The authors then apply these theoretical understandings to their opposition to euthanasia. The book is written primarily from the philosophical perspective and shows the in-depth research that is characteristic of Grisez's writings.[73]

In conclusion, Germain Grisez made a very significant contribution to Catholic moral theology. His creative intelligence and prodigious writings made him a major figure. Grisez himself, however, recognized that the vast majority of Catholic moral theologians writing today disagree with many of his characteristic positions.

Notes

1. For Grisez's own description of his life and work, see "About Germain Grisez" on the website The Way of the Lord Jesus, at www.twotlj.org/grisez_collaborators. Grisez's colleague and friend Russell Shaw has written two biographical sketches of Grisez: Russell Shaw, "The Making of a Moral Theologian," http://www.ewtn.com /library/homelibr/grisez.txt; and Russell Shaw, "Pioneering and Renewal in Moral Theology," in *Natural Law and Moral Inquiry: Ethics, Metaphysics and Politics in the Work of Germain Grisez*, ed. Robert P. George (Washington, DC: Georgetown University Press, 1998), 241–69.

2. Germain G. Grisez, *Contraception and the Natural Law* (Milwaukee, WI: Bruce, 1964). The text in this section will put in parenthesis the page numbers from this volume.

3. Shaw, "Making of a Moral Theologian," 6.

4. Grisez, "About Germain Grisez."

5. John C. Ford, "Review of *Contraception and the Natural Law* by Germain G. Grisez," *Modern Schoolman* 43, no. 4 (1966): 417–21.

6. "About John C. Ford, S.J.," The Way of the Lord Jesus, http://www.twotlj.org /Ford.html.

7. Shaw, "Making of a Moral Theologian," 9–11.

8. Grisez, "About Germain Grisez."

9. Germain Grisez, *The Way of the Lord Jesus*, vol. 1, *Christian Moral Principles* (Chicago: Franciscan Herald, 1983); vol. 2, *Living a Christian Life* (Quincy, IL: Franciscan, 1993); vol. 3, *Difficult Moral Questions* (Quincy, IL: Franciscan, 1997). Subsequent references will give just the title of the individual volume.

10. Grisez, *Christian Moral Principles*, title page.

11. Germain Grisez, "Colleagues: Joseph Boyle," The Way of the Lord Jesus, www.twotlj.org/grisez_collaborators.

12. Germain Grisez and Joseph Boyle, "Response to Our Critics and Collaborators," in George, *Natural Law and Moral Inquiry*, 213–37.

13. Grisez, "About Germain Grisez"; and Germain Grisez "Germain Grisez's Publications," The Way of the Lord Jesus, http://www.twotlj.org/other_works.html.

14. Russell Shaw, "Pioneering the Renewal in Moral Theology," in George, *Natural Law and Moral Inquiry*, 264.

15. Germain Grisez and Russell Shaw, *Fulfillment in Christ: A Summary of Christian Moral Principles* (Notre Dame, IN: University of Notre Dame Press, 1991).

16. Grisez, *Living a Christian Life*, 512–13.

17. Ibid., 507–13.

18. Ibid., 515.

19. Ibid., 510–11.

20. Edward C. Vacek, "Contraception Again: A Conclusion in Search of Convincing Arguments: One Proportionalist's [Mis?] Understanding of a Text," in George, *Natural Law and Moral Inquiry*, 50–81. For Grisez and Boyle's response, see "Response to Our Critics and Our Collaborators," in George, *Natural Law and Moral Inquiry*, 228–32.

21. Grisez, *Christian Moral Principles*, 184.

22. Ibid., 205–28.

23. Ibid., 216.

24. Grisez, *Fulfillment*, 56.

25. Grisez, *Christian Moral Principles*, 251–74; William E. May, "Germain Grisez on Moral Principles and Moral Norms," in George, *Natural Law and Moral Inquiry*, 15.

26. Grisez, *Contraception*, 60.

27. Ralph McInerny, *Ethica Thomistica: The Moral Philosophy of Thomas Aquinas* (Washington, DC: Catholic University of America Press, 1982), 50–62.

28. John Finnis and Germain Grisez, "The Basic Principles of Natural Law: A Reply to Ralph McInerny," *American Journal of Jurisprudence* 26 (1981): 21–31.

29. Grisez, *Fulfillment*, 5.

30. Grisez, *Christian Moral Principles*, 15–16.

31. Shaw, "Making of a Moral Theologian," 11.

32. Grisez, *Fulfillment*, 267–76; May, "Germain Grisez on Moral Principles," 17–18.

33. Grisez, *Christian Moral Principles*, 605.

34. Grisez, *Fulfillment*, 279.

35. Grisez, *Christian Moral Principles*, 654.

36. Grisez, *Fulfillment*, 256–66.

37. Grisez, *Living a Christian Life*, 297–98.

38. Grisez, *Fulfillment*, 291–301.

39. Grisez, *Christian Moral Principles*, 705–806.

40. Ibid., 661–64.

41. Ibid., 141–64.

42. Richard A. McCormick, *Notes on Moral Theology, 1981–1984* (Lanham, MD: University Press of America, 1984), 136.

43. Grisez, *Christian Moral Principles*, 159.

44. McCormick, *Notes, 1981–1984*, 136.

45. Grisez, *Christian Moral Principles*, 153.

46. Todd A. Salzman, *What Are They Saying about Catholic Ethical Method?* (New York: Paulist, 2003), 36–49.

47. For an analysis of this debate that tends to favor the proportionalist perspective, see Salzman, *Catholic Ethical Method*.

48. Grisez, *Fulfillment*, 92–98.

49. Ibid., 55–56.

50. Grisez, *Living a Christian Life*, 448–54.

51. John C. Ford and Germain Grisez, "Contraception and Infallibility of the Ordinary Magisterium," *Theological Studies* 39 (1978): 258–312. This article was republished in John C. Ford, Germain Grisez, Joseph Boyle, John Finnis, and William E. May, *The Teaching of Humanae Vitae: A Defense* (San Francisco: Ignatius, 1988), 117–219. Subsequent references will be to this book.

52. Francis A. Sullivan, *Magisterium: Teaching Authority in the Catholic Church* (New York: Paulist, 1983), 79–152.

53. *Lumen gentium*, no. 25 in *Documents of Vatican II*, ed. Walter J. Abbott (New York: Guild, 1966), 48.

54. Grisez, *Fulfillment*, 413.

55. Ford et al., *Teaching of Humanae Vitae*, 156–71.

56. Grisez, *Fulfillment*, 416–20.

57. Ibid., 421–37.

58. Ibid., 437.

59. Grisez, *Christian Moral Principles*, 847.

60. Grisez, *Fulfillment*, 420.

61. Sullivan, *Magisterium*, 150–52.

62. William Levada, "Infallible Church Magisterium and Natural Law" (STD diss., Pontifical Gregorian University, 1970).

63. Germain Grisez, "*Quaestio Disputata*: The Ordinary Magisterium's Infallibility," *Theological Studies* 55 (1994): 720–32, 737–38.

64. Home page, The Way of the Lord Jesus, www.twotlj.org.

65. Germain Grisez, *Abortion: The Myths, the Realities, and the Arguments* (New York: Corpus, 1970), 2–4.

66. Ibid., 333–46.

67. Germain Grisez, "Toward a Consistent Natural Law Ethics of Killing," *American Journal of Jurisprudence* 15 (1970): 64–96.

68. Grisez, *Living a Christian Life*, 488–504.

69. Grisez, *Abortion*, 338–39.

70. John Finnis, Joseph M. Boyle Jr., and Germain Grisez, *Nuclear Deterrence, Morality and Realism* (Oxford: Clarendon, 1987).

71. Germain Grisez, "The Moral Implications of a Nuclear Deterrent," *Center Journal* 2 (Winter 1982): 9–24.

72. For my description and analysis of the discussion, see Charles E. Curran, *Critical Concerns in Moral Theology* (Notre Dame, IN: University of Notre Dame Press, 1984), 135–40; and Charles E. Curran *Tensions in Moral Theology* (Notre Dame, IN: University of Notre Dame Press, 1988), 155–60.

73. Germain Grisez and Joseph M. Boyle Jr., *Life and Death with Liberty and Justice: A Contribution to the Euthanasia Debate* (Notre Dame, IN: University of Notre Dame Press, 1979).

6

Romanus Cessario

Romanus Cessario is a moral theologian who emphasizes Thomas's theological approach and understands this approach to be developed in the documents of the hierarchical magisterium of the Church, especially Pope John Paul II's encyclical *Veritatis splendor* and the *Catechism of the Catholic Church*. His *Sitz im Leben* helps to understand how he developed his moral theology.

Sitz im Leben

First, Cessario is a Thomist. This reality is intimately connected with his vocation as a Dominican priest. Thomas Aquinas himself was the most significant Dominican theologian, and the Dominican order has continued concentrating on, expanding, and developing his approach. Cessario, born in 1944, received his BA, MA, and STL (licentiate in sacred theology) from Dominican institutions in this country. He was ordained a priest in 1971 and received his doctorate in sacred theology from the University of Fribourg in Switzerland in 1980. In 2013, Cessario received the highest intellectual award of the Dominican Order—the STM (master of sacred theology). Cessario has taught at Providence College and as a member of the Pontifical Faculty of the Dominican House of Studies in Washington, DC, and for many years he has been professor of systematic theology at St. John's Seminary in Boston, Massachusetts.[1]

In all his major writings, Cessario has made clear that he is writing from a Thomistic perspective. His interest in Aquinas has focused primarily on moral theology, but he also has addressed many other historical and theological aspects of Thomism. The 2010 Festschrift presented to him on the occasion of his sixty-fifth birthday is titled *Ressourcement Thomism: Sacred Doctrine, the Sacraments, and the Moral Life*, thus showing the breadth of his published works.[2] Cessario, for example, has published a short history of Thomism, originally in French and then in English.[3]

One would expect that there has been a long history of Thomistic moral theologians, culminating in the present era, but such is not the case. As will be developed later, moral theology throughout the world and in the United States before Vatican II was identified with the manuals of moral theology, which employed a casuistic method to determine what was sinful and the degree of sinfulness. Cessario insists that these manuals, even those written by Dominicans, were not really Thomistic. In addition, in the United States, Thomism before Vatican II and even for years afterward was primarily developed from a philosophical perspective and not a theological one.

Cessario wrote his doctoral dissertation at the University of Fribourg, and ten years after finishing his dissertation he published a thoroughly revised version of it: *The Godly Image: Christ and Salvation in Catholic Thought from Anselm to Aquinas*.[4] Cessario here recognizes the fundamental importance of Aquinas's understanding of *sacra doctrina* (sacred teaching). He then deals in separate chapters with Aquinas's pertinent texts dealing with satisfaction in his biblical commentaries, his *Commentary on the Sentences of Peter Lombard*, the *Summa Contra Gentiles* and other writings, and finally the *Summa Theologiae*. The emphasis here is on divine grace, but Cessario also recognizes the importance of the created order and nature for the working of God's grace.

Cessario was most appreciative of the theological education he received at Fribourg. His first published scholarly article in *The Thomist* in 1987 discusses theology at Fribourg, with special attention to Servais Pinckaers's 1985 book *Les sources de la morale chrétienne: Sa méthode, son content, son histoire*.[5] Cessario claims, "no current English speaking author does moral theology the way Pinckaers does."[6] There is no doubt that Pinckaers has been the most important influence on Cessario's own theological development. Pinckaers (d. 2008) was a Belgian Dominican who, after receiving his doctorate in theology from the Angelicum, the Dominican university in Rome, taught moral theology at the Dominican *studium* La Sorte in Belgium. From 1975 until his retirement, he held the chair of moral theology in the French faculty of the University of Fribourg.

The focal point of Pinckaers's approach is the beatific vision with God. Aquinas first discusses the reality of beatitude in the second part of the *Summa*. For Aquinas, the end is first in intention and last in execution. The ultimate end of the beatific vision should specify all of moral theology. This loving union with the Trinity is the only true and complete happiness for every human being who comes to full human flourishing in knowing the truth and loving the good. The Christian life is specified and assisted by grace, the moral and theological virtues, and the gifts of the Holy Spirit. This beatitude and the journey toward it bring human nature to its fulfillment and happiness, but grace and beatitude are God's loving gifts that humans could never achieve on their own. Hence, an understanding of true human nature is most important for moral theology. According to Aquinas, grace builds on nature. Morality thus is based on true human flourishing and is not primarily a question of obligation deriving from some authority extrinsic to the human person.[7]

Cessario's General Approach

Cessario in his method and sources gives primacy to the theological understanding of Aquinas as proposed by Servais Pinckaers. He insists that scripture is the soul of moral theology.[8] His writings give a primary place to what he calls the classical sources that from the beginning have nourished the discipline of moral theology: the New Testament, the early Church fathers, and especially Saint Augustine.[9] His own theological writings show how often he brings in these sources in developing his moral theology. He sees these classical sources as supporting and grounding Thomistic moral theology. In addition, he sees his approach as carrying out the Vatican II mandate for a renewal of Catholic moral theology.[10]

What distinguishes Cessario's approach to Thomistic moral theology is his insistence that the encyclical *Veritatis splendor* of Pope John Paul II and the *Catechism of the Catholic Church* strongly support and enunciate the theory of Aquinas that he proposes. John Paul II wrote *Veritatis splendor* in 1993, and it constitutes a very different genre from all of his other encyclicals because it primarily concerns moral theory. In this document, the pope recognizes the crisis in Catholic moral theology and the widespread dissent from magisterial teaching.[11] Cessario likewise puts *Veritatis splendor* in relationship to the widespread rejection of Paul VI's 1968 encyclical *Humanae vitae* reiterating the Catholic condemnation of artificial contraception for married couples. The twenty-five years from 1968 to 1993, the year *Veritatis splendor* was written, represent a time in which only a limited number of Catholics accepted the teaching. He realistically realizes that the effective reception of *Veritatis splendor* among Catholic theologians remains to be evaluated.[12] There is no doubt throughout his writings that Cessario is very conscious that his own position is a minority position among Catholic theologians writing today.

On its very first page, Cessario's *Introduction to Moral Theology* highlights the importance of *Veritatis splendor* and its support for Thomistic realism. The book maintains that the understanding of the moral life proclaimed in the name of Christ by the Catholic Church is rooted in the moral realism developed by Thomas Aquinas. The book presents moral theology as integrally united with dogmatic and spiritual theology as the systematically ordered study of the journey of the human person created in the image and likeness of God back to the Father. The moral realism identified with the Thomist tradition and found in the ethical writings of John Paul II not only represents what is best in the Catholic moral tradition but also provides the most promising way to overcome the confusion and problems characteristic of much of Catholic moral theology today.[13] By giving such a prominent place to *Veritatis splendor*, Cessario thus indicates his position on the disputed issues in Catholic moral theology. He strongly supports the magisterial teaching on these issues that *Veritatis splendor* reasserted.

Cessario's emphasis on the importance of *Veritatis splendor* and the *Catechism of the Catholic Church* again also builds on the work of Pinckaers. Those who have studied with Pinckaers or carefully read his works recognize that the *Catechism of the Catholic Church* and *Veritatis splendor* indisputably bear the stamp of his moral theological outlook. These documents set out to redress the widespread errors in moral theology that gained ascendency in the immediate aftermath of Vatican II and the widespread negative reaction to Paul VI's 1968 encyclical *Humanae vitae*.[14]

In the very second paragraph of his article after Pinckaers's death discussing the Fribourg professor's place in the renewal of Catholic moral theology, Cessario points out that in 1987 few were aware "that the Holy See was turning to this distinguished University of Fribourg theology professor for assistance with two very important projects: the *Catechism of the Catholic Church* and Pope John Paul II's encyclical letter *Veritatis splendor*."[15] There is no footnote reference for this statement.

Moral Virtue and Theological Ethics

Romanus Cessario's primary contribution to moral theology has been the development of the role of moral virtue in a theological ethic. His 1999 book, which had a second edition in 2008, is a synthetic attempt to explain the moral virtues in theological ethics.[16] When he wrote, Cessario pointed out that virtue theory had a comparatively small place in recent Catholic moral theology. Casuistry, the study of individual cases often to determine what acts are sinful and the degree of sinfulness, was the approach of the manuals of moral theology, which became identified with the totality of moral theology in the four hundred years before Vatican II. Casuistry employed a legalistic approach, which saw morality primarily in terms of law and obligations. Efforts to renew moral theology after Vatican II have emphasized especially the role of proportionate reason. Although there are different varieties of this approach, proportionalist authors identify the moral life with ethical obligations concretized in norms or precepts, but as is well known they have wanted to relax the rigid moral legalism of the earlier casuistry of the manuals. Cessario proposes a virtue ethic as clearly distinguished and opposed to such ethics of obligation.[17] He sees virtue ethics rooted in the Gospel and the call of Vatican II for the renewal of moral theology. The New Testament frequently talks about the attitudes that should guide the life of the Christian. Cessario illustrates this reality with a long citation from the Letter to the Colossians 3:5–10. Put away what is earthly in you—anger, wrath, malice, slander, and obscene talk. You should peel off the old nature with the practices and acts of the new nature that is being received in knowledge after the image of the creator. As is well known, Vatican II also called for moral theology to be renewed by biblical teaching.[18]

Thomas Aquinas's development of moral theology carries out the biblical and Vatican II perspective. It is true that Aquinas has often been considered as a philosopher, but in his first question in the *Summa* he describes the work of theology as sacra doctrina based on God's revelation to us. Many see Aquinas's approach to ethics as focused only on the natural law. Yes, he does discuss the natural law but only in one question. Early in his book *The Moral Virtues and Theological Ethics*, Cessario cites a long excerpt from Aquinas on the New Law. The New Law is the gift of the Holy Spirit in the believer. This law is not something extrinsic imposed from the outside but is interior to the believer and constitutes a new heart. In the light of this New Law, theological ethics must affirm the transformation of the believer by grace.[19] Cessario, as mentioned above, frequently cites the Thomistic adage that grace perfects nature (*gratia perficit naturam*). Grace thus transforms nature and does not destroy it. Rather, it brings human nature to its fullest flourishing.[20]

To understand this relationship better, it might be helpful to see the relationship between nature and grace in light of Aquinas's insistence in the very beginning of the second part of the *Summa* that the ultimate end of human beings is happiness. Cessario often refers to this reality in many different places but without developing it in great detail. The Latin word used here by Aquinas is *beatitudo*—beatitude. The word beatitude obviously refers to the Beatitudes found in the Gospels of Matthew and Luke. Beatitude involves full human flourishing. Aquinas begins his discussion in the second part of the *Summa* with the question of happiness and what makes human beings happy. We are happy when our highest powers achieve their end. Throughout all his writings, Cessario rightly insists on the teleological nature of Aquinas's moral teaching. The higher God-given powers of human nature are the spiritual powers of intellect and will, which human creatures alone possess. The human intellect seeks the truth, and the human will seeks the good. Aquinas points out, as all recognize, that wealth, power, fame, and health do not make one truly happy. The human quest for the true and the good, however, can never attain its fullness in this world. In fact, human powers on their own remain incapable of achieving their ultimate end and fullness. The fullness of human flourishing—the attainment of the God-given end—can occur only in the beatific vision in love with God wherein the intellect and will come to embrace their ultimate end. God's gift of grace and glory alone can bring the human person to beatitude, but in the process this gift builds on, perfects, and transfigures the basic teleology found in all human beings.[21]

Cessario sees Aquinas as building on Augustine's famous statement from *The Confessions*: "You have made us for yourself, O Lord, and our hearts are restless until they rest in thee." Beatitude is the full realization of our human flourishing in which we fully know and love God in the beatific vision. This beatific fellowship with God and personal fulfillment still recognizes the limits of a created human nature. We come to the fulfillment of our human nature, but human nature is not done away with. Our created nature reaches its teleological fulfillment, which it cannot achieve on its own but only by the gracious gift of God.[22]

In keeping with his insistence on anthropology, Cessario points out that Thomistic theologians recognize three stages of the *imago Dei* (image of God) in the human person. First, there is the natural image of God based on creation that gives the aptitude of fully knowing and loving God. Aquinas rightly starts with what creation gives us and what can ultimately be achieved only by a gracious gift from God. What is potentially and aptitudinally an image of the divine person by the gift of creation is a historical reality frustrated by human sinfulness. The second stage of the image of God is the supernatural image through grace making the person a friend of God. In glory—that is, in beatitude—the image of God reaches its final and fullest existential state. This involves the final rest and fulfillment of human flourishing, thanks to the beneficent gift of God's full friendship and love.[23]

In his book on the moral virtues and Christian faith, Cessario builds on this Thomistic distinction of the relationship between nature and grace.[24] Aquinas defines virtue as a good operative *habitus*. Virtue is thus productive of good ends. Virtue signifies a class of qualities that are stable or "habitual" features of one's personality. Moral virtues are firmly rooted dispositions for specifically good human activity that both constitute and describe the moral character of the person. Virtue disposes the person to do good acts but also makes the person a better person. Virtues can and should grow and develop as part of true moral growth.[25] There is a problem with the English word "habit" as a translation of the Latin "habitus." The English word refers to a behavior pattern that operates almost in an involuntary way. Habitus in the scholastic sense means above all openness to creative activity and not mere repetition.[26]

Virtue has three characteristics: first, the promptness or readiness to do something; second, ease or facility in doing the action; third, joy or satisfaction while doing it. Thus, the generous person is ready to do generous deeds, has a facility in doing them, and enjoys doing such deeds. Virtues modify the basic powers of human nature. The two powers proper to human beings are the intellect and the will. Human beings share with all other animals the two sense appetites: the irascible appetite that strives to do what is difficult and the concupiscible appetite that desires what is good or pleasurable. Moral virtues differ from intellectual virtues, which do not affect the whole person but just the intellectual power. Thus, the virtue of geometry or the culinary arts helps one to think better or make a good meal, but they do not affect the whole person. One can encounter a gluttonous geometrician or a cheating chef. The moral virtues affect the whole person to do good in particular circumstances.[27]

Moral virtues are distinguished by Aquinas and many of those who went before him from the three theological virtues. The need of the theological virtues for Aquinas comes from his recognition of the twofold end of human life—the natural and the supernatural. The New Testament insists on the radical change that the grace of Christ brings about in one who is a friend of God and destined for beatitude. These theological virtues constitute the capacities given to the Christian to enable a personal relationship with the triune God through the grace and gift of the Holy Spirit. The three theological virtues of faith, hope, and charity are the gifts of a loving God so that the Christian person can enter into friendship with the triune God. These are called theological virtues because they have God's own self as their object. As scripture and tradition point out, charity or love is the greatest and most important of all the three theological virtues. Faith, however, precedes the other two virtues of hope and love in the order of their coming to exist in a person because the human will cannot hope or love unless it first knows the gracious God. Thus, faith modifies the human intellect, and hope and love modify the human will so that the person can truly be in a loving relationship with the triune God. The theological virtues thus are habits or qualities that enable the Christian to enter into loving relationship with God, with faith modifying the intellect and hope and love modifying the will to bring about such a relationship.[28]

Cessario shows that Aquinas develops the moral virtues on the basis of the cardinal virtues. Plato, Aristotle, and Cicero recognized the cardinal virtues. In the Christian tradition, Ambrose, Augustine, and Gregory the Great, as well as many fathers of the Church and the scholastics, also saw the moral virtues in light of the cardinal virtues.[29] "Cardinal" does not mean they are necessarily the most important virtues but that they are the logical hinges (*cardo* means hinge) for developing all the virtues. The four cardinal virtues modify the four human capacities or powers—the intellect and will that are proper to human beings and the sense appetites that humans share with animals. Prudence modifies the intellect, justice the will, fortitude the irascible appetite, and temperance the concupiscible appetite. All the other virtues in one way or another fit logically under one of these four virtues.[30]

In Aquinas there is a most important distinction of two types of moral virtues—acquired and infused. Acquired moral virtues are the work of human beings without the grace of God. We develop acquired virtues over a period of time by means of repeated instances or patterns of good human activity. These virtues influence the sphere of human action and decision-making. These are the virtues that the philosophers wrote about and continue to write about. These virtues, in Augustine's words, operate in the human city since they shape the moral character of the good citizen working in the political and social community. On the other hand, infused virtues are spiritual endowments that originate entirely in the sanctification that Christian theology attributes to the work of the Holy Spirit. They do not depend originally for their existence on the free exercise of human energy and capacities. Rather, they are freely bestowed graces that enable the believer, who nonetheless continues to act freely under their impulse, to undertake and persevere in the Christian life. These are the virtues that build up the city of God.[31] Cessario explains his moral theology on the basis of the infused moral virtues.

How then should we understand the infused virtues and their relationship and role in the supernatural life of grace and friendship with God?[32] For Aquinas, the substance of the soul remains distinct both conceptually and really from the capacities or faculties of the soul. Grace is what modifies the substance of the soul so that through the triune God's gift the person is now in friendship with God. Virtue qualifies directly the capacities of the soul, not its substance, so that each capacity—intellect, will, and sense appetites—operate on the level of our friendship with God. For Aquinas, grace or charity is not enough: The infused virtues as gifts contribute to the God-given character of the person and enable the person to perform supernatural acts based on the teleology of the individual virtues (e.g., justice or fortitude). The infused virtues that modify the rational and sense appetites integrate the great variety of individual goods into the perfection of choosing and loving God.

The infused moral virtues are another good example of the Thomistic recognition that grace builds on nature. Just as the acquired virtues help the person more readily and easily act in accord with the knowledge of the natural order, so in the supernatural order the infused virtues help the believer to act more readily and easily in accord with the human capacities that are now enabled by God to live in the world in accord with what friendship with God calls for. This emphasis on virtue and infused virtue also differentiates Thomistic ethics from all ethics of obligation and legalism. Thomistic ethics is intrinsic—based on what is in accord with true human flourishing and not dependent on some extrinsic law or obligation. There is a place for norms in moral theology, but they are the requirements of true human flourishing.

Cessario points out that John Duns Scotus, the thirteenth-century Franciscan scholar, disagreed with Aquinas on infused moral virtues. Scotus held that a person with theological faith and divine charity needs no other divine aid to direct one's life toward heavenly pursuits. For Aquinas, holiness suffuses and transforms the whole person. The grace of the infused moral virtues shapes and energizes the human operative capacities of intellect, will, and sense appetites so that the human person can act promptly, joyfully, and easily in all areas of life as a friend of God. Such an approach is definitely more in keeping with the New Testament insistence on the radical change that grace brings about in the human person.[33]

Some Catholic authors found it difficult to locate divine infused virtues in the concupiscible appetite because of the effect of original sin. Aquinas, however, recognizes the need for infused virtues even with regard to the sense appetites. A realist theology avoids any duality of the spiritual and the material. Virtue can and should transform all truly human behavior. The concupiscible and irascible appetites, which in themselves constitute the emotional life of the human person, possess the capacity for true virtuous formation also in the order of grace. These infused virtues are the cardinal infused virtues of fortitude and temperance.[34]

Cessario recognizes the relationship and the differences between the acquired and infused virtues. Christian realism maintains that basic human nature, with its inherent goodness through creation, is not destroyed by sin but is wounded. This wounded nature, however, cannot sustain a vigorous moral life for a very long time. Sin, however, affects acquired and infused virtues differently. An acquired virtue requires the conscious repetition of actions, so also its loss requires a certain number of contrary actions and not just one mortal sin. Infused moral virtues, however, are not compatible with mortal sin since the infused virtues rely on a graced relationship with God. One mortal sin involves the loss of grace and the infused virtues.[35]

Acquired and infused virtues comprise an organic unity in the believer. Since the infused moral virtues derive from divine grace, they form a specifically distinct habitus from acquired virtues. Acquired virtues are analogates of infused virtues. They are analogous, but they are not the same. Also, the infused virtues observe a different norm or measure than acquired virtues. The "form" (as distinct from the matter in hylomorphic theory) of infused virtue is a real participation in the imitation of Christ. This formal difference explains the reality of self-renunciation that goes even to the extreme of martyrdom for the believer.[36] To illustrate the relationship between the infused and the acquired virtues, Cessario develops two concrete alternatives: first, the case of the believer who enjoys the life of grace but does not possess a particular acquired virtue, and, second, the case of the person who possesses acquired virtues but does not enjoy the graced relationship with God.[37]

Cessario discusses prudence at great length—the only infused moral virtue that receives such treatment. Why? Cessario deals with theological ethics. He considers the other infused cardinal and moral virtues in general just to show how they are incorporated into the theological moral life. But realist moral theology assigns prudence a large and ambitious role because prudence must assure that each human act is both the complete form of moral goodness and at the same time in accord with moral science. Prudence is right reason about what is to be done. Prudence is both an intellectual and a moral virtue. Prudence remains a virtuous act of the intellect, but to bring this about prudence requires that the commanded action conform to the inclinations and ends of the rectified appetites. Christian wisdom develops in an individual as a result of both inclination and experience. For the moral theologian, human experience entails the proper interaction between the human subject and the world of created realities—that is, the specific objects of experience. The infused moral virtues and prudence exercise a causal influence on each other. Prudence has the role of a rational measure harmoniously directing and shaping the movements of the appetites toward the ultimate end of human flourishing. Cessario calls this the unitive function of prudence.[38] Prudence does not appoint the ends of the infused moral virtues but arranges actions to reach the ends. Prudence enables one to discover the right way to implement a particular moral virtue.[39]

Cessario raises an important theological question: Does an infused-virtue-centered moral theology made concrete for the individual by prudence fail to recognize the importance of divine grace in the practice of the Christian life? Authentic Catholic teaching on the life of divine grace asserts that the created will possesses no power to work onto salvation apart from a prior free exercise of the divine initiative. Scholastics call this a *gratia operans*. The infused virtues originally come from the freely bestowed grace of the Holy Spirit active in the lives of believers and not from the exercise of human willpower. The enduring human ability to live the virtuous life always requires the continued presence of divine cooperative grace. Aquinas insists that grace freely moves the human person.[40]

Cessario points out that Aquinas maintains that the gifts of the Holy Spirit complete and perfect the virtuous theological life of the Christian. The gifts represent the different ways in which the individual believer receives divine impulses and inspirations that assist one in performing virtuous activity and living out the Christian life. According to the traditional enumeration, going back to the book of Isaiah, the seven gifts of the Holy Spirit are wisdom, understanding, counsel, fortitude, knowledge, piety, and fear of the Lord. The gifts are different from the virtues. The gifts perfect the powers or capacities of the soul to receive the inspirations of the Holy Spirit, whereas the infused virtues perfect the rational and sense appetites to achieve their proper ends that are then ordered to loving union with God. The gifts thus are permanent spiritual endowments providing additional aids to live out the virtuous theological life of grace.[41]

A primary contribution of Cessario is to expound theological Christian ethics on the basis of the reality and role of the infused moral virtues in general. Here he is true to Aquinas but develops the infused virtues in much greater detail than Aquinas does in the *Ia IIae* of his *Summa*.[42] In addition, Cessario also takes great pains to show that this approach is in accord with scripture, especially the New Testament, and the earlier patristic writings, even though some scholastics such as John Duns Scotus do not recognize the existence of infused virtues.

Aquinas discusses what is today called moral theology in the second part of the *Summa*, which is divided into the *Ia IIae*, the first part of the second part, and the *IIa IIae*, the second part of the second part. In *Ia IIae*, Aquinas treats what today is called fundamental moral theology, which deals with aspects of moral theory that are common to all the particular areas of moral conduct. Special moral theology, which Aquinas develops in *IIa IIae*, deals with the particular areas of morality that Aquinas develops on the basis of the cardinal and moral virtues. As noted above, Cessario basically deals with the general discussion of the virtues in *Ia IIae*, except for the large section he devotes to the virtue of prudence in his book *The Moral Virtues and Theological Ethics*.

In 1994, Cessario wrote what amounts to a commentary on *IIae IIae* with a discussion of the theological and cardinal virtues. This book originally appeared in Italian in 1994 as part of *AMATECA*, an international series of handbooks in Catholic theology. An English version was published in 2002.[43] What is distinctive about this book is that all the moral virtues are discussed only as infused Christian virtues. Since this chapter deals primarily with the issues of method and approach, it will not discuss this book's discussion of the individual theological and cardinal moral virtues.

The Natural Law and Theological Ethics

A second contribution of Cessario is to consider the natural law in a theological context. Once more he recognizes a subordinate but significant role for the created or the natural (in this case, the natural law) in the context of his theological approach. For Aquinas, moral theology, like all of theology, is *sacra doctrina*, which embraces everything that God has revealed about Godself and about the created universe. It is the divine plan for our salvation. Aquinas's schema for developing his total theology is *exitus-reditus*—a downward procession of all things coming from God and the return of human beings to God. The disciplines often called dogmatic theology (theology that deals with the reality of God) and moral theology are distinguished only for pedagogical reasons with moral theology as the return of the rational and redeemed creature to God, which is developed in the second part of the *Summa*.[44]

Aquinas's realistic theological method is based on the foundational truth that the principles of the being and the truth of anything are the same. Realistic moral theology is based on the adage "*agere sequitur esse*"—actions follow from our being. The human being is an imago Dei, which, as mentioned in the discussion on virtue, has three stages: the natural image of God in creation, the image of God brought about by grace, and the full image of God in glory and beatitude. The created human person through intellect and will seeks the true and the good. The total flourishing of the human person—beatitude—comes only as a gift of God in heaven. Grace initiates the human person into this friendship with God. Our ultimate end remains uncreated good—God, who alone can fill the will of human beings to the brim because of God's own infinite goodness. In beatitude it is the human person who is fulfilled in loving union with the triune God. Thomistic moral theology is thus realistic and intrinsic. The good is what contributes to human flourishing, but true human flourishing that is grounded in created human nature can be achieved only by the gracious gift of God in grace and glory. The Church teaches something because it is true; it is not true because the Church teaches it.[45]

Moral realism operates within the framework of a highly refined teleology. Cessario describes Christian moral theology as one that explains and evaluates human behavior on the basis of whether a given human action properly and opportunely attains a good that conduces to the perfection of the agent. Broadly speaking, good moral action develops out of a proper love of those goods that constitute human flourishing. Cessario, however, does not develop a list of these goods. Recall that Germaine Grisez described in detail eight basic human goods. Such an approach is opposed to deontological approaches, which are based primarily on duty and obligation that comes from outside the person. But such an approach is also opposed to consequentialism and proportionalism, which are based on the consequences of the action.[46]

To engage seriously the task of discerning what constitutes human well-being requires that one conform to the divinely revealed wisdom that orders and shapes human conduct. There is a twofold reality in divine wisdom. It first refers to the image or exemplar that governs the activity of created things. Scripture and theology refer to this as the preexisting Logos, or Word of God, which is the true pattern according to which all things were made. Second, wisdom refers to the principle that moves every being to its proper end or goal through the sovereign attraction of the end or goal. In the sense of both exemplar and guiding principle, Thomists speak of eternal law as an analogical expression of the divine wisdom. Since human language always falls short of revealing divine truth, language is analogical and not univocal. The eternal law is how God wants the world to be—the full revelation of God for our salvation.[47] Those who do not have God's revelation, as Paul reminds us in Romans, can come to some knowledge of God's plan. The natural law for Aquinas thus is the participation of the eternal law in the rational creature. The natural law moves human conduct toward the human good. Such a natural law approach differs from secular humanism and idealism, which sees only human realities, because for the natural law the human person is an image of God, and the natural law finds its exemplar and model in the divine Logos. In addition, the Thomistic approach is based on God's wisdom and rational ordering, not on the will. The divine ordering through the intellect and not the divine will is primary. The Thomistic approach is not voluntaristic.[48]

In the post–Vatican II period, according to Cessario, classical natural law theory received little attention from Catholic moral theologians. Revisionist moral theologians rejected the classical theory because of its prescientific anthropology that does not recognize the role of historical consciousness, proposing a psychology absolutizing the faculties of the person rather than the person's own self, and because of its giving too much importance to the biological and physical aspects. On the other hand, exclusive Christocentric theologians, such as Hans Urs von Balthasar, reject the natural law and human reasoning because of this exclusive Christology.[49]

The natural law is not the only resource needed for a complete theory of Christian morality. It provides a starting point for discovering the concrete forms of moral goodness. The economy of salvation as a free and gracious gift of God alone can bring the human person to one's true fulfillment and beatitude.[50] In his *Introduction to Moral Theology*, Cessario has a long section on the New Law without going into detail about its precise relationship to the natural law.[51]

I think it is helpful to distinguish between the theological aspect of the natural law and the philosophical concept. The theological aspect refers to the role in the total theological picture. Cessario, as explained above, has seen both the need for and limitations of the natural law to be based on the concept of creation. There is a role for the natural law in moral theology, but it is not the primary source of moral theology, which comes from revelation and God's gift of grace. From the philosophical perspective, it refers to the meaning of human reason and human nature that has been extensively treated by Thomistic philosophers. In his basic introductory text on moral theology, Cessario briefly discusses this aspect.

The natural law involves a twofold participation in the eternal law. First, the natural law enables persons to participate cognitively in divine wisdom. Second, the natural law involves the structural tendencies or natural inclinations found in human nature. The natural law moves the person toward the particular goods that constitute true human flourishing and perfection. The practical intellect grasps the first principle of morality based on the nature of the good as that which all human beings desire. For Aquinas, the principles of the natural law embody inclinations to a course of actions that conform to the shape of our shared human nature. Thomas thus proposes a realist and naturalist approach to morality that differs from nonnaturalistic approaches (e.g., idealism) that base morality on mental structures and not on the being of human nature. Since Aquinas believes that human nature is sufficiently invariant across cultures, his morality claims a universal validity.[52]

Aquinas maintains there are three basic inclinations in human nature: the inclination to self-preservation, which humans share with all creatures; the inclination to procreation and the rearing of offspring, which humans share with animals; and the inclination to knowledge about God and living in human society, which is proper to humans as such. The commentators on Aquinas refer to these as the three primary precepts of the natural law. The natural law does not involve a materially exhaustive and closed set of instructions and deductive entailments governing every aspect of human conduct. The general precepts of the natural law articulate the basic inclinations to embrace the perfective ends of human flourishing. These inclinations, however, are only the foundation for the morally significant knowledge achieved connaturally through the contribution of the virtues. The previous section pointed out the need for all the virtues but especially the primary role of prudence. Notice here the synergy between the natural law and virtue. However, Cessario maintains that the natural law still furnishes some absolute norms that are binding on all human beings.[53] Recall in this context his insistence that the papal encyclical *Veritatis splendor* and the *Catechism of the Catholic Church* are true expositions of the Thomistic teaching.

Other Issues

In the course of developing his own approach, Cessario made scattered references to other approaches but only gave a sustained treatment to the casuistic method of the manuals of moral theology that came into existence after the Council of Trent in the sixteenth century and lasted until Vatican II. It seems somewhat odd to spend so much time on the manuals of moral theology since they have not been in use for over fifty years, but the discussion helps to illustrate the difference with his Thomistic approach. Here he recognizes that his own approach is based heavily on the work of Pinckaers. The primary problem with the manuals was their understanding of human freedom as the freedom or liberty of indifference. The person remains radically indifferent or undetermined when judging about the good to be done. This denies the basic Thomistic approach that human reason and human appetite are ordered to the true, the good, and human flourishing. Such an understanding of freedom was originally found in the nominalism of William of Ockham, which in its own way influenced the development of the manuals. The approach of the manuals is legalistic, with law replacing human goods; it is voluntaristic, based on divine law and not based on *recta ratio* and the ends of the rational and sense appetites seeking the good; and it is an ethic of extrinsic obligation and not of human flourishing that recognizes the inward attraction and intrinsic efficacy of divine and the natural law. Such an approach to morality is individualistic, minimalistic, concerned only with the morality of acts, and not interested in virtue and human flourishing.[54]

Some of the problems mentioned with regard to the manuals of moral theology are also present in almost all of modern philosophical ethics. Moral theories, which reject the understanding that the human person achieves its perfection through freely accomplished virtuous actions, are committed to developing ethical approaches that reject the realistic teleology found in Thomism. Consequentialism and utilitarianism with roots in the British moral tradition judge morality somewhat mathematically on the basis of consequences of the overall good accomplished for the largest number. Kantian deontology, which is typical of continental schools of ethics, grounds moral judgment in the duty or obligation to follow a moral imperative usually resulting from a priori moral reasoning.[55] The Enlightenment stressed the autonomous human reason of the human person, whereas the Thomistic natural law approach sees human reason and the natural law as grounded in the eternal law. In addition, Enlightenment thinkers also embrace the basic understanding of freedom as freedom of indifference.[56]

The Dominican theologian also strongly disagrees with the revisionist approaches in contemporary Catholic moral theology, which in this volume are represented by Bernard Häring and especially Josef Fuchs and Richard A. McCormick. Revisionist thinkers have objected to the traditional natural law approach by insisting on the centrality of the human person, and not human nature and the reality of historical consciousness, to explain human development and change. In addition, the revisionists maintain that the Thomistic approach absolutizes the physical and biological aspects of the human person. Without developing his argument, Cessario insists that since Thomistic natural law theory takes our physical being seriously, the basic grounds for the natural law are the built-in structures of human nature that ultimately participate in the eternal law.[57]

Cessario recognizes it is difficult to determine what denotes someone as a revisionist moral theologian, but in a general way they adopt some form of proportionate reasoning as a main feature of their moral methodology.[58] The exact meaning of proportionalism differs somewhat among various authors, but in general they recommend a greater flexibility with regard to norms based on factors such as weighing of results, the urgency of a particular situation, or the hierarchy of values. But such an approach, despite its flexibility, identifies the moral life with obligations concretized in norms or precepts (however flexible) and has little or no place for virtue.[59]

Cessario occasionally disagrees with compromise approaches. Some had proposed the reality of compromise because of the presence of sin in the world. Without mentioning this position, he insists that sin should not make us look for compromises.[60] A pragmatic and expedient spirit drives compromise moral theologies because of the alleged beneficial results coming from such action. Christians, however, recognize there will always be the reality of suffering in this world. As *Veritatis splendor* tells us, the unacceptability of consequentialist, proportionalist, and compromise approaches is evident in the witness of the Christian martyrs.[61]

Cessario holds on to absolute, universal, and exceptionalist moral norms, which the proportionalists tend to reject. Here again his primary aim is to develop his own approach and not to engage in in-depth discussion on this particular issue of absolute norms. For him such norms are based on human nature, which is common to all human beings. In one article he pays more attention to moral absolutes in the light of Pope John Paul II's teaching in *Veritatis splendor*, but here again it is mostly just a summary of the teaching of *Veritatis splendor* without any further reasoning or elucidation. *Veritatis splendor* stresses that freedom is not the freedom of indifference but that freedom must be seen in light of the truth and the good. There is a sort of connaturality between the human person and the true good. *Veritatis splendor* marks a new beginning for moral theology by unambiguously recognizing the need for "exceptionalist moral norms" that reflect divine truth. Such moral norms are important, but they are by no means the whole or even the primary aspect of the Christian moral life.[62]

The Dominican theologian is not engaged in a detailed analysis or defense of the sexual norms that the revisionists generally dispute. As a strong defender of *Humanae vitae* and *Veritatis splendor*, he obviously accepts the teachings of the papal magisterium on these issues. In his very short treatment of chastity in his book on specific theological and moral virtues, he summarizes Thomas's teaching in less than one page based on the inclinations of human nature. The sexual norms are invariable and precise. The only order for sexual activity exists between lawfully married man and woman; the measure for sexual gratification is that which respects both the unitive and procreative purpose of marriage. Thus, fornication, contraception, adultery, masturbation, and homosexual acts, among others, are always wrong.[63] Elsewhere in light of the fundamental importance of the object of the human act, he sees the object of the act as always condemning sexual acts such as adultery and masturbation.[64] In light of the very extensive discussion of these sexual issues, one wonders why Cessario does not treat them in great depth.

Cessario strongly differs from revisionists by not accepting the possibility and reality of dissent from noninfallible teachings of the papal magisterium on moral issues. Here again one is surprised by his short and brief discussion of such a controversial issue. He spends less than four pages on the magisterium in his *Introduction to Moral Theology*.[65] Elsewhere the Dominican theologian explicitly recognizes the existence of the contemporary debate about the role of the magisterium.[66] However, in the brief treatment in his *Introduction to Moral Theology*, he simply repeats the position generally accepted by all Catholic theologians that Catholics owe a religious assent of intellect and will to the noninfallible teaching on moral issues. Without any further explanation of this very controverted issue, such a statement settles the issue for him. There can be no dissent from such teaching. The fragility of human reason itself left to its own resources helps to appreciate the need for the Church's teaching office.

It is important to recognize why Catholics should accept the magisterium's teaching and not dissent. He does not explicitly mention the fact that for many the reason for accepting the teaching of the magisterium is based on the authority of the Church, as in the position of John Ford. The

Dominican theologian cannot accept this position, however, because it goes against his basic understanding that morality does not involve the legalistic framework of freedom versus authority. The ultimate basis for morality is truth. God guarantees the truth of what the Church teaches. One willingly accepts the teaching of the magisterium because its truth is guaranteed by God.[67] Elsewhere he emphasizes that the acceptance of the teaching of the Church's magisterium is not a form "of ecclesiastical moral positivism" (because the Church says so) but because the truth of the teaching is guaranteed by God.[68]

Cessario very briefly also criticizes fundamental option theories. These theories locate moral evaluation primarily in the subject's personal disposition toward God and not on the concrete moral acts themselves. The magisterium correctly warns that the fundamental option theories can foster self-deception.[69] In addition, fundamental option theories fail to recognize the distinctive formation that virtues give the moral powers to perform good actions.[70] In an article discussing the present pastoral scene, the Dominican theologian strongly criticizes the contemporary Catholic culture for forgetting about the reality of mortal sin and its consequences in the loss of grace and ultimate exclusion from everlasting happiness. Too many Catholics today think they can go to communion even if they have committed what a past generation knew were mortal sins. Cessario accepts the traditional teaching that mortal sin is the deliberate transgression of a grave precept of God, which turns us away from our ultimate end. Perhaps because of the pastoral nature of this article, he does not mention there the problems connected with fundamental option theories.[71]

In a number of places the *Introduction to Moral Theology*, especially in its footnotes, praises aspects of the approach of Germain Grisez and John Finnis.[72] While recognizing Finnis as a stalwart defender of objective moral norms, Cessario criticizes him for refusing to acknowledge that natural law is truly law.[73] But he does not appear to deal with Grisez's position of accepting the naturalistic fallacy that one cannot derive an "ought" from an "is." Grisez thus does not accept the metaphysical realism that is so central for Cessario. Recall that Grisez himself recognized that his position here was not truly Thomistic.

In conclusion, Romanus Cessario's major contributions are his insistence on the theological aspect of Thomistic ethics and the importance of the infused moral virtues for moral theology. Not all Thomists would agree with his strong support for John Paul II's encyclical *Veritatis splendor*. Cessario obviously disagrees with the revisionist approaches to moral theology, but he does not enter into a detailed refutation of the theory of proportionalism and many of its central positions, such as the legitimacy of dissent from noninfallible teachings and the denial of many of the negative absolute moral norms in the area of sexuality.

Notes

1. "Romanus Cessario," Saint John's Seminary, http://www.sjs.edu/wp-content/uploads/2014/08/Rev.-Romanus-Cessario-CV.pdf.

2. Reinhard Hutter and Matthew Levering, eds., *Ressourcement Thomism: Sacred Doctrine, the Sacraments, and the Moral Life: Essays in Honor of Romanus Cessario, O.P.* (Washington, DC: Catholic University of America Press, 2010). This volume gives a complete bibliography of his writings up to the time of publication (373–79).

3. Romanus Cessario, *Le Thomisme et les thomistes* (Paris: Cerf, 1999); Romanus Cessario, *A Short History of Thomism* (Washington, DC: Catholic University of America Press, 2003).

4. Romanus Cessario, *The Godly Image: Christ and Salvation in Catholic Thought from Anselm to Aquinas* (Petersham, MA: St. Bede's Publications, 1990).

5. For the English translation, see Servais Pinckaers, *The Sources of Christian Ethics*, trans. Mary Thomas Noble (Washington, DC: Catholic University of America Press, 1995).

6. Romanus Cessario, "Theology at Fribourg," *Thomist* 51 (1987): 361.

7. Ibid., 340–43.

8. Romanus Cessario, "Scripture as the Soul of Moral Theology: Reflections on Vatican II and Ressourcement Thomism," *Thomist* 76 (2012): 165–88.

9. Romanus Cessario, *Introduction to Moral Theology*, rev. ed. (Washington, DC: Catholic University of America Press, 2013), xvii.

10. Cessario, "Scripture as the Soul of Moral Theology," 168–71.

11. Cessario, *Introduction to Moral Theology*, xviii.

12. Romanus Cessario, "Moral Absolutes in the Civilization of Love," *Crisis* 13 (May 1995): 18–23.

13. Cessario, *Introduction to Moral Theology*, 1.

14. Romanus Cessario, "Hommage au Père Servais-Théodore Pinckaers, O.P.: The Significance of His Work," *Nova et Vetera* 5, no. 1 (2007): 12.

15. Romanus Cessario, "On the Place of Servais Pinckaers († 7 April 2008) in the Renewal of Catholic Theology," *Thomist* 73 (2009): 11.

16. Romanus Cessario, *The Moral Virtues and Theological Ethics* (Notre Dame, IN: University of Notre Dame Press, 1991).

17. Ibid., 12–14.

18. Ibid., 18–22.

19. Ibid., 15–16.

20. Ibid., 22–28.

21. Cessario, *Introduction to Moral Theology*, 175–83.

22. Ibid., 32–36.

23. Ibid., 28–29.

24. Cessario, *Moral Virtues*, 33.

25. Romanus Cessario, *Christian Faith and the Theological Life* (Washington, DC: Catholic University of America Press, 1996), 2.

26. Cessario, *Moral Virtues*, 36.

27. Cessario, *Introduction to Moral Theology*, 189–91.

28. Cessario, *Christian Faith*, 5–9.

29. Cessario, *Moral Virtues*, 31.

30. St. Thomas Aquinas, *Summa Theologiae*, vol. 2, trans. Fathers of the English Dominican Province (New York: Benzinger, 1948), *Ia IIae*, q. 61, 846–50.

31. Cessario, *Christian Faith*, 3.

32. Cessario, *Moral Virtues*, 52–59.

33. Cessario, *Christian Faith*, 4–5.

34. Cessario, *Moral Virtue*, 63–66.

35. Ibid., 96–102.

36. Ibid., 110–13.

37. Cessario, *Introduction to Moral Theology*, 117.

38. Cessario, *Moral Virtue*, 76–90.

39. Cessario, *Introduction to Moral Theology*, 130–31.

40. Cessario, *Moral Virtue*, 77–78.

41. Cessario, *Introduction to Moral Theology*, 197–203. It is interesting that Cessario does not develop the role of the gifts in his book on moral virtue.

42. Aquinas has scattered references to the infused virtues, such as *Ia IIae*, q. 63, a. 3c and q. 65, a. 2c and 3c.

43. Romanus Cessario, *Le virtù* (Milan: Jaca, 1994); Romanus Cessario, *The Virtues, or the Examined Life* (New York: Continuum, 2002).

44. Cessario, *Introduction to Moral Theology*, 1–8.

45. Ibid., 9–21.

46. Ibid., 42–43.

47. Ibid., 52–60.

48. Ibid., 61–65.

49. Ibid., 69–74.

50. Ibid., 75–77.

51. Ibid., 203–17.

52. Ibid., 77–85.

53. Ibid., 86–87.

54. Ibid., 219–32.

55. Ibid., 179–80.

56. Ibid., xv.

57. Ibid., 70.

58. Ibid., 68.

59. Cessario, *Moral Virtues*, 13–14.

60. Romanus Cessario, "On Bad Actions, Good Intentions, and Loving God," in Romanus Cessario, *Theology and Sanctity*, ed. Cajetan Cuddy (Ave Maria, FL: Sapientia Press, 2014), 191.

61. Cessario, *Introduction to Moral Theology*, 182.

62. Romanus Cessario, "Moral Absolutes," *Crisis* 13 (May 1995): 18–23.

63. Cessario, *Virtues, or Examined Life*, 193.

64. Cessario, *Introduction to Moral Theology*, 63.

65. Ibid., 119–23.

66. Cessario, *Moral Virtues*, 3.

67. Cessario, *Introduction to Moral Theology*, 119–23.

68. Ibid., 232.

69. Ibid., 181–82.

70. Cessario, *Moral Virtues*, 62; see also Cessario, *Theology and Sanctity*, 180.

71. Romanus Cessario, "Charity, Mortal Sin, and Parish Life," *Logos: A Journal of Catholic Thought and Culture* 19, no. 4 (Fall 2016): 86–100.

72. E.g., Cessario, *Introduction to Moral Theology*, 35n56.

73. Cessario, *Introduction to Moral Theology*, 67n45.

7

Margaret A. Farley

Margaret A. Farley shares with the authors examined thus far the *Sitz im Leben* of the significance of Vatican II and *Humanae vitae*. Since she received her PhD only in 1973, she was not immediately involved in the discussion over *Humanae vitae* but later dealt with the huge shadow that the encyclical cast on the ongoing world of Catholic moral theology.

Her Sitz im Leben includes other very different aspects.[1] As she has been a committed Sister of Mercy for more than sixty years, her religious commitment has influenced much of what she has done. This commitment also gave her a special interest in the Catholic Church. Farley received an MA in philosophy from Detroit University in 1960 and taught in the philosophy department of Mercy College in Detroit from 1962 to 1967. Her interest in philosophical ethics continued throughout her long career of teaching and writing on Christian ethics. Both her later education and the institution where she taught made her quite distinctive.

She went on to study for a doctorate in Christian ethics at Yale University, with her dissertation written under the direction of James M. Gustafson. Gustafson has had a lasting influence on her work and that of many other doctoral students. Gustafson at Yale and later at Chicago mentored many prominent professors in the field of Christian ethics today. In fact, no one has made a greater contribution in this area than Gustafson. (Protestant institutions generally refer to the discipline as Christian ethics, whereas the Catholic tradition calls it moral theology.) Gustafson's many students included Catholics as well as Protestants. He himself belonged to the United Church of Christ but was truly ecumenical and a very sympathetic and friendly critic of the Catholic tradition.[2] Gustafson was in dialogue with the most respected Catholic moral theologians in the post–Vatican II period and in 1978 published a very significant ecumenical study, *Protestant and Roman Catholic Ethics: Prospects for Rapprochement*.[3]

Margaret Farley began teaching at the Yale Divinity School in 1971 and continued until her retirement in 2007. She was the first woman to serve as a full-time faculty member there and in 1986 was appointed to the Gilbert L. Stark Chair in Christian Ethics. While at Yale, Farley, like her mentor and friend Jim Gustafson, trained a good number of significant future professors of Christian ethics. She had a widespread reputation as a very committed, excellent, and dedicated teacher. Two of her doctoral students in 2007 edited a Festschrift in her honor, *A Just and True Love: Feminism at the Frontiers of Theological Ethics; Essays in Honor of Margaret A. Farley.*[4] Not only with her doctoral students but also with her master's students, she was most generous with her time and attention. One former student and friend noted that Farley could have published much more if she had not been so generous and committed to all her students. She authored only two significant books and coedited three others, in addition to many significant journal articles and chapters in books. Her long tenure at Yale allowed her daily contact with the ethos and environment of a major Protestant divinity school in a world-renowned secular university. These relationships heavily influenced her own approach to moral theology.

Farley's major contribution is in the area of feminist ethics, which was obviously influenced by her environment at Yale and her dialogue with feminist authors in many academic disciplines. Truly a pioneer in Christian feminist ethics, she was chosen to write the articles "Feminist Ethics" in the *Westminster Dictionary of Christian Ethics* in 1986 and "Ethics and Moral Theology" for *Dictionary of Feminist Theologies*.[5] Her groundbreaking article "New Patterns of Relationship: Beginnings of a Moral Revolution" appeared in the 1975 issue of *Theological Studies*, the first major publication of Catholic feminist articles in the United States.[6]

Farley's Feminist Approach

Although Farley is recognized as a pioneering Christian Catholic feminist ethicist, she has never systematically developed her approach in a monograph. Her writings here are individual essays dealing with various aspects of Christian feminist ethics. Farley's article on feminist ethics in the *Westminster Dictionary of Christian Ethics*, which was republished as the first article in a collection of Catholic feminist ethics coedited by her, provides a summary overview rather than a systematic development of feminist Christian ethics.[7]

Feminist theory appears in a variety of disciplines, including theology. There are different approaches to feminism, such as liberal, socialist, and radical, but within this pluralism there are shared issues and values. Negatively, feminist ethics opposes sexism in all its forms—institutional structures and processes, attitudes and behaviors, and ideologies, beliefs, and theories—that establish and reinforce gender discrimination. Positively, feminism works for equality of respect and the concrete well-being of all persons regardless of gender. Feminism is for women but is not antimen. Feminism is based primarily on women's experience in coming to know what well-being means for both women and men.[8]

Christian feminist ethics shares this approach and relates it to Christian beliefs, theology, practice, and history. Negatively, it opposes the justification of the inferiority of women to men in all its different forms—male and female as total opposites (e.g., mind/body, reason/emotion, activity/passivity), the exaltation of dependence and suffering for women, and all Christian symbols that subordinate women. Positively, Christian feminism seeks true moral and religious development, the importance of virtues, a theory of love that recognizes a place for self-sacrificing love but always balanced by the principles of equality and mutuality, and more adequate theories of justice that can address the issues of power, violence, responsibility, and social cooperation.[9]

This section will try to develop in a more systematic way what Farley has written about feminist ethics in her various articles and essays. As mentioned in the survey article above, feminism relies heavily on experience as a fundamental source of moral wisdom and knowledge. Farley has addressed the fundamental importance of experience. Experience is essential for every form of knowledge, whether deliberation is a rational process or discernment is a more complex process involving the imaginative and the affective. In Christian theology and ethics, there was a turn to experience in the twentieth century.

Christian ethics commonly recognizes a number of sources of moral wisdom and knowledge: scripture, tradition, secular disciplines as various specifications of human reason in all its forms, and experience. Farley analyzes experience in dialogue with Gustafson and feminist uses of experience.[10] Experience is not just one source among others; it is an important part of the content of each of the other sources. Scripture, for example, is the record of some people's experience of God, tradition represents a community's experience through time, and humanistic and scientific studies are shaped by the experience of those who engage in them. Not only does past experience provide content for the other sources, but present experience also ultimately interprets all of them.

But the priority of experience raises problems. Whose experience counts as authoritative? Deconstructive approaches have rendered the appeal to experience more and more suspect as a guide for choice.

Farley explains how feminist theological ethics deals with experience.

Experience tests the other sources of moral wisdom and knowledge. In a somewhat paradoxical way, experience itself needs to be interpreted, but it also validates the interpretation it achieves. This is not the case of an unacceptable circular reasoning but rather a hermeneutic circle that involves a number of tests.

Feminism begins with the experience of women and the awareness of the dissonance between their interpretation of this experience and the interpretation given in culture and religious traditions. As a liberationist approach, feminism gives voice to those whose voices were absent in the other sources focusing on women's experience of injustice and the need to change the structures and systems that caused the injustice. Religious symbols have also incorporated injustices that need to be changed. By claiming their own interpretation of their own experience, women now claim a new identity—gender equality, a capacity for mutuality, genuine agency, the right to bodily integrity, new evaluations of sexuality, and gender justice in the family and society. The category of gender has been socially constructed and needs to be deconstructed in the light of women's experience. Feminists strongly oppose the gender complementarity traditionally associated with the Christian tradition because this complementarity (active/passive, reason/emotion) has subordinated the roles of women. Here Farley just hints at the problem in the Catholic tradition of claiming that our existing understandings of gender are based on human nature and that human nature is unchangeable and true in all times and circumstances. Throughout her writings, Farley has consistently recognized the danger of the Catholic tradition of claiming too much truth and certitude based on an unchanging human nature. In addition, Christian feminists call for critical reformulations of doctrines and symbols in the religious order itself. God, for example, too often has been an oppressor who uses women for the sake of men.

Farley as a perceptive academician realizes there are serious problems in learning from experience, but these problems are not intractable. Yes, experience may be socially constructed, lodged in a hermeneutic circle, and layered with meanings never fully understood, but deconstructive methods can help to arrive at some moral truths. There are processes of discovery, of consciousness-raising, of interpreting more accurately our experiences both past and present, of making explicit what was previously implicit. There are ambiguities, but feminism has shown the importance of women's experience of injustice.

Some criteria exist for deciding whose experience and which interpretations of experience should count. These criteria include coherence with generally accepted basic moral norms, intelligibility of experience in relationship to fundamental beliefs, some agreement with other sources, the integrity of the testimony of the one who is experiencing, harmful and helpful consequences of interpretations of experience, and confirmation in a community. Moral discernment can and should use these criteria in trying to arrive at truth, but experience might also challenge some of the existing norms and understandings. The ultimate authority for the priority of experience in moral discernment despite the problems is that moral truth must make sense to us. Even where there are significant differences, even contradictions, about different experiences, there are some possibilities of adjudication through communication. Sometimes the differences are only apparent, but sometimes they can be very real and disagreements will continue to exist.

Does the feminist approach admit any common or universal morality? Farley recognizes that some feminists have denied a common morality. From the practical perspective, theories of universal morality have been harmful to women and even some men. Theoretically the influence of postmodernism and deconstruction in some feminist circles argues against any universalism.[11]

In particular, Farley recognizes more specific arguments that some feminists have raised against common morality. As mentioned earlier, Farley herself pointed out a plurality of approaches to feminism. Socialist and Marxist feminists, for example, maintain that their understandings of human nature and society are socially constructed and that the prevailing worldviews reflect the power of the dominant classes. Radical feminism makes women themselves the focus of exploitation and the organizers of their own liberation. Two developments in feminist theology also argue against any universalism. Major feminists have reclaimed their bodies and insisted on the importance of embodiment. Such a focus indicates that feminist analysis is irrevocably committed to the historical, the particular, and the situated and is not open to the universal. A second development in feminist theology recognized that the experience of the Western writers of early feminist liberation did not represent the experience of all women. They were generally somewhat middle-class white women. Nonwhite, poor, black, and Hispanic women had very different experiences, thus feminism itself is not something universal. There is no doubt that for feminists the social construction of moral norms is nowhere more evident than in the historical interpretation of women's roles and duties in the family and in society.

Despite all the problems with universalism, Farley still recognizes the need for what I call "a chastened universalism." As a Roman Catholic, Farley comes from a tradition that, despite its gross failure to recognize the social construction of the norms it has often proposed as universal, has at least recognized the need for some catholicity and universality. As a social ethicist,

Farley is very much concerned about a just society or a just love in which there are some shared moral concerns. In Farley's words, "since feminism deals with the wellbeing of women and men, it has an important interest in understanding what is truly for the benefit of human persons and in arguing for the basic intelligibility of that good."[12]

Theories of unmitigated relativism are no less harmful than a universalism that claims too much certitude and universality. To adopt historical and cultural relativism abandons the field to the powerful or to conflict as the only ultimate in human existence. Farley's approach stands on the conviction that human persons can and ought to experience moral claims in relation to one another and that at least some of these claims can and ought to cross (though not ignore) the boundaries of time, culture, and history. Human persons can and should weep over commonly felt tragedies, laugh over commonly recognized incongruities, and yearn for common hope. It is possible across time and place to condemn commonly recognized injustices and act for commonly desired goals. The content of universal morality is more modest and much narrower than universal morality was in the past, but it is not empty.[13]

In her discussion of common universal morality, the Yale professor dialogues especially with postmodernist approaches. Farley recognizes that postmodernism is amorphic—a mixture of heterogeneous theories about art and architecture, literary criticism and logistics, philosophy and religion. There exists, however, some agreement about what postmodernism is against in philosophy: the universalizing tendency of the Enlightenment, the search for a stable reality behind historical contingencies, the possibility of establishing moral norms, and an ahistorical subject and moral agent. In her usual way, she first recognizes the positive contribution of philosophical postmodernism: the deconstruction of theoretical idols, the importance of particularity and difference, historical situatedness, the dynamics of power, and the false security of settled understandings of society and the world. She especially appreciates the recognition of and importance of the virtue of epistemic humility.[14] Later she would apply the virtue of epistemic humility to the Catholic hierarchical magisterium in calling for the grace of self-doubt.[15]

In some postmodern approaches, the centered self disappears and individual experience is illusory; even our bodies so important for our situatedness appear boundariless and disembodied. Rather than reject all postmodernist approaches in general, she chooses to dialogue with postmodernism in developing her own positive aspects while rejecting its denial of any communality or universalism. She defends the existence of a self capable of moral agency. In the experiences of love and suffering of others, we encounter reality of self and the other. In these experiences, we encounter reality in ourselves and in the other. In all types of love, we are awakened and touched by the lovableness of what is being loved. In the experience of accepting others, we experience the reality of ourselves and of others.[16]

No Catholic moral theologian has dialogued in such depth with post-modernism. Farley's Sitz im Leben influenced the need for such a dialogue. In a nondenominational divinity school and in a major secular university, postmodernism was an important approach that occasioned much discussion. But there is also something distinctively Catholic about this dialogue. The Catholic tradition has insisted on the compatibility between faith and reason as exemplified in the tradition of Thomas Aquinas's dialogue with, and learning from, Aristotle.

Farley's dialogue with postmodernism shows her deep knowledge of philosophy and philosophical ethics. Many of her writings show this same interest in philosophy, influenced no doubt by her early career as a professor of philosophy and her involvement in the academic life of Yale. Ironically, her most extended dialogue with postmodernism came in her presidential address to the Society of Christian Ethics in 1993.[17] Such an address, however, could have been given to any philosophical audience because there are very few references to distinctively Christian aspects.

Farley's Feminist Method

Recognizing the fundamental importance of experience and the need for some communality, Farley then develops her methodology in a twofold approach of a critique of existing realities and a reconstruction of a better reality. Such an approach has been distinctive of the feminist method.

Farley describes the first negative step as unmasking experience, deconstructing women's experience, and resisting complicity in a generalized false consciousness. She unmasks the old claims, which include the intellectual superiority of men; the innate suitableness of women and men for gender-specific roles; the physiologically determined psychology of patterns of women and men, such as the identification of men with intellect and women with emotions; the gender roles that go against equality and justice for women in the family (the husband is the head, and the wife is the heart); gender-specific variations in a right to education, work, access to occupational roles, participation in political life, and just wages; and gender differences that result in an unequal share in the burdens and responsibilities of society and church.[18]

In keeping with the acceptance of a chastened universality or common morality, Farley develops her reconstruction on the basis of respect for persons.[19] She insists even from a feminist perspective on the obligating features of the human person. There are intrinsic grounds that establish the general principle of respect for persons and specify its content. The two fundamental aspects of the human person are autonomy and relationality. With regard to autonomy, Farley recognizes the validity of God's claim that every human being is absolutely valuable as an end and not simply as a means or series of means precisely because persons are autonomous. But there are problems with an absolutized autonomy. Farley insists on a more integrated and social view of the human person. She thus proposes a second obligatory feature of persons: relationship.

There is need for both autonomy and relationality. An emphasis on autonomy alone involves a devaluation of the other and of community. Freedom here becomes only "freedom from," resulting in an excessive individualism. As a result of past history, one recognizes why autonomy is so important for feminist theory since society, culture, and the Church have denied such an autonomy, but autonomy alone is not sufficient. The danger in relationality is to give too much importance to community. The past has shown how traditional communities have perpetuated the tyranny of unequal roles and patterns of domination and subordination.

To bring together autonomy and relationality in the proper manner, Farley appeals to the Catholic understanding of the common good, which stands as a middle position between individualism and collectivism. Individualism gives too much importance to the individual person and denies the possibility of community, whereas collectivism so stresses the community that it denies the autonomy, dignity, and diversity of the individual. The theory of the common good insists that the good of the individual contributes to the good of the whole, and the good of the whole redounds to the good of individuals.[20]

On the basis of this understanding of the common good, Farley brings together autonomy and relationality. She quotes Pope Pius XII's saying that the origin and primary scope of social life is the conservation, development, and perfection of the human person. To deny women their equality and fundamental human rights harms the common good. Today the good of family, the Church, and society are better served by a model of leadership that includes a degree of collaboration among equals. Family structures that give responsibility for the rearing of children solely to the mother do not provide the greatest good to the children. Ecclesiastical structures that deny leadership roles to women do not provide the needed context for all persons to grow in their faith. The model of the relationship of the Trinity well illustrates this theory. Interpersonal communion, characterized by equality, mutuality, and reciprocity, constitutes the ideal and grounds norms that measure every human relationship.[21]

Against modernist rationalism, her approach can show that autonomy is ultimately for the sake of relationships. Against conservative forms of communitarianism, it can argue that relationships without regard for individuality and autonomy are destructive of persons and historically especially destructive of women. Against postmodernistic fusion of the self as subject into a network of systems in the womb of language, it can maintain that enduring relationships make an autonomous self ultimately possible.[22] The possibility and task of our freedom is to become truly one with our loves, and in that process shaping them—sustaining or changing, strengthening or weakening, integrating or fragmenting. Freedom then arises out of relationality and serves it. Freedom is for the sake of relationship with ourselves and with all that can be known and truly loved.[23] Farley further developed this notion of freedom in chapter 3 of *Personal Commitments*.[24]

Farley gives great importance to both love and justice in her understanding of human relationships. She recognizes that love has different meanings: equal regard for all persons, self-sacrifice, and mutuality. Unfortunately, the understanding of love within the Catholic and Christian traditions needs to be deconstructed. Yes, in that tradition all who are loved are equal before God but not as equal before one another. The reality of women was lesser than the reality of men; women were subordinated to men. Theology appealed to extrapolations from biological and sociopsychological data to support this relationship. This subordination and lesser stature of women were embedded in the totality of Western culture. A love that fails to respect persons and their needs as persons cannot be a Christian love of equal regard. Equal regard requires that women be affirmed and respected no less than men.[25]

Love as self-sacrifice also had a very negative influence on women and their roles by tying self-sacrifice to a pattern of subordinating women to men. Farley ties this understanding of self-sacrificial love as submission of women to men to the culturally accepted notion of women as passive and men as active. This active-passive dichotomy itself was rooted often in the understanding of the reproductive functions of women and men. However, the receptivity that is at the heart of Christian love is not just passivity. The receiving by the Son of his Father's love is an infinitely active receiving. So, too, is the Christian receptivity of God's love and the active receptivity of the love between humans. In true self-sacrificing love, receiving and giving are both two sides of the one reality that is the true other love. Farley goes on to say there are theological grounds for naming each of the persons in the Trinity as feminine as well as masculine. The love of women and men likewise should be truly equal and mutual.[26] Farley treats this understanding of love in her pioneering article, calling for changed relationships between women and men. Consequently, she is here limiting her understanding of love to this context.

In developing the relationships among human persons, Farley also appeals to justice. Her theory of justice, however, sees justice as the form of love. Justice means that each should be given her due. Justice requires that we affirm for all persons, women and men, what they reasonably need so that they may reasonably live as full human persons within the human and Christian communities. A just love rejects any subordination of women to men in personal relationships and opposes the institutions and structures in which such subordination is embedded.[27]

Farley's major monograph deals with sexuality under the title of *Just Love*, but the understanding of just love was part of her thinking all along. In the pioneering article that appeared in *Theological Studies* in 1975, she mentions just love at least three times.[28] A section of her 1986 volume on personal commitments also deals with just love.[29]

Personal Commitments

Although Margaret Farley is widely recognized as the leading Catholic feminist moral theologian, she has never published a monograph developing a systematic study of feminism. As mentioned, she has published only two true monographs. In 1986, she wrote *Personal Commitments: Beginning, Keeping, Changing*. The cover of the book refers to Farley as "a leader in the field of feminist ethics." But the book is not written from the perspective of feminist ethics. What happened here? The book is a development of the dissertation Farley wrote at Yale University under James M. Gustafson and defended in 1973—before her turn to feminism and feminist ethics. Farley in this book recognizes the explicit theological and even religious language of commitment only in the last chapter dealing with biblical covenant, but she assumes a Christian theological framework from the beginning. Note that she does not write out of a specifically Catholic framework but rather from a general Christian approach.[30]

Commitment is based on the possibility of making a free choice. The book focuses on interpersonal commitments, but Farley also recognizes even here the existence of a social dimension. Virtually all our commitments have limits, as illustrated by the existence of competing moral claims. Freedom, desire, love, and fidelity are all essential for relationships of commitment. Since we must be present to our commitments, chapter 5 develops a way for "free choice to prevent the loss of our love to the past and to sustain its engagement (even if a spontaneous response) in the future we have promised."[31] Chapters 6 and 7 deal with the obligations of commitments and release from the obligations. Release from the moral claim of commitment arises in three situations: (1) when it is impossible to sustain the commitment-relationship,

(2) when the specific commitment-obligation no longer fulfills the purpose of the larger commitment it was meant to serve, and (3) when a more important obligation comes into conflict with a commitment-obligation. In chapter 7, Farley uses the content of just love as the criterion in discerning the obligation. The last chapter explicitly explores the connection between the Jewish and Christian concept of covenant and commitment. In an earlier article, Farley discussed the commitment of Catholic religious.[32]

This book deals with many of the concepts that characterize her writings in feminist ethics as well with what will be found in the second major monograph, *Just Love: A Framework for Christian Sexual Ethics*. In the very first sentence, the preface states the evident concern from the beginning of the book to its end to take seriously the experience of concrete individuals. Thus, here experience is also the primary source but not the only source of moral wisdom and knowledge. *Personal Commitment* illustrates Farley's familiarity with and frequent use of philosophical ethics in developing her thought. Here, as in much of her other work, the role of moral choice is basic.

In her various articles and essays, Farley has written on a number of ethical issues. Her own interests as well as the invitations to write on various topics obviously influence what she has written. Sometimes she addresses issues from the broader Christian perspective in keeping with her role at the Yale Divinity School, but at other times in keeping with her religious and Catholic commitments she writes from a specifically Catholic perspective. This chapter will now consider her consideration of the family.

The Family

On a few occasions, Farley directly discussed the family from the Catholic perspective. Her primary analysis and criticism of the Catholic teaching on the family as found in official Church documents comes from her feminist perspective. Catholic teaching is suspect because it assigns roles in the family between the wife and the husband on the basis of different gender roles: the female as the heart, the male as the head, the male as embracing the approach of justice, and the female as embracing the approach of care. The Catholic perspective maintains that nature has designed these different roles but they are complementary. Farley, with most feminists, argues that gender is socially constructed and not based on human nature. These roles have to be deconstructed. Complementarity always involves subordination, giving the lesser role to the woman and keeping women from occupying most roles that are more important and public.[33]

Farley repudiates the three reasons that have been proposed in the past in Catholic teaching for the subordination of marriage and family life to celibacy and religious life. First, marriage and family were believed to belong to the "things of this world," which must be transcended for the sake of the kingdom of God. However, contemporary Catholic theology recognizes that the things of this world are also very much the things of God. Second, marriage is inextricably bound up with human sexuality, which itself is suspect. Theology today rightly recognizes that sexuality as created by God is fundamentally good, even though like all other things created it can be abused. The ultimate aim of sexual desire is not simply pleasure but relationship. Third, the sphere of the family is primarily women's sphere, which makes it historically and in principle subordinate to men's sphere. From her feminist perspective, she argues that such an approach is based on the faulty complementarity of gender roles so often found in Church teaching. This early article on family also emphasizes the need for justice in marriage and family and sees these primarily in terms of family violence, family structure, family stability, and the role of the family in the world.[34] Farley returns to this understanding of the need for norms of justice with regard to marriage and family in her later major work, *Just Love*.

In a discussion about the family and in other places, Farley has considered the question of the indissolubility of marriage in light of her understanding of commitments ceasing to oblige in three situations: impossibility to sustain the relationship, the marriage no longer serving the purpose it was meant to have, and a higher obligation conflicting with it. Pope John Paul II proposed both anthropological and sacramental reasons for his teaching on the indissolubility of marriage. By their ultimate gift to one another, wife and husband become one in such a way that they can no longer be separated. Such a position, however, according to Farley, fails to appreciate the limits of human freedom and is based on a very questionable concept of complementarity that involves subordination of the wife, and its emphasis on self-giving involves a loss of the autonomy and full personality of the spouses. Unfortunately, the marriage commitment can morally break down. Marriage is not indissoluble, and remarriage can be morally acceptable.[35]

In her more systematic study of sexuality, *Just Love*, Farley also considers the issues of marriage, family, and divorce. With respect to marriage and family, her perspective is more ecumenical and includes a historical overview, Christianity's influence in shaping historical and cultural approaches to marriage, the diversity of families today, and the need for justice in marriage and family in keeping with the norms of justice developed in the book for just love.[36] Her treatment of divorce in the context of the three aspects of commitment—making, keeping, changing—closely follows what she wrote earlier.[37]

Bioethics

Both in her work in the Yale Interdisciplinary Center for Bioethics and in her writings, Farley has addressed issues of bioethics and medical ethics. An article originally published in 1985 and subsequently republished in a number of places deals with feminist theology and bioethics, with most of the attention going to the theoretical aspect, which has already been described in this chapter in her approach to Christian feminist ethics. Feminist theology insists on three central considerations: relational patterns among humans, human embodiment, and correct human assessment of the world of "nature," pointing out that much of what was associated with the demands of nature in the past must now be deconstructed in light of approaches such as gender studies. Feminist theological ethics insists on the primacy of women's experience in light of the all-pervasiveness of patriarchy. The approach insists on the well-being of all persons but takes account of the historical and cultural reality of their embodiment today. The practical consideration involves only reproductive technologies. Women's experience with regard to reproduction has often been one of great pain and suffering in light of patriarchy. The medicalization of pregnancy and childbirth has added to this suffering and oppression. Consequently, as a feminist she approaches artificial-reproduction technologies with some suspicion because of this history. Farley does not condemn in vitro fertilization, the one aspect she considers in any depth, but points out that there are possible limitations, such as using the child to be only a means, and the requirements of distributive justice that might limit what one spends on in vitro research.[38]

Farley's 2002 Madeleva Lecture, *Compassionate Respect: A Feminist Approach to Medical Ethics and Other Questions*, developed the understanding of the need for compassionate respect. The Sitz im Leben of this lectureship dealing with spirituality also influenced Farley's topic and the way she treats it. Medical ethics is directly dealt with only in chapter 1 with regard to the specific issue of HIV/AIDS and there only to point out that compassion has to be normatively shaped to deal with the real needs of people in their concrete situations. In the case of HIV/AIDS, one must also recognize the importance of dealing with the understanding of sexuality, the role of women, and poverty. In this comparatively short discussion, she gives an overview of how care takes the form of love when one is suffering and in need but that care needs to be guided and formed in a way analogous to how justice structures love in a truly loving relationship.[39]

In the process of developing compassionate respect, she dialogues with both theologians and philosophers. Religions and theologians have emphasized compassion but have not given enough importance to respect;

philosophers have been better about respect but not given as much attention to compassion. Compassion sheds light on the person suffering or in
need (e.g., the patient) with all her complexity and particularity, illuminates
the situation of suffering and illness, reveals the form of relationship needed
between caregiver and patient, and is not blind to the vulnerability of those
in need and the asymmetry of caregiving relationships. Respect sheds light
on what compassion should require: the maximization of autonomy as far
as possible, protection of bodily integrity, provision of knowledge and com-
petent care, fidelity to commitments, honor to personal story, and deeply
human hopes.[40]

Farley has written extensively on HIV/AIDS, especially in the African
context, elaborating in greater detail some of the aspects mentioned in the
Madeleva Lecture. In addition, she has devoted much time and effort part-
nering with women in Africa working on the front lines to relieve the HIV/
AIDS pandemic. Farley has spelled out in great detail the depth and breadth
of her practical involvement with HIV/AIDS in Africa, carrying out in practice a preferential option for women in need and the poor.[41]

The Yale professor has also addressed the issue of abortion. In a very early
article, without revealing her own position, she addresses the impasse between antiabortionists and proabortionists by pointing out the existence of
bad faith on both sides of the debate. She discusses three significant issues:
the nature of the fetus (the proabortionists often see it as merely a part of
the woman, whereas the antiabortionists admit no ambiguity or uncertainty
about the status of the fetus); the needs and claims of a pregnant mother
(proabortionists give no importance to the relationship involving the mother
and fetus, whereas antiabortionists often do not recognize the needs of the
mother); evaluations of human life and the moral terms assigned to the act of
abortion (antiabortionists often call abortion murder even though their own
tradition is much more nuanced, whereas proabortionists often see it as just
another form of contraception). Farley hopes that both sides, with greater
clarity and modesty of claims, can transcend the present impasse and come
to a shared position arguing for a social context in which abortion becomes
unnecessary.[42]

Farley has also briefly discussed the Roman Catholic approach to the status of the fetus and the early embryo. Within the basic values that Catholics
share, there is some disagreement about the status of the embryo and fetus.
She herself points out that the human embryo in its earliest stages (before the
development of the primitive streak or implantation) is not an individualized
human entity and therefore not a person. In making this claim, she relies
heavily on the work of the Australian moral theologian Norman Ford. Farley
recognizes, though with her customary epistemic humility and modesty, that

her position is not certain. However, the weight of the evidence against there being an individualized human in the early embryo is great and more persuasive than the evidence for it. Consequently, both within the Catholic tradition and in the public forum, she supports embryonic stem cell research.[43]

Just Love

Her major monograph *Just Love* develops a framework for Christian sexual ethics. Her ecumenical approach begins with extended discussion of various interpretations of sexuality, the historical development of sexual ethics in the West, and a chapter dealing with cross-cultural perspectives, showing a great diversity of understanding.[44] The chapter on sexuality discusses embodiment, especially from the perspective of embodied spirits and gender. In keeping with her earlier writing, Farley recognizes a role for gender but argues that gender should not divide people from one another or determine roles in both the public and private spheres and that gender differences should not be seen in terms of complementarity. How do love and sex relate to one another? Sexual love involves an affective response, an affective way of being in union with the one loved, and an affective affirmation of the beloved.[45]

Her methodology for elaborating a framework for Christian social ethics follows the approach that she developed earlier. There are four sources of moral wisdom and knowledge for the Christian: scripture, tradition, secular disciplines and knowledge, and experience, with heavy emphasis on the latter. Her anthropology based on autonomy and relationality serves as the foundation for her approach. As already mentioned, love has to be formed and guided. Love is the problem, not the answer. Sexual desire and love must be just. Farley here depends on and develops the concept of just love that she used in her earlier writings. Just love requires close attention to the concrete realities of the person loved, of the one loving, and of the relationship between them. Justice has the practical meaning of rendering her or his due. We can and should shape love and desire by our free choices.[46]

Norms for just sex are based on respect for the autonomy and relationality that characterizes persons as an end in themselves and hence the promotion of their well-being. Farley proposes seven such norms: do no unjust harm, free consent of persons, mutuality, equality, commitment, fruitfulness, and social justice. These norms are truly norms, but they admit of degrees. She develops her understanding of each of these norms in some detail, but others can and do dispute her understanding of them, especially commitment and fruitfulness.[47]

In this book, Farley proposes a framework for thinking about sexual issues and limits her consideration to only three sexual issues: marriage and family,

same-sex relationships, and divorce and second marriages. The only issue we
have not yet discussed is same-sex relationships.

The structure of the book is different and even a bit odd. Her focus
throughout has been when sexual activity is appropriate in human relationships (i.e., involving different- or same-sex relationships). Farley followed
somewhat the same basic approach in an earlier article on same-sex relations,
which contains many of the ideas developed here.[48] Her primary focus has
not been on whether same-sex relations can be justified. Because of the very
intense debate on the subject, however, she now considers just three issues
related to the justification of same-sex relations. First, she discusses the four
sources and concludes that none of the sources provides much light on the
issue understood as whether same-sex relationships are always permitted or
prohibited. Second, the book applies here the just norms previously developed to same-sex relationships to show that they can truly be just, true, and
good. In the process, she explains in somewhat greater detail some of the
norms, especially that of fruitfulness and how it applies. A third consideration
focuses on whether the sexual orientation is given or chosen. Most have
justified same-sex relationships because of the given sexual orientation of
the person. Farley, however, concludes that same-sex relationships can be just
even if the person does not have a homosexual orientation but freely chooses
to engage in such a relationship.[49]

Since the book focuses on just a framework for Christian sexual ethics,
Farley does not discuss any other issues, such as the much debated issue of
premarital sex. In keeping with her own method of paying attention to
particular and concrete historical realities, such a discussion would be helpful in elaborating her own method by putting flesh and blood on her seven
norms in light of many sexual issues. However, one cannot do everything
in one book.

Feminist Theologian in the Service of the Church

Farley's Sitz im Leben helps to explain that she has used her academic expertise to speak to an ecumenical and secular audience in her role at the
Yale Divinity School and Yale University, but, as a committed Catholic and
religious in the Sisters of Mercy, she also has addressed the Church.

Farley presented a major paper at the first national meeting of the Wom-
en's Ordination Conference in Detroit in November 1975. From her feminist perspective she insists that there is a moral imperative for the Church
to ordain women. The reasons for not ordaining women to the priesthood
are false: Women lack the capacity for leadership, they cannot represent God

to the community and the community to God, and they are unworthy to approach the sacred.[50]

Farley reflected on power and the powerlessness of women in the Church in light of an incident involving her religious community, the Sisters of Mercy, who run many hospitals in the United States. After a five-year study, the Sisters concluded that in their hospitals they would do tubal ligations when required for the overall good of the patient. Hierarchical and papal Catholic teaching forbids such procedures. The Vatican and the US bishops declared that these policies of the Sisters go against Church teaching. The administrative team of the Sisters of Mercy responded that it had personal disagreements with the existing teaching, but in the present circumstances it would not take a stand in public against it and would withdraw its proposed policy. Farley personally concluded that the Sisters apparently accepted this silencing in order that their and other similar voices might prevail in the future.[51]

Farley addressed the tension between moral theologians and the hierarchical magisterium in the Church in light of the Congregation for the Doctrine of the Faith's declaration in 1986 that I, a tenured professor at Catholic University, was neither suitable nor eligible to teach Catholic theology because of my dissent from certain specific moral teachings. Farley explains my position that on complex and specific issues one cannot claim a certitude that excludes the possibility of error. The Yale professor points out that in the Catholic tradition, with its acceptance of the natural law, moral truths must make sense to those seeking the truth. Since moral insight comes from the recognition of a moral truth, persons cannot experience moral obligation just because they are told they should obey. All in the Church—laity, clergy, theologians, and church leaders—need "the grace of self-doubt." Yes, there are important things we should never doubt, but all the Church, especially leaders, needs the grace of self-doubt as the basis of epistemic humility, which itself is necessary for individual and communal moral discernment. A genuinely discerning Church must listen to all in the Church and not claim a certitude where it does not and cannot exist.[52] Farley in her own writing very often speaks of the modesty of her approaches and conclusions. She well exemplifies what it means to have the grace of self-doubt.

In this context she strongly opposes the silencing of theologians by Church authorities. The argument for silencing is based on the divinely ordained authority of the Church to teach the truth and to protect the members of the Church from error. Farley's argument against silencing again comes from the Catholic natural law tradition recognizing that moral teachings must make sense to those searching for the truth. Consequently, everyone in the Church, not just Church leaders, should participate in the discernment of moral truth.

Public moral discourse is a necessary condition for a faithful search for truth, even in the Church, precisely because of the presence of the Holy Spirit in all people in the Church. Silencing also can cause unjust injury to persons in the Church and to the common good of the Church.[53]

In a presidential address to the Catholic Theological Society of America in 2000, Farley pointed out two problems of credibility affecting the way in which the Church in the United States carries out its role in the public forum to work for a more just society. First, the placing of abortion at the center of the Church's public policy and agenda creates problems. It fails to recognize some of the uncertainties on this issue within the Church itself, but above all it overshadows so many other important moral and social issues that the Church supports for the good of society. The second obstacle to the credibility of the church in the public forum comes from the Church's prohibiting a free and responsible exchange of ideas within its own boundaries. The public perception of this silencing weakens the effectiveness of the Church as a voice trying to work for justice in our pluralistic society.[54]

Farley on two occasions had her own run-ins with Vatican authorities. In 1984, she was one of twenty-four religious women signers, along with others, of an advertisement in the *New York Times* saying there was a diversity of opinions in the Catholic Church on abortion and that a large number of Catholic moral theologians held abortion sometimes could be a moral choice. The Vatican congregation dealing with religious demanded that the nuns take back their support for the statement.[55] In the end cooler heads prevailed, and the Vatican congregation seemed to back down somewhat. Farley, through her religious superior, was in contact with the congregation and never publicly retracted her signature.[56]

In 2010, Farley was informed by the Congregation for the Doctrine of the Faith that she was under investigation because of positions she had taken, especially in her book *Just Love*. She responded in writing regarding these concerns of the congregation. However, on June 4, 2012, the congregation made public the decree condemning the book for being in opposition to the Church's magisterium—this included her positions on masturbation, homosexual acts, homosexual marriage, indissolubility of marriage, and divorce and remarriage. Consequently the book "cannot be used as a valid expression of Catholic teaching."[57] The sentence was not as severe as that meted out to many other moral theologians in the past, but that does not justify it. In addition, the process itself remained unjust, with the congregation acting as prosecutor, judge, and jury.

Margaret Farley, despite the fact that she did not publish that many monographs, has made a singular contribution to Catholic moral theology in the United States. With the other authors already considered, she wrote in light of the influence of Vatican II and *Humanae vitae*. She was, however, the pioneer Catholic feminist ethicist in this country. In light of her situation at Yale University and the Yale Divinity School, she often wrote about particular issues from a general Christian perspective, but in light of her commitment to her religious community and Catholic faith, she also often wrote from a specifically Catholic perspective.

Notes

1. For biographical information, see her curriculum vitae on the website of the Yale Divinity School, https://divinity.yale.edu/faculty-and-research/yds-faculty /margaret-farley. See also Maura A. Ryan, "Introduction," in *A Just and True Love: Feminism at the Frontiers of Theological Ethics; Essays in Honor of Margaret A. Farley*, ed. Maura A. Ryan and Brian F. Linnane (Notre Dame, IN: University of Notre Dame Press, 2007), 1–19; and Margeret Farley "Love, Justice, and Discernment: An Interview with Margaret Farley," *Second Opinion* 17 (October 1991): 80–91.

2. For a Festschrift in Gustafson's honor from his former doctoral students, see Lisa Sowle Cahill and James F. Childress, *Christian Ethics: Problems and Prospects* (Cleveland, OH: Pilgrim, 1996).

3. James M. Gustafson, *Protestant and Roman Catholic Ethics: Prospects for Rapprochement* (Chicago: University of Chicago Press, 1978).

4. Ryan and Linnane, *Just and True Love*.

5. Margaret A. Farley, "Feminist Ethics," in *Westminster Dictionary of Christian Ethics*, ed. James F. Childress and John Macquarrie (Philadelphia: Westminster, 1986), 229–31; Margaret A. Farley, "Ethics and Moral Theology," in *Dictionary of Feminist Theologies*, ed. Letty M. Russell and J. Shannon Clarkson (Louisville, KY: Westminster John Knox, 1996), 88–91.

6. Margaret A. Farley, "New Patterns of Relationship: Beginnings of a Moral Revolution," in Margaret A. Farley, *Changing the Questions: Explorations in Christian Ethics*, ed. Jamie L. Manson (Maryknoll, NY: Orbis, 2015), 1–23.

7. Margaret A. Farley, "Feminist Ethics," in *Feminist Ethics and the Catholic Tradition: Readings in Moral Theology No. 9*, ed. Charles E. Curran, Margaret A. Farley, and Richard A. McCormick (New York: Paulist, 1996), 5–10.

8. Ibid., 5.

9. Ibid., 9–10.

10. Margaret A. Farley, "The Role of Experience in Moral Discernment," in Farley, *Changing the Questions*, 47–68.

11. Margaret A. Farley, "Feminist and Universal Morality," in Farley, *Changing the Questions*, 88–111.

12. Ibid., 88.

13. Ibid., 201.

14. Ibid., 146–47.

15. Margaret A. Farley, "Ethics, Ecclesiology, and the Grace of Self-Doubt," in Farley, *Changing the Questions*, 161–81.

16. Margaret A. Farley, "How Shall We Love in a Postmodern World?," in Farley, *Changing the Questions*, 148–54.

17. Ibid., 143–60.

18. Farley, "New Patterns of Relationship," 9.

19. Margaret A. Farley, "A Feminist Respect for Persons," in Farley, *Changing the Questions*, 125–42.

20. See, e.g., Jacques Maritain, *The Person and the Common Good* (New York: Charles Scribner's, 1947).

21. Farley, "New Patterns of Relationship," 21–23.

22. Margaret A. Farley, "Feminism and Universal Morality," in Farley, *Changing the Questions*, 107.

23. Farley, "Respect for Persons," 141.

24. Margaret A. Farley, *Personal Commitments: Beginning, Keeping, Changing* (San Francisco: Harper & Row, 1986), 23–37.

25. Farley, "New Patterns of Relationship," 8–9.

26. Ibid., 10–20.

27. Ibid., 20–23.

28. Ibid., 20–21.

29. Farley, *Personal Commitments*, 80–109.

30. Ibid., 1–11.

31. Ibid., 53.

32. Margaret A. Farley and Doris Gottmoeller, "Commitment in a Changing World," *Review for Religious* 34 (November 1975): 846–67.

33. Margaret A. Farley, "Family," in *New Dictionary of Catholic Social Thought*, ed. Judith A. Dwyer (Collegeville, MN: Liturgical, 1994), 375–79.

34. Margaret A. Farley, "The Church and the Family: An Ethical Task," *Horizons* 20, no. 1 (1983): 50–71.

35. Margaret A. Farley, "Divorce, Remarriage, and Pastoral Practice," in *Moral Theology: Challenge for the Future; Essays in Honor of Richard A. McCormick*, ed. Charles E. Curran (New York: Paulist, 1990), 213–39.

36. Farley, *Just Love*, 245–71.

37. Ibid., 296–311.

38. Margaret A. Farley, "Feminist Theology and Bioethics," in *Theology and Bioethics: Exploring the Foundations and Frontiers*, ed. Earl E. Shelp (Dordrecht, Netherlands: D. Reidel, 1985), 163–86, reprinted in *On Moral Medicine*, 2nd. ed., ed. Stephen E. Lammers and Allen Verhey (Grand Rapids, MI: Eerdmans, 1998), 633–38.

39. Margaret A. Farley, *Compassionate Respect: A Feminist Approach to Medical Ethics and Other Questions*, 2002 Madeleva Lecture in Spirituality (New York: Paulist, 2002), 1–21.

40. Ibid., 42.

41. Margaret A. Farley, "Partnership in Hope: Gender, Faith, and Responses to HIV/AIDS in Africa," *Journal of Feminist Studies in Religion* 20 (Spring 2004): 133–48. See also Lisa Sowle Cahill, "Feminist Theology and Sexual Ethics," in Ryan and Linnane, *Just and True Love*, 40–43.

42. Margaret A. Farley, "Liberation, Abortion, and Responsibility," *Reflection* 71 (May 1974): 9–13, reprinted in Lammers and Verhey, *On Moral Medicine*, 633–68.

43. Margaret A. Farley, "Stem Cell Research: Religious Considerations," in Farley, *Changing the Questions*, 311–18; Margaret A. Farley, "Roman Catholic Views on Research Involving Human Embryonic Cells," in *The Human Embryonic Cell Debate: Science, Ethics, and Public Policy*, ed. Suzanne Holland, Karen Lebacqz, and Laurie Zoloth (Cambridge, MA: MIT Press, 2001), 113–18.

44. Farley, *Just Love*, 17–109.

45. Ibid., 109–74.

46. Ibid., 182–206.

47. Ibid., 207–32.

48. Margaret A. Farley, "An Ethics for Same-Sex Relations," in *A Challenge to Love: Gay and Lesbian Catholics in the Church*, ed. Robert Nugent (New York: Crossroad, 1984), 93–106.

49. Farley, *Just Love*, 271–96.

50. Margaret Farley, "Moral Imperatives for the Ordination of Women," in *Women in Catholic Priesthood: An Expanded Vision; Proceedings of the Detroit Ordination Conference*, ed. Anne Marie Gardiner (New York: Paulist, 1976), 35–57.

51. Margaret A. Farley, "Power and Powerlessness: A Case in Point," *Proceedings of the Catholic Theological Society of America* 37 (1982): 116–19.

52. Farley, "Ethics, Ecclesiology, and the Grace of Self-Doubt," 161–81.

53. Ibid., 69–87.

54. Margaret A. Farley, "Presidential Address: The Church in the Public Forum; Scandal or Prophetic Witness?," *Proceedings of the Catholic Theological Society of America* 55 (2000): 87–101.

55. Kenneth A. Briggs, "Nuns, Expressing Dismay, Ponder Vatican Threat," *New York Times*, December 19, 1984, www.nytimes.com/1984/12/20/us/nuns-expressing-dismay-ponder-vatican-threat.html.

56. David E. Anderson, "Nun Denies Retracting Signature on Abortion Related Ad," UPI, February 19, 1986, www.upi.com/Archives/1986/02/19/nun-denies-retracting-signature-on-abortion-related-ad/1843509173200/.

57. Congregation for the Doctrine of the Faith, "Notification on the Book *Just Love: A Framework for Christian Sexual Ethics* by Sr. Margaret A. Farley R.S.M.," March 30, 2012, www.vatican.va/roman_curia/congregations/cfaith/documents/rc_con_cfaith_doc_20120330_nota-farley_en.html.

8

Lisa Sowle Cahill

Lisa Sowle Cahill is a prolific and very highly regarded moral theologian who has taught at Boston College from 1976 to the present and holds the J. Donald Monan Professorship. As with the other moral theologians already discussed, her *Sitz im Leben* helps to explain her approach to moral theology. Five aspects are most significant in this regard.

Sitz im Leben

First, Cahill, having obtained her PhD in 1976, was in the second wave of Catholic moral theologians after Vatican II.[1] Unlike all the scholars previously discussed, with the exception to some degree of Margaret Farley, she was not directly and immediately involved in the response to *Humanae vitae*. The first wave of Catholic moral theologians in the post–Vatican II era dealt both with the reforms brought about by Vatican II and especially with the encyclical *Humanae vitae* in 1968, which had such a profound influence on the Catholic Church. Catholic moral theologians at the time of the encyclical and immediately afterward focused on this document and its ramifications with regard to moral norms in moral theology. As a result, most other considerations faded into the background. Cahill did not directly and immediately deal with *Humanae vitae*, but later she considered many of the aspects and issues that came to the fore in the 1970s and following.

Second, Vatican II stressed the importance of ecumenism for Catholic life and theology. The first post–Vatican II moral theologians were somewhat ecumenical and used their ecumenical interests in dealing with their primary focus on *Humanae vitae* and especially the issue of moral norms. Cahill is ecumenical in a deeper and broader way, beginning with her training at the University of Chicago under James M. Gustafson. Gustafson comes out of the Protestant tradition but is also very knowledgeable about and appreciative of many aspects of the Catholic tradition and the development in Catholic moral theology after Vatican II. In 1978, Gustafson wrote a very significant ecumenical book, *Protestant and Roman Catholic Ethics: Prospects for Rapprochement*.[2] Cahill's doctoral dissertation under Gustafson discussed Protestant and Catholic approaches to euthanasia. Cahill's ecumenical approach comes through in all her many writings. Three of her books were published by Fortress Press, which is associated with the Lutheran Church.[3] Her first book on Christian ethics of sexuality began as a series of lectures given at the Pacific School of Religion in Berkeley, California, a Protestant graduate school of theology.[4] Only one of her full monographs was published exclusively by a Catholic publisher—Georgetown University Press. Cahill especially appreciated the theological emphasis in Protestant Christian ethics.

Cahill, however, always identifies herself as a Catholic moral theologian. She has addressed many of the aspects and issues that have come to the fore in Catholic moral theology and enthusiastically embraces a modified Thomistic approach in all her writings. Cahill has published fifteen articles in *Theological Studies*, the premier Catholic theological journal in the United States. In addition, she has edited nine volumes in *Concilium*, a liberal, international, Catholic theological publication begun by many of the outstanding theological figures in Vatican II that continues to publish to this day.[5] There is no doubt, therefore, that Cahill is truly both Catholic and ecumenical.

Third, Cahill is the first Roman Catholic married woman theologian to play a significant role in moral theology. Her first interest in moral theology centered on bioethics, as illustrated in her doctoral dissertation. Her original interest in bioethics "was soon almost overwhelmed by invitations to speak, write, and teach about issues related to sex, marriage, family, and women's roles."[6] However, she continued to write in many other areas as well.

A fourth important influence coming from her Sitz im Leben is feminism. As mentioned in the last chapter, Margaret Farley is the mother of Catholic feminists in this country and was writing on the topic even before Cahill finished her doctoral dissertation. Cahill, however, as a woman theologian and especially with her interest in sexuality and women's roles, was naturally open to the feminist approach. She has often described herself as a feminist and a Thomist.

Fifth, her study of and writings in feminism opened the door for recognizing the importance of doing theology from the margins and from the experience of those who suffer injustice and inequality in human culture and society. This interest in injustice and inequality ultimately embraced more than just the issue of feminism. In her later writings, she has focused on those who are on the margins of society and victims of injustice and inequality, especially the poor. As a result, she has stressed the importance of the mission of Jesus and the mission of the Christian Church to work for justice and equality, especially in the contemporary global context.[7] Not only is she interested in social justice as an important topic in moral theology, but she has also insisted on the social aspect of all moral issues today. This approach comes to the fore especially in her more recent writings on bioethics, which in the past had usually been treated almost exclusively from the individualistic perspective. Cahill insists that the individual perspective is not enough in light of the social and global realities of the present world.[8]

Method

According to the description on her Boston College webpage, Cahill's first interest is "method in theological ethics," while her second interest is the "New Testament and ethics."[9] She has never written a monograph on method, but her writings frequently refer to it. Her first book dealt with both the sources of ethics and ethical methodology.[10]

Early Treatment of the Sources of Moral Theology

A primary aspect of the method of moral theology involves the sources of the discipline. In these early writings, she deals with the sources of Christian ethics (note that here she uses the Protestant terminology of "Christian ethics" to refer to the discipline) and their interrelationality.[11] The four complementary sources are the foundational texts of scriptures of the faith community (the Bible); the community's "tradition" of faith, theology, and practice; normative philosophical accounts of essential or ideal humanity; and descriptions of what actually is and has been the case in the past and the present that involves the role of the empirical sciences.

These four sources spell out in some detail the traditional question of revelation and reason as the sources of moral theology. The Catholic tradition has tended to give priority to the role of reason, as illustrated in the work of Thomas Aquinas, whereas the Protestant tendency has given priority to revelation, as illustrated in the approach of Martin Luther. She does not refer to the well-known Methodist quadrilateral that recognizes the four sources of scripture, tradition, reason, and experience.[12] Cahill does not make experience a separate source, but she incorporates experience into all the other sources.[13] She proposes that fidelity to these four mutually correcting sources and success in judicially balancing them is a standard for measuring the adequacy of how the tradition has dealt with an issue and how we should deal with an issue today. The relationship between the sources is ever dialectical, circular, and critical.

What happens if the four sources are not in agreement? In a final brief chapter in her first book, Cahill in a somewhat sketchy manner shows how on the basis of her method she deals with sexuality and differences among the sources.[14] The Christian scriptures and tradition reveal the social nature, and not only the individual aspect, of sexuality with its relationship to marriage, procreation, the family, and the broader human society. Note here her early emphasis on the social aspect of moral issues. A dominant stream of contemporary Western philosophy and culture since the Enlightenment stresses the freedom, autonomy, and rationality of the individual. Throughout her writings, Cahill, on the basis of her scriptural, theological, and philosophical understanding, opposes this individualistic emphasis. In her quite brief consideration of moral norms in this first book, *Between the Sexes: Foundations for a Christian Ethic of Sexuality*, she deals more with the contemporary scientific approaches, especially with regard to the test case of homosexuality. Scientific studies show that sexual orientation is not something freely chosen by the individual, a reality that was unknown to the biblical authors and the Christian tradition. Also, psychiatry and psychology today no longer see homosexuality as a psychic disorder. Gay and lesbian people can be and often are mature, well-balanced human beings.

In light of the sources, especially the scripture and the contemporary scientific understandings, she holds on to what she proposes as the biblical and Christian norm of sexuality involving a permanent commitment of heterosexual partnership and love open to procreation. However, she recognizes some departures (described as rare) that are acceptable if they represent the most morally commendable course of action concretely available to individuals caught in tragic and ambiguous situations. On this basis Cahill accepts committed homosexual relationships. This involves the moral dilemma of causing some evil for what is perceived as an obligatory good. Cahill concludes by pointing out that in the Christian community the Spirit is the primary reference and determiner of moral evaluation.[15]

Questions abound about this approach. Is the biblical and Christian norm of sexuality too narrow and too tight? How does one determine when there are exceptions to the norm that are acceptable? If divorce and homosexual relationships are acceptable, why not premarital sex? However, one cannot expect a comparatively short treatise to consider and solve all these complex issues.

In retrospect, Cahill's first book sets the trajectory for her future work, especially in four significant areas. First, she continues to develop and work out the basic method and its importance in her subsequent work. Second, her later writings continue to recognize the importance of scripture as a primary source for moral theology. Third, opposition to individualism and autonomy characterizes her writing to the present. In this context she develops in more detail her feminist and modified Aristotelian-Thomism as her philosophical understanding of truly human flourishing. Fourth, her writings continue to return to, or at best mention, the question of exceptions and conflict situations.

The New Testament and Today

In her 1994 book on discipleship, pacifism, and just war theory, *Love Your Enemies: Discipleship, Pacifism, and Just War Theory*, Cahill basically follows the method previously mentioned.[16] Her emphasis in this book is primarily on the theological aspect. Here she considers in greater depth the development of tradition through the early Church, Augustine, Aquinas, and Luther, with contrasting chapters on war in God's name and pacifist witness to the Gospel, concluding with two chapters on the ongoing American debate. This book is primarily a scholarly explanation of the Christian approach to discipleship, pacifism, and war down through the centuries that can serve as a standard resource for all those who are interested in this subject. The volume itself does not develop Cahill's own moral evaluation of the issues.

For our purposes, this book develops in a somewhat different way the role of the scriptures in moral theology. In so doing, it also emphasizes the theological aspect of her methodology. Cahill's approach in the book situates itself in the context of contemporary debates over pacifism and just war, in particular in light of the broader methodological issue of specifically Christian sources and human rational sources as the primary fount of Christian ethics. In this book Cahill accepts the challenge to take seriously the New Testament witness of Jesus's call to peacemaking and the rejection of violence. The question for the Church and the individual Christian believer today as ever is how the mandate of Jesus to live in love, peace, and forgiveness is to function in our contemporary public moral life. In this context Cahill emphasizes the primacy of the biblical notions of discipleship, the kingdom of God, and the Sermon on the Mount, while recognizing the eschatological reality that the fullness of God's reign or kingdom will come only at the end of time.[17]

Cahill's approach to the use of scripture begins with the radical community of discipleship that Gospel preaching and kingdom values create, and not with the specific norms governing peace and the resort to violence. The issue for us now, as it has always been for Christians, is analogous to that faced by the earliest community of the disciples of Jesus developed in the New Testament: how to relate the demands of the Gospel to the public life and situation in which one lives. This volume attempts to show how Christians down through the centuries have responded. We should challenge our culture with the message of Jesus analogously to the challenge the Gospel of Jesus posed to the culture of his time. Since Christian disciples and the Christian communities live in the midst of the so-called secular world, the Sermon on the Mount will not be the only relevant source in determining how to respond to the injustices and conflicts of our world. Just as the New Testament community borrowed some forms of moral knowledge, instruction, and exhortation from its culture, so Christian communities today must be in conversation with their culture and contemporary approaches. But the final criterion of appropriate Christian action must be the experience of discipleship itself.[18]

In the mid-1990s, Cahill revisited the issues of sexuality, marriage, and gender and adopted an understanding of the New Testament approach similar to what was developed with regard to peace. The teaching of Jesus and the reign of God primarily present a vision and not a set of norms, as has so often been thought to be the case in the history of Christianity. The positive biblical vision of sex focuses on faithful, heterosexual marriage, and sex outside of that context is clearly not part of the normative pattern for the early disciples and the Christian community. The function of this vision is to encourage and support disciples in building up relationships within the community. Unfortunately for most of our tradition, sexual teaching has been used to reinforce the types of boundaries of judgment and exclusion against which original discipleship stood. A Christian sexual ethic's first function is not to mark off or condemn but to inspire and encourage the disciples to do good.[19]

This vision transforms human relationships by reordering relations of dominance and violence toward greater compassion, mercy, and peace and by acting in solidarity with the poor. A constant New Testament theme is the transformation or reversal of ordinary human relationships so they better reflect God's presence and power as disclosed in Jesus Christ. The recognition of values such as equality, reciprocity, and the individuality and sociality of every person represents an advance in human moral consciousness and the critical possibility for social reform. However, these new patterns of social relationship can in no way simply be equated with and supportive of modern liberal values of equality, freedom, self-determination, and mutual respect. The New Testament values are not so much the protection of personal choice and the furtherance of effectively fulfilling relationships but rather the integration of all persons in a new sense of communal unity and inclusiveness in Christ.[20]

New Testament values challenge existing cultural criteria of inclusion and exclusion and call for moral relationships to dislodge power and include the poor. New Testament values liberate from oppressive constraints on sexual and gender behavior and propose an understanding of the body that is central to the liberative practice. But early Christian practices existed in a hierarchically ordered patriarchal structure, and these biblical values did not and could not totally transform the existing cultural realities. The moral challenge for the first disciples of Jesus was to devise a set of strategies to break the grip of existing societal norms on the quality of their own communal relationships. The existing social order recognized women's sexual and reproductive capacities, and to a lesser extent even men's, to serve a stratified, controlled, and dominative social order. Patriarchy formed a central part of that order. Christians did not always successfully meet the challenge, but neither did they totally fail.[21] For example, virginity was not so much a negative response to human sexuality as it was a commitment to communal solidarity and a rejection of the hierarchical and state-controlled functions of the patriarchal family.[22]

Take also the example of the *Haustafeln*, the famous household codes repeated a number of times in the New Testament, which commend to Christians the existing relationship among the paterfamilias, women, children, and slaves. Many have seen here the New Testament conformity to the existing culture and even the endorsement of slavery and second-class status for women. Cahill points out even in this regard there was some transformation occurring. In the early Christian Church, some women (Prisca, Phoebe, Junia) had leadership roles. Concerning slaves, the deutero-Pauline writings integrate slaves as moral agents to whom the Gospel is directly preached. In somewhat of an understatement, Cahill notes that the changes brought about in the New Testament regarding women and slaves were not a high-water mark for subsequent efforts, but at least there was a process of transformation toward compassion (personal) and solidarity (social).[23]

With regard to the family, the Christian faith calls families to a new existence in which marital and kin bonds are the basis for affectionate, mutual, just, and general internal family relations and for compassionate and sacrificial outreach to those beyond one's family, especially the powerless and those in need. This ideal brought about some transformation in the existing cultural understanding in New Testament times, but the hierarchical and exclusionary aspects of gender and household structures continued to exist.[24]

Further Development of the Theological Aspect

In the twenty-first century Cahill developed the theological aspect of her method in Christian ethics in her *Global Justice, Christology, and Christian Ethics*. The context of the book comes from the present situation that the global realities of human inequality, poverty, violence, and ecological destruction call for a Christian response. Such evil and suffering are unjust, wrong, and unacceptable and need to be challenged and transformed. The kingdom of God proclaimed by Jesus shows that salvation is also corporate and political. The fullness of the kingdom is future, but even now the kingdom is inbreaking to transform social and political life to a more equal, just, and inclusive reality. Cahill develops her position by examining in great detail the Christian understandings of creation and salvation while developing both a Word and a Spirit Christology. She shows a deep understanding of the theological literature on these issues. The Genesis account of creation calls humans to responsibility; Jesus's ministry of the kingdom makes possible a new way of existence stressing justice, equality, peace, and the preferential option for the poor; humans are redeemed and empowered through the incarnation, cross, and resurrection; the spirit of the risen Jesus through the Church converts persons and communities to bear witness to this inbreaking kingdom, which by definition has significant political and social dimensions. In this book she gives only the broad theological parameters and does not develop the social ethical approach to justice.[25]

In another volume in the twenty-first century, *Theological Bioethics: Participation, Justice, Change*, Cahill introduces two new elements to her theological methodology. The first is "adverse virtue," a way to understand when choices represent human attempts to act with integrity in the midst of unavoidable conflict and adversity.[26] Such actions are not virtuous in the full sense because they are not fulfillments of what human beings are called to be. But, on the other hand, they are not examples of "sinning bravely," because the actor does not think they are wrong. (Earlier Cahill had accepted this sinning bravely approach to such conflict situations.)[27] Nor are they true exceptions to moral rules that would minimize the ambivalence in the situation itself. In my judgment, a further ethical discussion is necessary to determine exactly when and how such actions are expressions of adverse virtue.

The second new aspect is participatory theological ethics. Theoretical discourse becomes relevant to the practical order only by making present patterns of relationship and structures that match the intellectual discourse. The role of participatory Christian ethics is to promote social arrangements that are consistent with the values of human dignity, the alleviation of suffering, cooperative realities, and a preferential option for the poor. The global level requires working with other theological and religious approaches that share the same values.[28]

The Philosophical Understanding of Human Flourishing

Most important is the philosophical understanding of the normatively human. What contributes to true human flourishing? Cahill describes her approach here as feminist and realistic in the Aristotelian-Thomistic tradition.[29] There is no need to discuss feminist methodology in detail since the last chapter has done so in its discussion of Margaret Farley's approach. Cahill's Sitz im Leben is in the second wave of feminism in the Christian and Catholic contemporary situation. From her earliest writings, she frequently cites Farley, Elisabeth Schüssler-Fiorenza, and Rosemary Radford Ruether. Cahill does not describe her feminist approach in as much detail as she does her realistic Thomistic understanding. The feminist method involves the twofold step of unmasking the patriarchy and then developing a hermeneutic of recovery or retrieval to show what is a just understanding of human flourishing for all people. Feminism for Cahill is committed to equal social power for women and men. Whatever differences there might be between women and men, they cannot be accepted and warranted for social systems that give men authority and power over women.[30]

To fully appreciate Cahill's philosophical understanding of the human and truly human flourishing, it is helpful to recognize the problems she finds in other approaches. Most problematic is modern philosophical liberalism that puts primary emphasis on individualism and comes close to absolutizing human freedom and autonomy. This approach is very prevalent in the culture and ethos of the United States today. In addition, Western and American culture today give great importance to the role of the sciences. However, when a scientific view of knowledge and argument is combined with a liberal commitment to personal freedom, the result for social theory or public policy is a "hands-off" attitude to moral judgments except when individual autonomy is infringed on or measurably bad consequences prove it. Cahill also strongly opposes subjectivism and relativism.[31]

Cahill recognizes some positive aspects in the philosophical approaches of antifoundationalism and postmodernism. There can be no doubt that there have been too many claims for universality at the expense of the legitimate diversity and pluralism that can and should exist. However, postmodernism and antifoundationalism cannot provide ways for understanding the needs of justice, solidarity, and the common good in our world today. The postmodern sensibility is marked by randomness, fragmentation, and distrust of all "metanarratives." Postmodernism celebrates pluralism and differences and rejects any objective moral foundations. With regard to sexual ethics, postmodernism rejects the Western "bourgeois" norms of sexual behavior. Pluralism, freedom from restraint, and the unavailability of any master plan for understanding sexuality have become watchwords. Some feminists have accepted such postmodern approaches, but there is no possibility of proposals for justice and human solidarity in society without some recognition of moral foundations. In my terminology, postmodernism helps to unmask the patriarchy, but it cannot provide the foundations for building a truly just society and world based on communal bonds of solidarity and a capacity to care for strangers and the other as well as oneself. What is needed today is a critical, realistic philosophical approach.[32]

Cahill advocates a Thomism that generalizes from human experiences of basic human needs, of fulfilling goods, of well-ordered societies, and of human happiness. Her approach draws not on abstract rationality but on reasonable interpretations of historical existence to global and normative proposals about the goods human action should seek to realize and ends to which it ought to conform. A vision of the essential elements in human flourishing is inductively inferred from the data and facts of human experience and held up as a standard for action.[33] She strongly disagrees with the neoscholastic Thomism that permeated Catholic thought in the pre–Vatican II period.[34]

Cahill's understanding of the natural law is teleological—human actions and morality are purposeful; realistic—the basic human values are objective and shared among culturally different human beings; and inductive—a moral epistemology that is experientially based and formed on the basis of a broad consensus.[35] The virtue of prudence here is key. At the practical level all knowledge of the natural law and all applications of its requirements of justice are perspectival, including the influences of historical and social location.

The natural law does not require that humans or the human species are unchanging, but basic human characteristics such as intelligence, imagination, contextual freedom, and sociality and relationality perdure even within change. There are basic goods constitutive of human flourishing, but there is no complete categorization of such goods. For Aquinas these basic human goods are human life and health, the institutionalization of procreation to socialize children, the economic and political organization of society, and the formalization of religious expression. Experience reminds us that all cultures can agree on the need to be cared for and loved and to reciprocation in kind; the need for food, clothing, education, and health; and the need for a healthy environment in which we can live peaceful, just, and meaningful human lives.

Describing these basic human goods is not difficult—the difficult step is showing that all persons are entitled in principle to equal access to such basic goods. Aquinas himself did not recognize such equality to be a basic human good because he was living in a very hierarchically structured society. Arguments for equality can be based on the need for human persons to recognize that all persons share in a common humanity: They are like us as subjects capable of human suffering and transcendence. The human capacity for empathy and compassion help all to recognize the basic equality of all others.

Sociology points to the fact that societies of greater equality are more successful. The recognition of human equality seems to require more than just intellectual arguments. Narratives, personal histories, anecdotes, and aesthetic media such as the visual arts and poetry and even photographs bring home the humanity and dignity of those who suffered due to social inequalities. Think of the powerful photographs of starving children and the body of a dead child washed ashore after the sinking of a boat full of immigrants fleeing from violence and injustice.

Knowledge of the natural law must be developed through inductive consensus-building that identifies patterns of continuity within change, incorporates new insights such as the fact of human equality, and recognizes that bias and vested interests will work against basic equality and must be countered. Knowledge of human goods, needs, and obligations approaches universality only to the extent that the reasoning process involved is expansive, inclusive, and critical.

The natural law requires prior dispositions to know reality, persons, and goods truthfully and in their proper relationships. It also requires good judgment about what to do in a given situation. (I frequently remind students that a big heart does not excuse a stupid ass!) Even more important, one needs a practical determination to put judgment into effect. To judge an act well requires a practical desire and thrust to appreciate and achieve these basic goods that are reasonable and not being dissuaded by concupiscence or disordered desire. This tendency to act on behalf of human goods and basic equality is called virtue, which is a tendency to seek and do the good. In this context Aquinas developed the cardinal virtues and the moral virtues. Of the four cardinal virtues, Aquinas gave by far the longest treatment to justice.

Such an understanding of the natural law thus enables all human beings today to recognize the sufferings, injustices, and inequalities that so often characterize our present world. In addition, the characteristic virtues predispose all to work to overcome such injustices.

Cahill has also expressed an appreciation of the realistic version of pragmatism, which holds a number of things in common with the natural law: To know things one has to be open or disposed to them, to desire to know; the self, knowledge, and agency are social and practical; practices shape and validate knowledge as correspondence to reality; and true knowledge is not detached but issues in consequences. However, the natural law emphasizes more clearly than pragmatism the following important aspects: the objective nature of the good as a normative criterion of moral realities and of true proposals or practices that correspond to them. For the natural law it is not enough that moral knowledge be true in the sense of corresponding to reality—it must also be virtuous in the sense of corresponding to and acting for the reality of the good. The objectivity of some basic goods, priorities among them, their amenability to reasonable yet inductive inquiry, and their appeal across cultures despite local variations are the contributions of natural law ethics.[36]

Cahill thus holds on to the need for both the theological and philosophical approaches. In this light, she disagrees with the approach of Stanley Hauerwas, who has written extensively on virtue. Hauerwas's basic thesis is that the Christian character or virtue is formed in and only in the Church understood as a countercultural community constituted by the vision, narrative, and practices of Jesus Christ. Her differences with Hauerwas are threefold. First, Cahill sees the theological as involving the transformation of all society through the inbreaking of the kingdom. Second, she sees the Church working with all others for the common good. Hauerwas sees the Church as a particular community within the broader human community that bears witness to the work of Jesus. Third, Cahill, like Aquinas, has a positive and constructive view of reasonable human morality, with a recognition that the goods that constitute human flourishing can be known across communities, cultures, and religions.[37]

In sum, Cahill's criticism of contemporary US culture stems from the individuality and absolutization of freedom and autonomy. She opposes injustices and inequalities that exist because of the failure to recognize that every human being has an equal right to the basic needs of food, clothing, shelter, education, and health care. In the economic sphere, she insists on the preferential option for the poor. The kingdom values are thus truly consonant with the understanding of true human flourishing developed in her Thomism.

Cahill wants to see the kingdom values and human flourishing working together in the Christian person and in the Christian community. Recall that the previous wave of Catholic moral theologians, as illustrated in the work of Fuchs and McCormick, was involved in international discussion about whether the Christian perspective adds any material content to what is based on reason. Cahill refers to that debate but does not enter into discussion about it. Lately she has illustrated the relationship in terms of her emphasis on participatory theological bioethics.[38] A participatory, theological ethics joins its narrative, prophetic, ethical, and policy discourses to participatory intervention in social structures. Using theological symbols and claims such as creation, image of God, love of neighbor, and care for the poor, theological bioethics relates these to mediating concepts such as solidarity, common good, and distributive justice. It develops and learns by means of practices in which Christians join with members of other faith traditions and with institutions and organizations founded around types of identity other than religious. Note here also the mutual relationship of theory and practice affecting one another. Christians thus work with other religious groups and nonreligious groups. The implication is that what Christians propose can be accepted by others, religious or not, on the basis on both religious claims and the mediating concepts of human flourishing developed in her case from her modified Thomistic approach.[39]

Tradition and Human Sciences

Without doubt, of the sources of the discipline, Cahill gives most attention to the biblical-theological and the philosophical and to the relationship between these two. What about the other two—tradition and the descriptive aspects of the human coming from the sciences? With regard to tradition, she understands tradition as based on the experience of the Church and the Christian in responding to the times, by an analogy with the way in which the biblical authors responded to the circumstances of their times. As noted, her books frequently develop in detail the topic by tracing the historical Christian tradition with special emphasis on Aquinas and Luther. In the process, she analyzes and criticizes the different historical approaches. These figures are significant but not normative for Christians today. In discussing Christology, Cahill deals with the early councils of Nicea and Chalcedon, recognizing, however, room for a plurality of theological approaches today. The two councils, in accord with Catholic self-understanding, authoritatively set the bar for contemporary Christologies. They accept the fact of intellectual paradox (Jesus as fully God and fully human), prioritize practical unity in the Church over the coherence of theological systems, and leave much room for substantially different approaches. The parameters of this pluralism are that Christologies must affirm the full humanity and divinity of Jesus in a Trinitarian framework.[40] Cahill spends comparatively little time dealing with the fourth source for the discipline: descriptive accounts of the human based on experience and the sciences. In fact, as mentioned previously, she gives the most attention to this source in her very early discussion of homosexuality.[41]

Bioethics

From the very beginning of her academic career, Lisa Sowle Cahill has specialized in the area of bioethics. Her theological ethical method was often developed in relationship to bioethics. Three characteristics of her method stand out: (1) the importance of both theology and philosophy, but especially the role of theology in light of the Catholic tradition's penchant to use only the natural law; (2) the social aspect and dimension of every ethical issue, especially in light of the previous methodology in bioethics to look only at the individual aspect of one act; and (3) a participatory theological approach to the public sphere that recognizes the need to deal with all the intermediate institutions and realities of public life and not just governmental or professional policies.[42]

Cahill often, and even as late as 2003, developed her approach to bioethics on the basis of commentaries on the work of Richard A. McCormick. In the process, she commented on McCormick's methodological approach. McCormick employed a modified natural law approach, but, in response to later criticism that he failed to recognize the role of faith, he gave more attention to faith and the specifically Christian. He referred to his approach as "reason informed by faith." To the end, however, McCormick insisted on the reasonableness of his ethical conclusions, but he tried to show that faith gives ethics an added dimension. The Christian tradition assists reason in perceiving, disposing, and directing how reason functions, but Christian insights are confirmatory, not originating.[43]

Cahill interprets McCormick's proportionalism as a move to see moral action in a more contextual way recognizing the conflicts individuals face in their social context, but there is a need to go further and recognize the cause of conflicts that individuals face in the disordered world in which they live and the social practices in which we all participate. McCormick in his proportionalism opened the door to moving in the direction of recognizing the social dimension of all reality and the negative influences of existing structures and institutions. However, Cahill is unpersuaded by McCormick's proportionalism precisely because it attaches all the social causes and consequences of actions to specific moral decisions in themselves and not to the broader societal and structural analysis. In addition, she is not persuaded by McCormick's position that by going against the associated good of freedom, one also goes against the good of life itself. If this were true, it would seem that one could never go to war at all.[44]

Cahill elaborates the public role of theological bioethics in keeping with her methodological approach. She objects to the reigning "liberal consensus" that the primary criteria of law and public policy are individual liberty and rights and that the only acceptable public language for bioethics is neutral, secular, and rational.[45] With regard to method, there should be an important role for religious narrative, symbols, and understanding. With regard to content, public theological bioethics clearly challenges the existing consensus stressing the unquestionable belief in science, the economic market, and liberal individualism. Cahill insists on distributive justice, health care reform, the common good in a global context, and the preferential option for the poor. With regard to the means theology uses, not only is there a place for

policy statements and professional guidelines, but also participatory theological ethics works to transform the intermediate institutions, structures, and
groups in the broader civil society in accord with the principle of subsid-
iarity. She gives special concern to a focus on empowering the heretofore
marginalized groups.[46]

Her book *Theological Bioethics* focuses in depth on many examples of this
activist, public, participatory, theological approach. She develops examples
of successful local and international religious-theological action for health
equity. These include Catholic health care ministry and its mission to the
poor and underserved; the hospice movement as an answer to physician-
assisted suicide; religiously sponsored pressures for health care reform, both
nationally and internationally; religious networks supporting the availability
of AIDS drugs, AIDS education, and condoms; care for persons with AIDS
and care for AIDS orphans; adoption as an alternative to expensive, low-
success reproductive technologies; and international networks resisting in
the name of social justice the implementation of innovations in human and
agricultural genetics. Cahill calls for national and international health-access
reform recognizing that health is a basic human and social good. Change will
only come about, however, through organized efforts from below.[47]

A number of times Cahill has visited the issues of death and dying.[48] Coming out of the Catholic tradition, she is committed to the famous distinction
between ordinary and extraordinary means and insists on the important role
of palliative care because death and dying are much more than just medical
issues. The best response to movements for suicide and euthanasia is to create
a social ethos that accepts dependency and decline as part of the human condition and that employs the best medical knowledge to ameliorate physical
and emotional suffering while drawing on spiritual traditions and guidance
to offer patients and caregivers hope in transcendent meaning beyond their
present condition. Given the ambiguity in the distinction between allowing
death to occur and directly causing death, it is difficult if not impossible to
insist on an absolute boundary between the two. A particular case of direct
killing might even be an example of adverse virtue, but this does not mean
that theologians should not resist the direct killing of the elderly, especially
when it is proposed as a legally protected social institution.[49]

The morality of abortion in a narrow (and therefore inadequate) context
raises two issues: the nature and value of the embryo-fetus and the solution
of conflict situations. With regard to the first, one confronts the two aspects
of the descriptive scientific knowledge and the normative philosophical aspects that are based on the descriptive. Cahill recognizes that there is uncertainty about the moral status of the embryo and early fetus. The integral
relation and interdependence of human embodiment and human identity

recommend the conclusion that the moral status of developing life also develops. She worries that those who hold similar developmental approaches or give a precise biological criterion for the beginning of personhood fail to give enough importance and value to the early fetus. As mentioned above, she has expressed her recognition that the direct-indirect solution to problems of conflicts involving human life is not totally absolute. With regard to abortion and the law, the debate also includes many other aspects, especially the equality of women and the proper role of law in a pluralistic society. In this country, Cahill strives for a mediating position. An adequate solution must recognize the importance of sexual responsibility and equality for women and men; the responsibility of both parents for children, born or unborn; and the responsibility of every community to ensure that no woman chooses abortion because she lacks housing, food, or necessary health care or because bearing a child would destroy her educational and employment goals and hopes. She critically points out that the US Catholic bishops have overstressed the personhood of the fetus and have failed to recognize the equality and needs of women, thus affecting the credibility of their own position on the abortion issue.[50]

Theological Bioethics deals extensively with biotechnology, especially in the light of justice. With regard to artificial reproductive technologies, as in the case of abortion, Cahill recognizes the danger of seeing the moral argument only in terms of free choices. She argues with regard to these artificial reproductive technologies that low success rates, disproportionate expense, the priority of other medical needs, and the availability of other solutions should be a part of public deliberations about the ethics and practice of assisted reproduction.[51]

Sexuality

The understandings of the body and of gender play a significant role in the discussion of sexuality. Cahill strenuously opposes the Manichean and Augustinian approaches that see the body, especially in terms of sexuality, as something evil. In addition, as is often the case, she develops her understanding of the body today as a middle position between two contemporary extremes. Current interest in the body seems to take one of two directions: the affirmation of the body as constitutive of personhood or the deconstruction of the body as produced by social discourse and consciousness. Cahill's approach is "both-and"—the body and culture.[52] Humans are embodied beings, so there can be no dualism between body and soul, between physical capacities and social accomplishments. Embodiment itself, however, is thoroughly historical, so we can never identify any cultural mediation of the body as an unchanging given of human existence. Her middle position recognizes both that biology is not destiny and also that human freedom is not disincarnate.[53]

Gender refers to the personality characteristics, behaviors, and social roles that are assigned to the female or male sex.[54] As a Christian feminist, Cahill strenuously defends the basic equality of women and men based on the equal beginning coming from creation. She is highly critical of patriarchy and the subordination of women to men that has been a part of the human and Christian traditions. As a Roman Catholic, she strongly opposes recent Catholic papal teaching. The documents of Pope John Paul II see the true fulfillment of women in terms of motherhood. No such claim is made for the true fulfillment of men in fatherhood. Likewise, Pope John Paul II, despite some positive developments with regard to the equality of men and women, still proposed a complementary relationship between women and men that in reality enforced the subordinate social roles for women.[55]

Cahill vigorously opposes domestic and parental roles for women and public, political, and economic roles for men. Yes, there are obvious physical differences between women and men, but these differences do not bar women from social, public, political, and economic roles. The obvious physiologically different roles of women and men in reproduction do not call for or demand different social roles for women and men. Based on both empirical studies and her own understanding of embodied human existence, Cahill recognizes there can be cognitive (e.g., women are more verbal) or affective (e.g., women's experience of sexuality) differences between women and men. But these differences do not take away from the basic equality of women and men and their ability to fulfill the same public roles in social life.[56]

Cahill also writes extensively on sexual morality. Her Sitz im Leben definitely influences her approach. She started writing in moral theology more than a decade after Humanae vitae. Thus, unlike John C. Ford, Richard A. McCormick, Josef Fuchs, and Germain G. Grisez, she was not directly involved in the debate over Humanae vitae. Although, as pointed out above, she dealt with the aftermath of Humanae vitae in terms of absolute norms and theories of proportionalism and utilitarianism, by her own admission the sexual issues involved in Humanae vitae were not the sexual issues she was facing when she wrote. However, she briefly and strongly agrees with the revisionist criticisms of the sexual teaching of Humanae vitae and the neoscholastic tradition. This approach was too deductive, claimed too much certitude in dealing with complex specific issues, and concentrated only on the sexual act seen especially in terms of its physical structure and its relationship to procreation.[57] She also notes some developments in contemporary Catholic understanding as found in hierarchical teachings, especially those of John Paul II. The current teaching puts more stress on the interpersonal understanding of sex and the importance of love and intimacy but still employs a patriarchal procreative model focused on the sexual act.[58]

What is the approach and understanding of sex that Cahill is reacting to? It is the contemporary cultural understanding present in the United States and other first-world countries that affects Catholics as well as all other Christians. Our contemporary culture views sex in an individualistic and even narcissistic framework and disassociates sex from parental fulfillment and social responsibility, thus marginalizing the role of commitment in sex and making sexual privacy and free choice serve as a front for continuing oppressions and violence toward women.[59] In regard to the last point, as noted earlier, she has raised questions about some artificial reproductive technologies.[60]

Her later approach to sexuality differs somewhat from her earlier method. Her primary purpose now is not to develop sexual norms and a casuistry to deal with particular issues but to develop a vision of sexuality that inspires Christian people. As will be developed shortly, this ideal consists of committed, pleasurable, loving, and parental sex. She does not, however, intend to use this ideal to exclude or necessarily condemn gay and lesbian persons, divorced persons, or those desirous of a permanent relationship who enter tentative sexual liaisons hoping for eventual love and permanency.[61] Cahill maintains that Christian communities have expended disproportionate energy debating issues such as homosexuality that affect a smaller number of Christians and have not given enough attention to the sins that lurk close to the tradition's heterosexual, marital, and procreative heart. Think, for example, of domestic violence, emotional manipulation of spouses, narcissism within the family, and drug and alcohol abuse.[62] Thus, she is primarily interested in what she has experienced as a married, heterosexual spouse who is a mother of five.[63]

Cahill brings her biblical, feminist, and revised Thomistic method to develop her understanding of sexuality. Her feminist and biblical method points out the patriarchy and subordinationist aspects in the scripture, but it also reveals other, more positive values and how the biblical tradition in its own way tried to transform to some extent the existing cultural realities. She also considers at some length the historical tradition giving greater attention to Augustine, Aquinas, and Luther. These three figures in the tradition itself were to somewhat different extents very negative about sexual pleasure and insisted on the primacy of procreation, but they also strove to transform some of the existing cultural understandings and approaches.[64] Cahill tries to follow the best of the tradition today by trying to transform the existing cultural understanding of sex described earlier.

On the basis of her biblical investigation, Cahill concludes that the biblical vision focuses on faithful, heterosexual marriage. The body plays an important role in this vision, but procreation is not primary. The purpose of such a vision is to support community members to build up the community. The guiding biblical moral vision for all human realities is an ethic of compassion and solidarity that brings into the community those who have been excluded and marginalized. A Christian sexual ethic's first function, despite the contrary practice of much of the Christian community, is not to mark off boundaries or condemn but to inspire and encourage the disciple to do good. Cahill also applies her feminist method to the biblical evidence and to the historical tradition to insist on the evil of patriarchy and the need for basic equality between women and men across the board.[65]

Cahill recognizes that to fill out and expand the biblical vision, one needs an understanding of what human flourishing brings to the vision.[66] On the basis of her Thomistic understanding of human flourishing with regard to sexuality, she builds on an embodied anthropology recognizing a significant role for the body. Human sexual flourishing depends on the realization of the equality of the male and female sexes and in their union based on the values of reproduction, pleasure, and intimacy. Human sexuality has these values of reproduction, pleasure, and intimacy elaborated in personal relationships over time and in the social institutions of marriage and family.[67]

Despite her insistence on a sexual vision and not casuistry, Cahill briefly engages in casuistry in one paragraph of her two later books on sexuality. The three values of sexual intimacy, committed love, and parenthood can be prioritized with loving commitment in the first place as the one inviolable value. The realization of the other two values depends on changing concrete conditions. Thus, sexual expression and shared biological parenthood can in some instances be sacrificed to the priority of a love relationship.[68]

In a later article, Cahill does address the issue of same-sex marriage. In this case, as often happens to moral theologians, Cahill was asked to participate in a conference to discuss this issue. Her conclusion is that both Church and society should give such unions "legal recognition and ecclesial respect." Her essay develops, however, in a somewhat curious way and does not employ a casuistic approach. Cahill recognizes two opposing positions coming from official hierarchical Church documents and the writings of some theologians supported by the attitudes of many Roman Catholics. Her basic concern reflects her often developed position that the Catholic understanding of marriage should oppose a truncated understanding of marriage as a one-on-one loving relationship involving little or no broader relationship with the larger parental, familial, and social responsibilities of the couple. The magisterium has somewhat played into this truncated understanding by focusing on marriage as a total self-gift. With regard to same-sex marriages, it is generally recognized among many Roman Catholics today that gay persons are capable of "marital" love, and the quality of the love between same-sex couples is in no way inferior to the marital love of straight spouses, but the understanding of heterosexual marriage and same-sex marriage must go further than this because the approach is too individualistic. Same-sex couples, like heterosexual couples, must recognize not only a responsibility for the spouse but also important responsibility for children (if any), the larger family, and the broader social community.[69]

In a 2000 monograph, Cahill developed her approach to the family from a Christian social perspective, once again emphasizing the family's role in trying to transform the world. Her approach to family follows some patterns found in her earlier writings on sexuality and other topics. She wants to advance an inclusive and supporting approach to family life—one that can hold up ideals such as male-female coparenting and sexual fidelity without berating and excluding other forms of family today, including gay and lesbian families. The ideals of Christian family life should focus on fostering the role of Gospel-informed commitments and behavior and not on the form that the family takes.[70] Once again, she gives importance to the biblical and historical tradition, recognizing their shortcomings as well as their attempt to transform the existing culture, but she also develops the metaphor of the family as domestic church. There can be limitations and problems resulting from the understanding of the family as domestic church, but Cahill also points out the positive aspects of such an approach.[71] One creative chapter illustrating her concern with the particular and the marginalized deals with lessons to be learned from African American families.[72]

Cahill focuses on the values of the kingdom or reign of God proclaimed by Jesus to structure the family as an inclusive community united in love of neighbor and enemy that should strongly resist the worldly hierarchies of gender, race, and class and the failure of contemporary society to recognize the preferential option for the poor. In historical practice, unfortunately, Christian families have often tended to support socioeconomic hierarchies of privilege. The Christian vision of family strives to overcome self-promoting and exclusionary tendencies and to enhance the family's ability to teach affection, empathy, and altruism. The Christian family's threefold responsibility is to form children, to serve the Church, and to try to transform the world.[73]

Social Ethics

In her book *Global Ethics, Christology, and Christian Ethics*, Cahill elaborates biblical and Christian reasons for Christian commitment to justice in light of the inequality, poverty, sexism, racism, and violence in our contemporary world. Not only are these problems today an affront to the Christian biblical and theological vision, but they also stand in some opposition to the fundamental goodness of human nature. This book thus proposes a basic Christian and human framework for developing a social ethics.[74]

As already pointed out, in dealing with bioethics and sexuality, which are very often considered under the rubric of personal or individual ethics as distinguished from social ethics, Cahill has insisted on the social ethics dimension of these areas. In a true sense she recognizes the social dimension of all Christian ethics. In the very first paragraph of a 2012 article, Cahill refers to herself as a feminist, liberationist, and biblical social ethicist. Later in the same essay, she refers to herself as a "Catholic, feminist, liberationist, social ethicist." Note that all the other adjectives in her description of herself modify social ethicist.[75]

One illustration of her work in the traditional area of social ethics is her analysis of two social encyclicals of Benedict XVI: *Deus caritas est* and *Caritas in veritate*.[76] Here again, as in all of her work, the emphasis is on the role and importance of method. Benedict's first encyclical, *Deus caritas est*, assigned political work to the laity and restricted the Catholic Church's social involvement to the laity. In this encyclical, Benedict emphasizes the Word Christology that he had employed in his earlier writings, especially in his book *Jesus of Nazareth*. This Word Christology coheres with his long-standing vision for a countercultural approach in Europe in opposition to the forces of secularism. For the Church to function as a countercultural alternative, its identity and voice must be clear and strong. A Word Christology is biblically attested, theologically coherent, and ethically necessary, but it is not enough. The problem is that such a Christology limits the understanding of the human based on the incarnation only to the spiritual realm with its relationship to the divine. To be human also involves the material, embodied, relational, social, and political dimensions. In her book *Global Ethics, Christology, and Christian Ethics*, Cahill insists on the need for a Spirit Christology in addition to a Word Christology and on the primary significance of the kingdom values proclaimed by Jesus.[77] In the later writings of Benedict from 2005 to 2009, Cahill sees Benedict's approach moving in this direction. As a result, there is no sharp contrast between the work of the Church and the work of the laity.

Cahill deals more extensively with peace and violence than with any other issue of social ethics. Recall her 1994 monograph that tries to take very seriously the biblical approach to these issues as well as the historical development down to the present. The reader is somewhat surprised that Cahill, however, does not develop and expound her own position in this book.[78]

Later, however, Cahill briefly developed her own position. Again there is some surprise because, whereas the book stresses the importance of the biblical emphasis, she basically accepts the natural law approach of Thomas Aquinas to the issue of violence. Her general acceptance of Aquinas's natural law approach has already been discussed. In the case of war, Aquinas begins by recognizing a prima facie wrongness to war that can be overridden by a dire threat to the common good. His basic just war criteria are developed in terms of reason and the cardinal virtues, but the integration of Christian insight is evident in the way Cahill discusses the issue. She modifies the Thomistic approach in two areas. First, Aquinas in general recognizes the role of sin in human affairs, but he does not explicitly recognize that just war thinking can easily be perverted and fail to serve the common good. Recent history certainly demonstrates this fact. Second, Aquinas does not fully acknowledge the tension or conflict that arises when immediate justice calls for measures that contradict the basic moral vision of the Gospel.[79]

Cahill recognizes that conflict and war will not be eradicated and at times can be ethically justified. However, based on her understanding of discipleship and eschatology, recognizing the tension between the now and the not yet, she insists on the importance of the strategy of peacebuilding for Christians. Peacebuilding is an important way to reduce conflict and its causes and is a good illustration of the Christian expression of the politics of salvation and advocacy for inclusive human flourishing. Peacebuilding also demonstrates how hope is engendered from within human suffering, as illustrated in a number of narratives she develops.[80] Notice how similar her position is to what Bernard Häring proposed.

In conclusion, it is impossible to discuss adequately all that Cahill has written in her vocation as a Catholic moral theologian. The breadth and depth of her writing are most impressive. This chapter has tried to deal with the most significant aspects of her work.

In my judgment, the most outstanding contribution of her work is to carry on in her circumstances and Sitz im Leben what is perhaps the most characteristic aspect of the Catholic ethical tradition—the insistence on a "both-and," and not an "either-or," approach. Cahill insists on both the theological and philosophical aspects of moral theology and shows how this approach enables her to be in dialogue with Christians, followers of other religions, and those who rely simply on human reason. Too often in the past, moral theology has distinguished and even separated the areas of individual ethics and social ethics, but Cahill recognizes that all ethics has a significant social dimension. As a feminist and a Thomist, she holds on to the importance of both the particular and the universal. There is a tendency among some to see the new and the old in opposition, but Cahill finds truth in both the older and the newer approaches while continuing to criticize both. Such an approach well illustrates what it means to work with a living tradition.

All have to admire the depth and breadth of her work. In light of the ongoing specialization in moral theology, generalists such as Lisa Sowle Cahill are probably a dying breed. In some ways, however, her dealing with method, fundamental moral theology, sexuality and family, bioethics, and various aspects of sexual ethics contributed to her lasting contribution that even the so-called individual ethics of sexuality and bioethics have significant social dimensions.

Notes

1. "Lisa Sowle Cahill, Resume," https://www.bc.edu/content/dam/files/schools/cas_sites/theology/pdf/lcahill_cv.pdf.

2. James M. Gustafson, *Protestant and Roman Catholic Ethics: Prospects for Rapprochement* (Chicago: University of Chicago Press, 1978).

3. "Lisa Sowle Cahill, Resume."

4. Lisa Sowle Cahill, *Between the Sexes: Foundations for a Christian Ethics of Sexuality* (Philadelphia: Fortress, 1985), ix.

5. "Lisa Sowle Cahill, Resume."

6. Lisa Sowle Cahill, *Family: A Christian Social Perspective* (Minneapolis: Fortress, 2000), xiii.

7. Lisa Sowle Cahill, *Global Justice, Christology, and Christian Ethics*, New Studies in Christian Ethics (Cambridge: Cambridge University Press, 2013). Cahill, in this book and in some other books, reworked essays and articles she previously wrote. As a result, one does not have to consider those articles that previously appeared in journals and edited books.

8. Lisa Sowle Cahill, *Theological Bioethics: Participation, Justice, Change* (Washington, DC: Georgetown University Press, 2005).

9. "Lisa Sowle Cahill," Boston College Theology Department Faculty, https://www.bc.edu/bc-web/schools/mcas/departments/theology/people/faculty-directory/lisa-cahill.html.

10. Cahill, *Between the Sexes*, 1.

11. Ibid., 4–7.

12. Stephen W. Gunter et al., *Wesley and the Quadrilateral: Renewing the Conversation* (Nashville, TN: Abingdon, 1997).

13. E.g., Lisa Sowle Cahill, *Women and Sexuality*, 1992 Madeleva Lecture in Spirituality (New York: Paulist, 1992), 42.

14. Cahill, *Between the Sexes*, 139–52.

15. Cahill takes a similar approach to method and scripture in an earlier article: Lisa Sowle Cahill, "Moral Methodology: A Case Study," *Chicago Studies* 19, no. 2 (1980): 177–87.

16. Lisa Sowle Cahill, *Love Your Enemies: Discipleship, Pacifism, and Just War Theory* (Minneapolis: Fortress, 1994).

17. Ibid., 1–14. Cahill generally uses the word "kingdom," which most feminists tend to avoid using.

18. Ibid., 15–38.

19. Lisa Sowle Cahill, *Sex, Gender, and Christian Ethics*, New Studies in Christian Ethics (Cambridge: Cambridge University Press, 1996), 155–60.

20. Ibid., 121–23.

21. Ibid., 141.

22. Ibid., 152–53.

23. Ibid., 160–62.

24. Cahill, *Family*, 18–47.

25. Cahill, *Global Justice, Christology, and Christian Ethics*, 201–3, 247.

26. Cahill, *Theological Bioethics*, 117–20.

27. Cahill, *Between the Sexes*, 149.

28. Cahill, *Theological Bioethics*, 43–69.

29. Cahill, *Sex, Gender, and Christian Ethics*, 1–3.

30. Cahill, *Between the Sexes*, 68–100; Cahill, *Sex, Gender, and Christian Ethics*, 14–45.

31. Cahill, *Sex, Gender, and Christian Ethics*, 14–17.

32. Ibid., 17–35.

33. Ibid., 36–37, 46–55.

34. Ibid., 49.

35. Cahill develops her understanding of the natural law especially in Cahill, *Global Justice, Christology, and Christian Ethics*, 247–89. See also Cahill, *Sex, Gender, and Christian Ethics*, 46–55.

36. Cahill, *Global Justice*, 10–18, 273–75.

37. Ibid., 272–73.

38. Lisa Sowle Cahill, "On Richard McCormick: Reason and Faith in Post–Vatican II Catholic Ethics," in *Theological Voices in Medical Ethics*, ed. Allen Verhey and Stephen E. Lammers (Grand Rapids, MI: Eerdmans, 1993), 85–86.

39. Cahill, *Theological Bioethics*, 250–57.

40. Cahill, *Global Justice, Christology, and Christian Ethics*, 138–47.

41. Cahill, *Between the Sexes*, 145–52.

42. Cahill, *Theological Bioethics*, 1–12.

43. Cahill, "On Richard McCormick," 85–89.

44. Lisa Sowle Cahill, *Bioethics and the Common Good*, Père Marquette Lecture in Theology 2004 (Milwaukee: Marquette University Press, 2004), 26–31.

45. Lisa Sowle Cahill, "Theology's Role in Public Bioethics," in *Handbook of Bioethics and Religion*, ed. Daniel E. Guinn (New York: Oxford University Press, 2006), 37.

46. Cahill, *Theological Bioethics*, 13–69.

47. Ibid., 69ff. Cahill briefly summarizes these aspects of her public participatory theological approach on p. 69 and develops them in much greater detail throughout the book.

48. See especially two important articles: Lisa Sowle Cahill, "Sanctity of Life, Quality of Life, and Social Justice," *Theological Studies* 48 (1987): 105–23; and Lisa Sowle Cahill, "Bioethical Decisions to End Life," *Theological Studies* 52 (1991): 107–27.

49. Cahill, *Theological Bioethics*, 70–120. This is her most developed and systematic discussion of the topic.

50. Ibid., 170–92. For her many other articles on this issue, see "Lisa Sowle Cahill, Resume."

51. Cahill, *Theological Bioethics*, 170–92.

52. Cahill, *Sex, Gender, and Christian Ethics*, 73–77.

53. Cahill, *Women and Sexuality*, 66–67.

54. Lisa Sowle Cahill, "Gender and Christian Ethics," in *The Cambridge Companion to Christian Ethics*, 2nd ed., ed. Robin Gill (Cambridge: Cambridge University Press, 2012), 112.

55. Cahill, *Women and Sexuality*, 49–54.

56. Cahill, *Between the Sexes*, 83–104; Cahill, *Sex, Gender, and Christian Ethics*, 82–90.

57. Cahill, *Women and Sexuality*, 8–14; Cahill, *Sex, Gender, and Christian Ethics*, 50, 68–69.

58. Cahill, *Women and Sexuality*, 49–54; Cahill, *Sex, Gender, and Christian Ethics*, 201–7.

59. Cahill, *Sex, Gender, and Christian Ethics*, 116–17.

60. Cahill, *Women and Sexuality*, 71–79.

61. Cahill, *Sex, Gender, and Christian Ethics*, 116.

62. Ibid., 160.

63. Ibid., 116.

64. Cahill, *Sex, Gender, and Christian Ethics*, 166–94; Cahill, *Women and Sexuality*, 7.

65. Cahill, *Sex, Gender, and Christian Ethics*, 154–65.

66. Ibid., 163.

67. Cahill, *Sex, Gender, and Christian Ethics*, 109–14; Cahill, *Women and Sexuality*, 70.

68. Cahill, *Women and Sexuality*, 70–71.

69. Lisa Sowle Cahill, "Same-Sex Marriage and Catholicism: Dialogue, Learning, and Change," in *More Than a Monologue: Sexual Diversity and the Catholic Church*, 2nd ed., ed. J. Patrick Hornbeck II and Michael A. Norko (New York: Fordham University Press, 2014), 141–55.

70. Cahill, *Family*, xi.

71. Ibid., 83–110.

72. Ibid., 111–29.

73. Ibid., 4, 18–50.

74. Cahill, *Global Ethics*, 1–31.

75. Lisa Sowle Cahill, "Theological Ethics as Political Ethics: A Conversation with Raymond Geuss," *Studies in Christian Ethics* 25, no. 2 (2012): 153–59.

76. Lisa Sowle Cahill, "*Caritas in veritate:* Benedict's Global Reorientation," *Theological Studies* 71 (2010): 291–319.

77. Cahill, *Global Values*, 122–203.

78. Cahill, *Love Your Enemies*.

79. Cahill, *Global Justice*, 275–80.

80. Ibid., 290–303.

9

Ada María Isasi-Díaz

Feminist theology in the United States, carrying on the liberationist approach of beginning with the experience of the oppressed, opened the door for two later theologies likewise beginning with the *Sitz im Leben* of the oppressed: Latina theology and black theology. The two most recognized theological ethicists writing in these two approaches are Ada María Isasi-Díaz, the mother of *mujerista* theology, and Bryan N. Massingale in black Catholic theological ethics.

The distinction between systematic and moral theology is somewhat abstract and does not recognize the reality that all theology is one, and there is much overlap between systematic and moral theology. A good example of this overlap is the consideration of theological anthropology, which is often developed by systematic theologians but has important ramifications for moral theology. While there is overlap, the distinction between systematic and moral theology still retains some meaning and importance in both these theological traditions. Both Isasi-Díaz and Massingale consider themselves to be theological ethicists or moral theologians. Both were trained in theological ethics and identify themselves as such and write from that perspective. This chapter will discuss the work of Isasi-Díaz, while the next chapter will consider Massingale.

Ada María Isasi-Díaz writes from the Latina perspective in the United States. Hispanics make up a relatively large segment of the US Catholic Church. According to the Pew Research Center, 59 percent of Catholics are white, while 34 percent are Hispanic. In addition, the percentage of Hispanic Catholics grows every year. Since blacks constitute only 3 percent of the Catholic population, one logically expects a much greater theological activity among Latina and Hispanic theologians than among black theologians.[1]

The Academy of Catholic Hispanic Theologians in the United States (ACHTUS) came into existence in 1988 and has met annually ever since.

In 1993, ACHTUS began publishing the *Journal of Hispanic/Latino Theology*, In the first ten years (1993–2003), Liturgical Press contributed to publishing the journal, but such a venture became too expensive. The journal was published online until 2015 but no longer exists.[2] As a result of the work of the academy and the journal, there definitely exists a good nucleus of Hispanic Catholic theologians writing in the United States.

The late Virgilio Elizondo is looked on as the "father of US Latino religious thought." Elizondo, a priest of the archdiocese of San Antonio who received a doctoral degree from the Institute Catholique in Paris, cofounded the Mexican American Cultural Center to prepare those ministering to Hispanic people. In 1983, he published *The Galilean Journey: The Mexican American Promise*, tracing the similarities between Jesus's Galilean background and the mestizo experience of Hispanics in the United States. Every year, ACHTUS confers the Virgilio Elizondo Award on an outstanding Hispanic theologian in the United States. In 2007, the Catholic Theological Society of America gave Elizondo its highest award—the John Courtney Murray Award.[3] His writings contain some ethical aspects, as is true of most Hispanic theologians in the United States, but he did not consider himself an ethicist.

There is no doubt that Ada María Isasi-Díaz is the most significant theological ethicist among US Latina theologians. In 1989, she coined the term "mujerista theology," which she did not use in her earliest writings. In a 1988 book coauthored with Yolanda Tarango, she referred to her topic as "Hispanic women's liberation theology."[4] The development of womanist theology by black feminists in the United States helped her in her search for a name. To name oneself is one of the most powerful abilities a person can have. In love songs and protest songs, Hispanic women are often called *mujer*—woman. Those who make a preferential option for *mujeres* should be called "mujeristas." The name "mujerista theology" has been generally accepted to describe the theology done by and for Hispanic women in the United States.[5] In the very first issue of the *Journal of Latino/Hispanic Theology*, she published an article, "Praxis: The Heart of *Mujerista* Theology."[6]

Sitz im Leben

Mujerista theology emphasizes the importance of Latinas telling their own story. In a number of different places, Isasi-Díaz has told her own story.[7] She was born in Havana, Cuba, in 1943 but came to the United States in 1960 as a political refugee. She joined the Ursuline Sisters and was sent to Peru as a missionary for three years. There she first lived with and heard the stories of poor women. After returning to the United States and leaving the Ursuline community, she realized that religion was the central aspect in her life but wondered exactly what to do. She participated in the first Women's Ordination Conference in 1975, and there became a feminist. Isasi-Díaz worked for the conference and also began participating in the meetings of Las Hermanas, a Hispanic Catholic organization.

She then committed herself to the struggle of Latinas for liberation. Realizing the need for theological education, she enrolled in 1983 at Union Theological Seminary in New York. There, under the tutelage of Beverly Harrison, acknowledged as a leading feminist ethicist in the United States, and with the support of a good number of women struggling for liberation in various areas, Isasi-Díaz wrote her doctoral dissertation, which was published in a modified form in 1993 as *En la Lucha: In the Struggle; A Hispanic Women's Liberation Theology*.[8] She started teaching social ethics at Drew University in 1993 and stayed at that institution until her untimely death from cancer in 2012. Having decided to study for a PhD and to work later as an academician, she had to deal with the fact that it is the work she did with Latinas that was most life-giving for her. Through the years she has learned the difficult task of straddling both worlds, the academy and the grassroots Latina community. Even while teaching at Drew, she regularly worked with a community of Latinas in East Harlem in New York. The need to be an activist working in the neighborhoods with Latinas was not something she did in addition to her theological ethics. Her theological ethics was intimately connected with her grassroots liberation activism. This Sitz im Leben in being both an activist and an academic theological ethicist is what is distinctive about her approach.

Three contexts are important for understanding the Sitz im Leben of Ada María Isasi-Díaz: the historical and cultural, the theological, and the contexts of her own writing. The historical-cultural context is the situation of Hispanic women in the United States. Isasi-Díaz uses "Hispanic" to refer to the three most populous groups of Hispanic women—Mexican American, Puerto Rican, and Cuban. These mujerista or Hispanic women face a threefold oppression: sexism, racism, and, for many, economic deprivation. Their lives thus are a struggle for liberation from these oppressions, but survival means much more than merely living. Survival involves the struggle (*la lucha*) to *fully* be—to have the power to decide about one's history and one's vocation or historical mission.[9]

Another important aspect of the culture has to do with *mestizaje-mulatez*, a term that mujerista theology employs to refer to the coming together of races and cultures, including religion as an element of culture. In Latina communities we find people from many different countries of origin. Mujerista theology emphasizes the importance of the African and Amerindian strands in their culture. This broad racial–cultural richness has made mujeristas realize the need to insist on similarities rather than on differences among them.[10]

The theological-ethical context involves primarily feminist and liberation theology. Isasi-Díaz described herself after 1975 as a feminist and wrote her dissertation under Beverly Harrison, acknowledged as a leading feminist ethicist in the United States. Feminist theology, as noted in the discussion of Margaret Farley and Lisa Sowle Cahill, takes as its starting point the oppression of women by patriarchy. Feminist theology itself is a form of liberation theology that arose among Catholics in Latin America and also black Protestant theologians in the United States. While she was working with the poor in Lima, Isasi-Díaz came into contact with Gustavo Gutiérrez, who is generally acknowledged as the father of liberation theology. Like feminist and liberation theologies, mujerista theology begins with the experience of the oppressed, but now there is a threefold oppression: sexism, racism, and economic deprivation. Sexism comes from the patriarchal attitudes of many, especially Hispanic men. Racism comes from the dominant white culture in the United States. Economic deprivation characterizes the lives of most mujeristas, although some, especially Cubanas, are often in the middle class.[11]

Liberation theology gives an important role to the metaphor of the kingdom or reign of God, especially its social, political, and historical dimensions in this world. Isasi-Díaz, from the very beginning of her writings, recognized the importance of the concept but changed its name to "kin_dom of God." The kingdom-of-God metaphor had often been misused, as illustrated by the identification that pre–Vatican II Catholic theology made between the Church and the kingdom of God. At its best, the kingdom of God is a metaphor for the alternative world order based on the teaching of Jesus. But the metaphor of the kingdom does not work for us today for two reasons: It emphasizes the hierarchical structure of God's reign and is a patriarchal term. Isasi-Díaz avoids these two problems by changing its name.[12]

The third context is the nature of her writing. The only systematic monograph written solely by her is her revised doctoral dissertation, *En la Lucha*. This book, like the earlier *Hispanic Women: Prophetic Voice in the Church* coauthored with Yolanda Tarango, summarizes in Spanish the English chapters. The essay was her primary writing genre. These essays appeared in journals and very often in chapters of edited books. Two of her books are collections of essays. In light of her grassroots involvement and her theological ethical teaching and writing, she managed to write a good number of essays explaining and developing her mujerista theology. These essays are somewhat repetitive as they try to explain mujerista theology to different audiences in different contexts. In the last years before her death, she published a number of essays on justice that she had planned to publish as a book.

Method

Isasi-Díaz maintains that praxis is at the heart of mujerista theology. It is the method that distinguishes mujerista theology from other theologies, especially the classical theology that begins with ideas about God and the world and then applies them to how people should act.[13]

Liberation theology by definition involves the struggle for the liberation of the oppressed group.[14] Such liberation is a personal, self-actualizing struggle that is the moral responsibility of all those engaged in that struggle. Moral agency and moral responsibility characterize the roles of those struggling for liberation. The oppressed are not just objects for the pity, concern, or help from others. They, above all, are not objects acted on by oppressors. They are subjects and moral agents struggling for liberation.

Mujerista theology is a praxis grounded in and arising from the lived experience of Latinas. Latinas in our society are oppressed by their ethnicity, sex, and often poverty. As moral subjects, they reflect on the experience of their liberating struggle. Latinas' lived experience is not the same as other oppressed groups, including Latinos. Latinas do not find their values and understandings reflected in the broader society. In fact, the understandings and structures of the broader society have been imposed by the strong and powerful and serve to keep Latinas in their place. The cultural and andro-centric biases of contemporary US society do not support the participation of Latinas in the broader society and actually oppose it. The lived experience of Latinas in their struggle to be liberated from their oppression is a true *locus theologicus* and the primary source of mujerista theology. This theology begins with the lived experience of Latinas struggling against their oppression. This primary source differentiates mujerista theology from all other theological approaches, especially the classical moral theology that begins with principles and then applies them to action.

The Bible does not play an important role in the experience of Latinas. They generally do not read the Bible, and know only the popularized versions of biblical stories.[15] In one essay in an edited book, *The Bible and the Hermeneutics of Liberation*, Isasi-Díaz does discuss a mujerista use of the Bible. When the Bible is used, it must promote true liberation. This essay focuses on the proper interpretation of the parable of the owner of the vineyard, who, in the generally accepted interpretation, generously gives to those who work only an hour the same pay as those who have worked the whole day.

Isasi-Díaz, depending on Frederick Herzog, insists on reading the parable from the perspective of the whole-day workers, who rightly feel insulted by the owner. He has not respected them in their labor. They therefore properly protest what he had done. Their protest is not accepted, but they have retained their honor, self-respect, and dignity by standing up to the owner.[16]

Praxis is critical reflective action. The reflective part does not follow the action. Action and reflection are inseparable moments, though neither is reduced to the other. Liberative praxis combines reflection with action. This understanding points to an anthropology different from the anthropology of much modern theological ethics, which begins with a bourgeois subject characterized by a freedom based on rationalization and individualism. Mujerista theology begins with poor, oppressed Latinas—those who suffer, have been ignored by history, and treated by the power elites as not belonging. Latinas' conscious involvement in this liberation struggle involves their own moral agency and responsibility in the liberative struggle. Reflection is an important part of praxis. There is no dichotomy between reflection and action. Thus, Latinas are, in the words of Antonio Gramsci, "organic intellectuals." In their involvement in liberative praxis, they contribute to a conception of the world and thus bring into being new modes of thought. Since the source of mujerista theology is the lived experience of Latinas, and since Latinas involved in the liberative practice are organic intellectuals, grassroots Latinas *are* mujerista theologians.[17]

Such an understanding differs from the approach taken by many other liberation theologians. Gustavo Gutiérrez sees theology as a second step of reflection after praxis. For Isasi-Díaz there are not two steps. Praxis is reflective action, and hence for believing people the liberation struggle involves theology. Note how this is a fundamentally different understanding of theology rooted in reflective praxis. For mujerista theologians, the ongoing revelation of who God is and what God is like is to be found in their struggle for survival, justice, and liberation. They do not live differently as Christians from the way they live as mujerista theologians. There can be no distinction between the first step of action and the second step of theologizing. Doing mujerista theology is their way of life. To insist that grassroots Latinas are theologians recognizes their moral agency, their responsibility, and their ability to cause what happens. Being conscious of the causality of their lives means that Latinas can speak for themselves and explain their own reality.[18]

Thus, mujerista theology as a praxis is done by the community as each Latina contributes to the process of doing theology according to her own gifts. In light of particular times and needs, one gift may be more useful than another, but that does not mean it is more important. Those who are "theological technicians" with academic training and degrees are not more fully theologians than the Latinas who lead the action component of liberating praxis or those who are gifted in expressing the beliefs of the community through ritual. There is no such thing as academic mujerista theology on the one hand and grassroots mujerista theology on the other.[19]

What precisely is the role of the theological technician in mujerista theology? In the 1988 book Isasi-Díaz coauthored with Yolanda Tarango, the authors describe how they gathered diverse groups of Hispanic women together for weekend retreats in which they talked about their experience in the struggle against racism, sexism, and economic deprivation. The theological technician has two roles. The first is as an enabler to lead the participants in the group to grasp the knowledge they all have. Second, as a writer-recorder, the theological technician has the task of being faithful to what the Latina community has said and being accountable to the community for making what is said understandable to other communities of struggle and even to the dominant group, in order to challenge it.[20]

In her revised doctoral dissertation published in 1993, Isasi-Díaz now used more academic terms to describe the role of the professional theologian or the theological technician.[21] Her method does not begin with the same old questions proposed by the classical theology. Nor does it begin with an analysis of the scriptures or the teaching of the Christian tradition. Her method begins with the experience of the Latinas in their struggle against oppression. The problem with most sociological studies is that they objectify the objects of their study and often come up with abstract types. It is important to deal with the Latinas as subjects and recognize the importance of their individual particularities. She uses ethnographic interviews and acknowledges she has been using this method for the last ten years. The interviews often take place after the retreats mentioned above or independently of them, but Isasi-Díaz in the second case already is familiar with the women she interviews.

This intensive interviewing provides an opportunity for the interviewees to articulate their lived experience, to tell their story in a way that makes them understand what being agents of their own history is all about. Ethnographical principles call for the participation of the women being interviewed in developing the method itself. There should be as little mediation as possible in describing and making known the culture in question. Ethnography involves an emic approach, which seeks to understand and appreciate the lived experience of those being interviewed. It does not judge the religious understanding and practice of Hispanic women, nor does it try to make them fit into traditional theological frameworks or categories. The emic approach is holistic because it takes into account the cultural context of Hispanic women.

To bring together multiple ethnographic accounts, she uses the basic understandings and techniques of metaethnography. This method does not attempt to aggregate the information gathered in the interviews but to interpret it. To properly and accountably interpret the interviews, the mujerista professional theologian must be an insider. Note how this fits in with her own self-description as an activist and a theologian. In *En la Lucha*, Isasi-Díaz, after describing her method, then includes in a long, separate chapter the very words of Latinas as moral agents involved in the liberative praxis of their struggle.[22] Such a method has a much thinner understanding of theology than the other approaches discussed in this book.

Content of Mujerista Theology

Isasi-Díaz uses five Spanish terms—*la lucha, lo cotidiano, el projecto histórico, la familia/communidad*, and *religiosidad popular*—to describe important aspects of mujerista theology. As the titles of two of her books indicate, la lucha is the central element of mujerista theology. It is the main experience in the lives of the majority of Latinas. Life for Latinas facing their threefold oppression is difficult and involves much suffering, but suffering is not the central element in their lives. Latinas also celebrate with fiestas and in other ways and recognize, in the words of an old Latino/a song, that the good life is one that one enjoys. They develop rituals to celebrate and help them in their struggle. Yes, suffering is part of their struggle, but it is not the basic reality of their lives.[23] God is present to Latinas in their daily lives and struggles. In the fiesta celebration on the feast of Our Lady of Guadalupe on December 12, they sing with great fervor, "Come walk with us, holy Mary, come." This presence gives them the strength to carry on the struggle. Notice how their spirituality is very much a community spirituality.[24]

Cotidiano does not appear in the index of her revised dissertation but is developed in subsequent writings. It refers to the liberative daily experience of Hispanic women's everyday struggle and is more than a descriptive category. Cotidiano also has the hermeneutical importance of referring to the stuff and processes of Hispanic women's lives. Finding ways to struggle against oppression is part of cotidiano. It is also the epistemological framework of the theological enterprise and refers to Latinas' efforts to understand and express how and why they live and function as they do. Cotidiano rescues Hispanic women's daily experience from the category of the unimportant and argues against the false universalism of the dominant culture that ignores Latinas' daily experience. It is a way to understand theology not as academic and churchy attempts to see theology as being about God but rather as what we humans know about God.[25]

Mujerista theology uses the term "projecto histórico" to refer to the preferred future of liberation for Latinas and the historical specific means to bring it about. Salvation and liberation are two aspects of the one process involving our relationship to God and neighbor. Liberation refers to being agents of their own history, which will never be fully achieved in this world. It involves three different but interrelated aspects: *libertad* (freedom), *comunidad de fe* (faith community), and *justicia* (justice). Libertad emphasizes Latinas as agents of their own history involving the process of conscientization, opposing a narrow self-promotion while recognizing commitment to the struggle involves true self-realization. Communidad de fe is the goal of rejecting sin, both personal and social, and is also the community that makes rejecting sin possible. Justicia refers to the political, economic and social structures we seek to build to make oppression impossible.[26] From the very beginning, Isasi-Díaz insisted on the importance of justice but developed it in much greater detail at the end of her life. This chapter will consider her understanding of justice later.

In discussing the projecto histórico as the preferred future, Isasi-Díaz mentions the importance of social structures, beginning with a rejection of existing socio-political-economic structures, which are based on an oppressive understanding of power as dominion and control. These structures also aim to set one oppressed group against another. Isasi-Díaz insists on the slogan made famous by feminists that the personal is political. Latinas need to set up strong community organizations and work for economic democracy.[27]

The fourth aspect of mujerista theology is the emphasis on familia/communidad. Familia plays an important role for Hispanics. In the United States the word "machismo" connotes the idea of extreme chauvinism. Behind this approach, however, is an attempt by the dominant culture to consider itself as superior. This underlying reality does not, however, take away from the fact that Latinas have much struggling to do in their families when they strive to be agents of their own future. For Latinas, communidad is an extension of the family. Familia/communidad constitutes the first and primary area where Latinas are historical protagonists. Isasi-Díaz, however, cautions against any attempt to romanticize Latino/a families and communities or to downplay conflicts and oppression that Latinas suffer in their own domain. But with all its problems, familia/communidad as a grounding element for Latinas and their self-understanding must be a central element in mujerista theology.[28]

The emphasis on familia/communidad opposes the emphasis on individualism and the anthropology of the contemporary dominant culture. Such an emphasis coheres also with the important role given to solidarity. Isasi-Díaz calls for a paradigmatic shift involving solidarity as the appropriate present-day understanding of the Gospel call to charity and love. Solidarity recognizes the interconnection between oppression and privilege, between rich and poor, between the oppressed and the oppressors. It also refers to the cohesiveness that should exist among all communities of struggle. The goal of solidarity is to participate in the ongoing praxis of liberation. Solidarity in its broadest perspective seeks the ultimate mutuality of oppressor and oppressed. Oppressors who are willing to listen to the oppressed by that very listening leave behind their oppression and become "friends" of the oppressed. Solidarity will not become a reality until we are totally committed to this mutuality. Isasi-Díaz recognizes that more than two-thirds of the people in the world live under terribly oppressive conditions and that unless we recognize the interdependence and mutuality of all persons, there will be no true liberation.[29] The question to be raised here is whether Isasi-Díaz recognizes the enormous complexity of the realities involved in the continuing role of personal and structural sin in our world.

A fifth important component of mujerista theology is religiosidad popular—popular religiosity. From her earliest writings, Isasi-Díaz dealt with this reality.[30] Popular religiosity for Latinas is central to their struggle and allows religion to play a very central role in their lives. The Christianity and Catholicism of Latinas have their origins and historical roots in the fact that the conquistadores brought their religion with them as a part of their domination. Over time there is no doubt that Latinas have accepted this Catholicity but incorporated into it some of the religious traditions brought to Latin America by African slaves and the Amerindian traditions bequeathed by the great Aztec, Maya, and Inca civilizations. Popular religiosity refers to the religious understandings and practices of the masses in contrast to the "official" Christianity or Catholicism of the Church. The popular religiosity of Latinas is thus syncretic, bringing in other elements to their understanding of Catholicism. For example, is Our Lady of Guadalupe the mother of Jesus, or is she Tonantzin the Aztec goddess? Catholic Latinas strongly consider themselves Catholics but are also open to other religious beliefs and practices.

Popular religiosity has often been a source of embarrassment for the official Church, which has tried to denounce it and work against it or to purify it by baptizing it into accepted understandings and practices. Isasi-Díaz mentions that most of what is now official Church teaching and practice arose from syncretic processes in the earlier history of Christianity but is now used as an orthodoxy to condemn popular religiosity today.

There are a number of ways in which the contemporary popular religiosity of Latinas differs from the understanding and practice of the official Church. The Bible does not play an important role in their lives. Likewise, Jesus is not that central to their beliefs and religious practices, and perhaps some do not even believe in the divinity of Jesus. In their religious practices the central part is given to what the official Church sees as marginal, such as popular devotions, processions, statues and altars in their homes, and fiestas. The Eucharist is not the primary way in which Latinas celebrate their faith. The Mass is seen as a public ceremony used to solemnize the most important moments in the life of a person or a group of people. Popular religiosity is willing to invest Catholic religious practices with meanings derived from other religions. Likewise, it changes the understanding and meaning of official Catholic realities so that baptism and first communion become rituals of passage. The only criticism Isasi-Díaz gives to the popular religiosity of Latinas is when it fails to support the liberative praxis.

On a number of occasions, Isasi-Díaz compared the approach of mujerista theology to the traditional or official theology and Christology.[31] Perhaps the best illustration of the difference is found in the article she wrote on Jesus Christ.[32] Mujerista theology is very different from the traditional Christology. It is respectful of the traditional approach with its emphasis on Jesus as truly God and truly human, but this is not the way mujerista theology understands Jesus. Mujerista theology does not begin with doctrines and applications of what the Church teaches about Jesus Christ but rather with the lived experience of Latinas. Christology, like all religious beliefs, follows the mujerista ethical stance and is based on it. The very understanding Latinas have in their family and community, even from a very early age, shapes what they believe about Jesus. Their knowledge of Jesus does not determine what they do, but rather their faith follows their practice. Belief follows the pattern that is sown in their consciences.

Mujerista Christology emerges from three key elements in the daily practice of Latinas: (1) Latinas hunger for deep personal relationships to sustain them in their journey; (2) they need God as a companion on the journey in their struggle, not as one who solves their problems; and (3) only insofar as Latinas become a part of God's family can they really say they believe in *Jesucristo*, melding "Jesus" and "Christ" into one word signifying the faithful companion in the struggles and the daily life of Latinas. Liberation-salvation is not the exclusive task of Jesucristo but the task of all who have Christ as their last name. Even the traditional Christian Christology recognizes we are all cocreators and coredeemers. Belonging to the family of God means being connected to the values and practice of God's family. Christology follows ethics. What we believe about Jesus follows from how we conduct our lives. Grassroots Latinas rarely experience a crisis of faith, precisely because Jesucristo walks with them in their everyday life and in their struggle for liberation.

Isasi-Díaz is widely recognized as the mother of mujerista theology. However, her understanding of theology is somewhat restricted. She is interested in praxis, not theory. Her insistence that all those engaged in the liberating struggle of mujeristas are theologians is a narrow approach to theology. Un-like Gutiérrez and most other liberation theologians, she rejects the un-derstanding of theology as a reflection on praxis. Theology is rooted in the reflective praxis itself. There is no need for a second step of theology as reflection on praxis.

Ethics

The very first paragraph of the prologue to her coauthored 1988 book in-sists on the intrinsic unity in mujerista theology of bringing together what has classically been called systematic theology and moral theology, or ethics. To speak of ethics separately is a heuristic device because of the inability to speak of several things at the same time in an intelligent manner. In treating ethics, Isasi-Díaz follows her method of listening to the lived experience of Latinas. The individual is a moral agent responsible for both individual and social life. The freedom of the individual is intrinsically linked to the self-determination of the community to which she belongs. The self-determina-tion of the person should not manipulate or diminish any other person or community. Enablement and relationality are guides for all ethical activity. Power is not understood as control and domination but as enablement and creativity. The struggle for survival-liberation guides moral judgments that arise inductively from lived experience and also involve important emotional and feeling aspects. Moral criteria are not dictated from above but are dia-logical, involving what is happening and to whom it is happening in light of the lived practice. What is important is not orthodoxy but orthopraxis. Mujerista theology critiques sexism, classism, and ethnic prejudice wherever they are found, especially in the official Church but also in feminism and Latin American liberation theology.[33] Her interest is primarily, but not ex-clusively, in social ethics.

Latinas often speak about "what my conscience tells me."[34] In small ev-eryday matters as well as in important matters, Latinas frequently refer to conscience, sometimes as a way to show others that one has thought deeply about the matter. The churches, however, oppose such an understanding of conscience and propose instead an authoritarian conscience imposed by a superior person or force from outside the person. The primacy of con-science has a long tradition in the Roman Catholic Church, but unfortu-nately the hierarchy insists on its moral teaching as coming from God. The authoritarian conscience thus curtails the freedom of conscience. Isasi-Díaz then develops in a comparatively long section the contemporary Catholic theological recognition of the legitimacy of dissent from hierarchical moral teaching. In this way, the primacy of conscience is supported.

The Catholic approach is not the only problem. About 20 percent of Hispanics in the United States belong to or relate to the Protestant tradition. Mainstream Protestant churches have downplayed the role of conscience as the guiding force of the moral life. In fundamentalist, Pentecostal, and store-front churches, the authoritarian conscience comes to the fore either because of the fundamentalist interpretation of the scripture or the authority of the pastor, who is often a patriarchal male.

Conscience in mujerista theology is understood holistically as the moral consciousness of the person as moral agent. The formation of moral consciousness involves the conscientization of the person, which is an integral part of the struggle for liberation. The reflection on action in praxis leads to critical awareness and becomes a building block in deciding the next action. The most important or overarching generative theme for Latinas is the struggle for survival-liberation, which gains specificity in the lived praxis. Yes, there are dangers in judging and deciding that come from human finitude and sinfulness, but the process of conscientization helps to overcome these dangers. Here, too, there is a rather restricted understanding of ethics.

Justice

Justice has always been a primary consideration for mujerista theology. In the last years of her life, Isasi-Díaz published a number of essays on justice that she was planning on putting together in a book of essays with the tentative title of *Justicia: A Reconciliatory Praxis of Care and Tenderness*. Her death unfortunately meant that the book was never published.[35] From the very beginning, Isasi-Díaz insisted that liberation is a single process involving three different levels or aspects: libertad, communidad de fe, and justicia.[36]

In keeping with Isasi-Díaz's message, justice is not a theory or philosophy of the principles to be applied to life. The goal of mujerista justice is not to build a theoretical system of justice but to establish justice in Latinas' lives. Justice involves overcoming the oppression that Latinas suffer. There are five different types of oppression for them: exploitation, marginalization, power-lessness, cultural imperialism, and systemic violence. Particularities of mujerista justice have also been spelled out in her analysis of the projecto histórico. Mujerista justice is concrete since it begins with the injustices suffered by Latinas. The history of salvation, the realization of the kin_dom of God, does not happen apart from the daily struggles of Latinas. The kin_dom of God is God's gift, but it transforms the actions of those who receive it. It is already present in history but does not ever reach its complete fulfillment here in history. A mujerista justice recognizes the importance of power, understood as both a personal and structural process. The person who is looked on as powerless must become self-defining and self-actualizing. Mujerista justice cannot be achieved at the expense of others. It goes beyond redistribution and calls for restitution. The mujerista concept of justice recognizes that the rights of Latinas are socioeconomic rights as well as civic-political rights. This approach calls for a new way of understanding power as enabling and not dominating, as well as redistribution of wealth and privileges coupled with restitution in our society.[37] (In a later essay, without mentioning her previous call for restitution, Isasi-Díaz rejects restitution and reparation as very often being a form of revenge that in its own way is a violence and thus stands in the way of reconciliation.)[38]

Her later essays dealing with justice develop the basic ideas mentioned in her earlier discussions. Two significant differences appear in the later writings. First, the reality of justice is developed in more depth and detail. Second, she recognizes the broader reality of justice and not just the situation of Latinas. The starting point for her understanding of justice and the face of justice in the twenty-first century stems from the reality that more than two-thirds of the world's population lives in situations of injustice.[39]

Justice involves a reconciliatory praxis of care and tenderness. The oppressed demand reconciliatory justice that moves them into the center of reality, not only to explain justice but also to provide a concrete guide to make justice a reality in our world today. Those who are not involved in a particular struggle against oppression can still share in this struggle through creative imagination fueled by a solidarity with victims.[40]

In a true sense, this understanding of justice is radically subjective, but Isasi-Díaz insists on redefining objectivity as the radical subjectivity of the victims of oppression in their struggle. Without much in-depth discussion, she insists that this radical subjectivity in no way skirts rational discussion. It uses weighty arguments that are persuasive and clear. It is valid because it is a straightforward, understandable, and commonsense approach. Since it is also particular, this radical subjectivity must be open to the critical challenge of others. Her approach to justice not only begins with the subjective but also the particular, but it does not deny the possibility and reality of some universals. Isasi-Díaz strongly opposes an abstract understanding of justice based on universal principles but does not want to deny that some universality can be obtained on the basis of the experience of particularities.[41] By insisting on the radical subjectivity of justice, Isasi-Díaz is logically developing her notion of justice in light of her basic method and approach.

Her approach, however, differs from the traditional approach to justice with its insistence on objectivity. The best illustration of the traditional understanding of justice is the famous symbol of the woman with the blindfold holding the scales. Lady Justice was based on the Roman goddess of justice

(Justitia) but with reference back to ancient Egypt and Greece. The scales she carries signify her weighing the pros and cons of the issue of justice involved. Images from the fifteenth century have included the blindfold, representing objectivity. Justice is objective, blind, and imparted without fear or favor.

Isasi-Díaz has one essay devoted to the contemporary approach to justice of John Rawls, who also developed his theory to oppose individualistic liberalism.[42] He built a theory of objective justice on the basis of what rational people behind the veil of ignorance, but not knowing any particulars (e.g., race, class, gender, age, health conditions, how they live), would choose as justice for a society. In a scholarly article, Isasi-Díaz points out her fundamental differences with Rawls but also appreciates how mujerista theology can use aspects of his approach. The fundamental disagreement is the fact that Rawls does not begin with the subjective experience of injustice by the oppressed. Also, he does not recognize the social construction of reality as proposed by Peter Berger and Thomas Luckmann. This understanding points out that oppressive reality has been socially constructed and can and should be changed. Rawls's concept of the United States as a liberal democracy is also detrimental to those who are not in the dominant group. There are aspects of Rawls's approach, however, that are compatible with mujerista theology. He does not propose one theory of justice that all should accept but recognizes the need for an overlapping consensus coming from different perspectives and starting points. His theory of the veil of ignorance was an attempt to reveal and overcome biases that blind people, a concept that calls for dialogue as a reciprocal engagement of all in society, which calls for voices of all to be heard.

Isasi-Díaz's approach of starting with the reality of injustice insists on the solidarity of all in an option for the poor. Here she strenuously opposes the concept of a preferential option for the poor, which, although she does not say so, is the accepted approach in Catholic social teaching. The liberal understanding of the preferential option for the poor allows the dominant group to hold on to its privileges and riches. The option for the poor makes the oppressors realize the change that they must make. Some defend the preferential option for the poor on the basis that God loves everyone but prefers the poor. Yes, God does love everyone, but God does not love oppressors as such. God's love for oppressors calls them to conversion and repentance.[43]

An underlying reason for injustice comes from our understanding of differences. Unless we reconceptualize differences in a positive way, we will continue to live in a world of injustice and violence. Our approach to difference brings about the existing exclusions, whereas inclusion is what we need. Yes, differences do exist in our world, but the problem is how the dominant group uses these differences to exclude and marginalize others.

The American melting-pot idea means that the dominant group of society sets the norms and standards and everyone else has to live accordingly, giving up their own realities. What the majority requires is itself very culturally specific and not an ideal of humanity as something universal and neutral. The privileged groups ignore their own particularity and specificity. A more insidious consequence is that the oppressed group internalizes the negative understandings of them proposed by the dominant group. Differences should be used to build bridges in an inclusive way and not to exclude and marginalize. Difference should mark the boundaries that make true relationships possible.[44]

The proposed subtitle for the book on justice she was never able to publish involves the three realities of reconciliation, care, and tenderness.[45] Her earlier essays had somewhat touched on these three aspects of justice, but a later essay developed them in greater detail.[46] Isasi-Díaz uses "care" and "solicitude" as somewhat synonymous. Solicitude shifts the focus of justice away from defending the rights of individuals in the light of principles and puts the focus on persons, especially oppressed people, within the context of communities, societies, and nations. Solicitude involves a dialogue of all concerned, but this dialogue centers on the oppressed. Dialogue with the oppressed is the best way to overcome the finitude, incompleteness, and prejudices of the privileged. Solicitude as sentiment, attitude, and action emerges as a response to injustice when we listen to the voices of the oppressed.

Reconciliation involves rebuilding what has been torn asunder and producing a new order of relationships as a basis for the true human flourishing of all. The work of reconciliation is a humble process, a road traveled together in dialogue one step at a time, and a process that involves risk, ambiguity, and uncertainty. Reconciliation forces all of us to recognize that at some times in our lives we have been oppressors and exploiters. Reconciliation is both a personal and a social virtue. It will not happen easily and requires a radical conversion. Reconciliation involves a process that begins with the cause and concerns of the poor and oppressed.

Tenderness keeps solicitude and reconciliation moving forward. It enables us to focus on working together in the cause of the common good of the community, to recognize our own vulnerabilities, and to overcome the temptation to be selfish and merely protect our own self-interest. Tenderness introduces into the theory and practice of justice the importance of emotions. Too often ethicists emphasize the role of reason as controlling emotions, but emotions can and should also tutor and test reason. Without tenderness, there is no possibility for truth, solicitude, or reconciliation. A reconciliatory praxis of care and tenderness is necessary to break the bonds of oppression and bring about justice and right relationships in our world.

Isasi-Díaz herself raises the question of whether her understanding of justice is naive.[47] There is no doubt, however, that she recognizes that justice involves a long, difficult struggle. She concludes one of her essays on justice by pointing out that as an activist she often feels discouraged because others do not listen to the call of the conscience of the poor and oppressed in our world. But she goes on to say that we cannot let these deaf ears silence our calls. Life is la lucha.[48]

In my judgment, Isasi-Díaz's approach provides important aspects of justice that all theories of justice should incorporate. On the other hand, her approach is limited. Specifically, I see three limiting aspects about her theory of justice. The first aspect is that she develops her thought in a few comparatively short essays. It is impossible to develop a full-blown approach to justice in such a genre.

Justice is a very complex reality with many dimensions. Two important areas of justice, for example, are the political and the economic. Political relations involve the relationships of individuals to one another, the relationships of individuals to their states, the relationship of states to one another, and all of these relationships in light of the global community. The complexity here is enormous. Reflect for a moment just on the international relationships of states between and among themselves. In today's world, all are conscious of the many existing complex issues. The problem of immigration is enormous and exists in many parts of the world. The questions of civil disobedience, violence, and war have been debated for centuries, and technological developments such as nuclear weapons and drones have added new dimensions. The issues of climate and pollution have come to the fore in recent years. In the economic area, issues often seem almost intractable. What are the requirements of just trade between and among nations? In our own country we cannot agree on what justice requires in this complex reality. In the midst of the present nation-state system, both in the political and economic realms, there will always be need for compromises and imperfect solutions.

A second factor limiting Isasi-Díaz's development of justice comes at times from her starting point. The title of her 2010 article "Reconciliatory Praxis: A Decolonial *Mujerista* Move" emphasizes this somewhat narrow starting point. She describes her proposal as a mujerista proposal, for it arises from the lived experience of Latinas living in the United States, committed to our liberation and the liberation of all peoples. In this article she starts from three cases or illustrations that are quite limited and limiting: the conflict between the archdiocese of New York's attempt to close a church that was home to Latinos and Latinas, the tensions in the relationships between Cubans living on the island and those living overseas, and the struggle of poor people in Chiapas to be consulted about where the Mexican government was going to build a road.[49] Such limited starting points do not provide the basis for a full-blown theory of justice applicable to all aspects of injustice in our world today but rather are quite narrowly focused issues that do not deal with the more complex realities of justice. However, at times she begins from the broader starting point of injustice.

A third factor limiting Isasi-Díaz's approach comes from the theological perspective of not explicitly developing the reality of the power of sin and sinful social structures in our world. There is no doubt that she implicitly recognizes the reality of human sinfulness by her insistence on the struggle—la lucha. But a more adequate theological approach to justice gives explicit development to the reality of sin in our world and the effects involved in our struggle against it.

There can be no doubt that the understanding of justice developed by Isasi-Díaz is limited. However, she points out very important aspects that to some extent should be present in every Christian approach to justice. Theories of justice must begin with, or at least recognize as most significant, the reality of injustice. There is no doubt that most of the theories of justice that have been proposed over the years have failed to really listen to the cries of the poor and the oppressed. Any adequate approach to justice must recognize the fundamental importance of the virtues, attitudes, and realities of solicitude, reconciliation, and tenderness.

Isasi-Díaz has made a creative and noteworthy contribution in proposing a mujerista theology based on her own activist involvement in the liberating struggle of mujeristas in the United States. Her understanding of theology, however, is quite restrictive and limited since it insists that all those involved in la lucha are theologians. Her theological method does not recognize the need for a second step of theological reflection on the praxis. Note the difference compared to the approaches of Cahill and Farley.

Notes

1. Michael Lipka, "A Closer Look at Catholic America," Pew Research Center, September 14, 2015, www.pewresearch.org/fact-tank/2015/09/14/a-closer-look-at-catholic-america.

2. ACHTUS, Academy of Catholic Hispanic Theologians of the United States, www.achtus.us.

3. "Father Elizondo, Nationally Known Notre Dame Theology Professor, Dies," Catholic News Service, March 17, 2016, http://www.catholicnews.com/services/englishnews/2016/father-elizondo-nationally-known-notre-dame-theology-professor-dies.cfm; Allan Figueroa Deck, "Introduction," in *Frontiers of Hispanic Catholic Theology*, ed. Allen Figueroa Deck (Maryknoll, NY: Orbis, 1992), ix–xxvi; Virgilio P.

Elizondo, *Galilean Journey: The Mexican-American Promise* (Maryknoll, NY: Orbis, 1983).

4. Ada María Isasi-Díaz and Yolanda Tarango, *Hispanic Women: Prophetic Voice in the Church; Toward a Hispanic Women's Liberation Theology* (San Francisco: Harper & Row, 1988).

5. Ada María Isasi-Díaz, "Mujeristas: A Name of Our Own!," *Christian Century* 106, no. 18 (May 1989): 560–62.

6. Ada María Isasi-Díaz, "Praxis: The Heart of *Mujerista* Theology," *Journal of Latino/Hispanic Theology* 1, no. 1 (November 1993): 44–55.

7. Ada María Isasi-Díaz, *Mujerista Theology: A Theology for the Twenty-First Century* (Maryknoll, NY: Orbis, 1996), 13–34; Ada María Isasi-Díaz, *La Lucha Continues: Mujerista Theology* (Maryknoll, NY: Orbis, 2004), 11–23; Isasi-Díaz, "*Mujerista* Theology: A Praxis of Liberation; My Story," in *Shaping a Global Theological Mind*, ed. Darren C. Marks (Aldershot, UK: Ashgate, 2008), 77–87.

8. Ada María Isasi-Díaz, *En la Lucha: In the Struggle; A Hispanic Women's Liberation Theology* (Minneapolis: Fortress, 1993). In subsequent citations, I will use the tenth-anniversary edition: Isasi-Díaz, *En la Lucha: In the Struggle; Elaborating a Mujerista Theology* (Minneapolis: Fortress, 2004). Notice here the change to *mujerista* theology in the subtitle.

9. Isasi-Díaz, *En la Lucha*, 31–34.

10. Ibid., 2–3; Isasi-Díaz and Tarango, *Hispanic Women*, xiii.

11. Isasi-Díaz, *Mujerista Theology*, 59–85; Ada María Isasi-Díaz, "Reading a Theology of Liberation from a *Mujerista* Perspective," in *Scholars and Their Books*, ed. R. S. Sugirtharajah (London: SCM, 2009), 143–57.

12. Isasi-Díaz and Tarango, *Hispanic Women*, 116n8. See also Ada María Isasi-Díaz, "Kin_dom of God: A *Mujerista* Proposal," in *Our Own Voices: Latino/a Renditions of Theology*, ed. Benjamin Valentin (Maryknoll, NY: Orbis, 2010), 171–89.

13. Isasi-Díaz, "Praxis."

14. This and the following paragraphs synthesize what is found in different places in her writings—e.g., Isasi-Díaz and Tarango, *Hispanic Women*, 60–73, 94–110; Isasi-Díaz, *En la Lucha*, 176–87; Isasi-Díaz, *Mujerista Theology*, 59–85.

15. Isasi-Díaz and Tarango, *Hispanic Women*, 66.

16. Ada María Isasi-Díaz, "A *Mujerista* Justice and Human Flourishing," in *The Bible and the Hermeneutics of Liberation*, ed. Alejandro F. Botta and Pablo Adriñach (Atlanta: Society of Biblical Literature, 2009), 181–95.

17. Isasi-Díaz, *En la Lucha*, 177–81.

18. Isasi-Díaz, "Reading a Theology of Liberation," 143–57.

19. Isasi-Díaz and Tarango, *Hispanic Women*, 104–5; Isasi-Díaz, *En la Lucha*, 184–87.

20. Isasi-Díaz and Tarango, *Hispanic Women*, 106–9.

21. Isasi-Díaz, *En la Lucha*, 85–96.

22. Ibid., 104–42.

23. Isasi-Díaz, *Mujerista Theology*, 129–31.

24. Isasi-Díaz, *La Lucha Continues*, 25–28.

25. Isasi-Díaz, *Mujerista Theology*, 66–73. See also Isasi-Díaz, "Communication as Communion: Elements in a Hermeneutic of *Lo Cotidiano*," in *A Gendered World: An Introduction to Feminist Biblical Interpretation in Honor of Katherine Doob Sackenfeld*, ed. Linda Day and Carolyn Pressler (Louisville, KY: Westminster John Knox, 2006), 27–36.

26. Isasi-Díaz, *En la Lucha*, 52–61.

27. Ibid., 59–61.

28. Isasi-Díaz, *Mujerista Theology*, 137–44.

29. Ibid., 86–104.

30. Isasi-Díaz and Tarango, *Hispanic Women*, 66–70. See also Isasi-Díaz, *En la Lucha*, 57–69.

31. E.g., Isasi-Díaz, *Mujerista Theology*, 59–85.

32. Ada María Isasi-Díaz, "*Identificate con Nostros*: A *Mujerista* Christological Understanding," in *Jesus in the Hispanic Community: Images of Christ from Theology to Popular Religion*, ed. Harold Recinos and Hugo Magallanes (Louisville, KY: Westminster John Knox, 2009), 38–57.

33. Isasi-Díaz and Tarango, *Hispanic Women*, 77–91.

34. For Isasi-Díaz's most complete treatment of conscience, see Isasi-Díaz, *En la Lucha*, 150–67.

35. Lisa Isherwood, "An Interview with Ada María Isasi-Díaz," *Feminist Theology* 20, no. 1 (September 2011): 8.

36. Isasi-Díaz, *En la Lucha*, 54.

37. Ada María Isasi-Díaz, "*Un Poquito de Justicia*: A Little Bit of Justice," in Isasi-Díaz, *Mujerista Theology*, 105–27.

38. Ada María Isasi-Díaz, "Justice as Reconciliatory Praxis: A Decolonial *Mujerista* Move," *International Journal of Public Theology* 4, no. 1 (2010): 42–45.

39. Ada María Isasi-Díaz, "Reconciliatory Praxis: The Face of Justice in the Twenty-First Century," *Apuntes* 30, no. 2 (Summer 2010): 44.

40. Ada María Isasi-Díaz, "Justice as a Post-9/11 Theory," in *The Impact of 9/11 on Religion and Philosophy: The Day That Changed Everything?*, ed. Matthew J. Morgan (New York: Palgrave Macmillan, 2009), 169–72.

41. Ibid., 172–75. See also Isasi-Díaz, "A *Mujerista* Hermeneutic of Justice and Human Flourishing," in Botta and Adriñach, *Bible and Hermeneutics of Liberation*, 183–84.

42. Ada María Isasi-Díaz, "John Rawls on Justice," in *Beyond the Pale: Reading Ethics from the Margins*, ed. Stacey M. Floyd-Thomas and Miguel A. De La Torre (Louisville: Westminster John Knox, 2011), 145–52.

43. Isasi-Díaz, "Justice as Reconciliatory Praxis," 42–43.

44. Isasi-Díaz, "Reconciliatory Praxis."

45. Isherwood, "Interview with Ada María Isasi-Díaz," 17.

46. Isasi-Díaz, "Justice as a Post-9/11 Theory," in *Impact of 9/11*, 175–83.

47. Isasi-Díaz, "Justice as Reconciliatory Praxis," 50.

48. Isasi-Díaz, "Reconciliatory Praxis," 58.

49. Isasi-Díaz, "Justice as Reconciliatory Praxis," 37–40.

10

Bryan N. Massingale

As a result of different sociological and ecclesiological factors, black Catholic theology has only recently emerged in the United States, and black Catholic theologians are comparatively few. In 2010, there were only about twenty Catholics of African descent with doctorates in Catholic theology, although there were others in related disciplines.[1] Black Catholic women were some of the first persons in this field employing black liberationist and feminist perspectives. Jamie Phelps edited two respected books in the area.[2] Phelps also rejuvenated and reconvened the Black Catholic Theological Symposium, which since her intervention has met annually from 1991 and which since 2007 has published the *Journal of the Black Catholic Theological Symposium*.[3] Diana L. Hayes has written a number of books developing a womanist theology from the Catholic perspective.[4] Both Phelps and Hayes contributed to the special December 2000 issue of *Theological Studies* dealing with black Catholic theology.[5] Another leading black systematic theologian in the Church today is Shawn Copeland, who in 2003 was the first black person to become president of the Catholic Theological Society of America. She was the editor of the 2000 symposium in *Theological Studies*. Her many writings, as exemplified in *Enfleshing Freedom,* coming from the perspective of black systematic theology with a special concern on theological anthropology, have significant consequences for moral theology.[6]

Sitz im Leben

Bryan N. Massingale is the outstanding black Catholic moral theologian writing today. He, too, served as president of the Catholic Theological Society of America, in 2009. Massingale is a priest of the Archdiocese of Milwaukee. He received his academic degrees in moral theology from the Catholic University of America (licentiate in sacred theology) and the Alphonsian

Academy in Rome (doctorate of sacred theology). Massingale taught at the diocesan seminary in Milwaukee before going to Marquette University and since 2016 has been a professor at Fordham University in New York. He has written more than eighty articles and in 2010 published *Racial Justice and the Catholic Church*. Likewise, he was one of the contributors to the 2000 symposium in *Theological Studies* on black Catholic theology.[7]

Catholic theologians recognize a threefold public that they serve: the Church, the academy, and the world. Some give more importance to one or another of these three. There is no doubt that Massingale has seen himself as a thinker for the Church.[8] Many aspects of his life show this concern for the Church. He is a diocesan priest who to this day is still heavily involved in the pastoral work of the Church. His writing has been primarily directed to the Church and for the good of the Church. Many Catholic theologians to some extent experience this tension, but Massingale experiences it much more than most. As a black Catholic theologian, he considers himself not only as a scholar-teacher but also and even primarily as a scholar-teacher-activist. He was raised and nurtured in the black community. He feels an important need to be an integral part of that community as he speaks to and for the black Catholic community to the rest of the Church.

This tension is felt in two ways. First, the academic world does not have any appreciation of or give any respect for one's involvement in the pastoral life of the Church or in the daily life of the black Catholic community. Respectability and the rewards of the academic life in terms of promotion and recognition come only from scholarly publication. For Massingale, this is not the most important reality in his life, but in an amazing way he has been able to satisfy the requirements of the academic world and for the last few years has been wooed to join some of the major Catholic theological faculties in the United States.

A second way in which this tension appears involves the demands on one's time. Academics by definition spend most of their time doing the work of scholarship. However, this is only a part of the work that Massingale and others like him do. There are many demands on him to speak to and write for the needs of the black Catholic community and for the Church as a whole. The tension is only heightened by the fact that Massingale is an excellent communicator. His talks and addresses are always clear, logically developed, and attentively received by his listeners. There are few people who can captivate an audience as well as Massingale does. He is constantly being asked to speak to black groups and to the broader groups, associations, audiences, and institutions (e.g., colleges and universities) within the whole Catholic Church. He also helps official Catholic groups, such as the Conference of Catholic Bishops, Catholic Charities, and the Catholic Health Association.

The fact that Massingale is *the* outstanding black Catholic moral theologian only adds to the many demands on his time.

A second source of tension comes from his identity as black, Catholic, and an intellectual. The history of the Catholic Church in the United States with regard to black Catholics is scandalous. The vast majority of Catholics once endorsed the reality of slavery. Segregation was rampant in Catholic life up until the 1960s. Black Catholics were not allowed in "white" Catholic schools on all levels and often not accepted in Catholic hospitals and health care facilities. Racism and prejudice marked the attitude of Catholics to their fellow black Catholics. The tension between being black and being Catholic in the United States is obvious. But this tension is further complicated by the role of the intellectual, who is called to speak truth in general and, in the theologian's case, truth to the Church. Even today many people in the Church do not want to hear this truth. Thus, the black Catholic theologian in the Catholic Church today experiences tremendous tensions in trying to carry out the vocation of being a black Catholic theologian.

Massingale has reflected on the personal struggles of being a black Catholic theologian as well as on the joys that come from such involvement. The struggles can bring him to depression and despair. He at times becomes weary to the depths of his soul and overwhelmed by the challenges of keeping his sanity in a white culture and in white institutions. Like all of us, he feels the temptation to "fit in" and "be like everybody else," but he realizes that the black theologian must often pay the price of speaking truth to power. Massingale often experiences his vocation as a continuing struggle. But in a truly paradoxical way, he has also experienced the joys of being a black Catholic theologian. He has been strengthened and buoyed up by the sacred trust of being an esteemed part of the black Catholic community. In his frequent relationships with ordinary black Catholics, he is renewed in his own vocation by their deep appreciation for what he is trying to do. In addition, he has experienced the joy of creating something new in the midst of the struggle and making some progress, even though at times the progress seems very little. One of the joys of this journey and struggle of a black Catholic theologian in the United States is that of sharing the theological vocation with a small supportive group of his colleagues in black Catholic theology.

Racism

In light of Massingale's understanding of the role of the black Catholic moral theologian, the most important issue is racism as it exists in American society and especially in the Catholic Church in the United States. His 2010 book

Racial Justice and the Catholic Church brings together in a more systematic way many of the points he has made in previously published articles on racism. The Catholic Church in the United States is white and racist.[9] US society, even after the election of Barack Obama, is still racist. In his book he uses some incidents connected with the aftermath of Hurricane Katrina to show that racism still exists in white society.[10] Later he shows the racism in the Trayvon Martin case and calls for the Catholic Church to support the Black Lives Matter movement.[11]

What is racism? Most Americans lack an adequate understanding of its depth, extent, and true nature. Racism is not simply a matter of interpersonal relations. Racism is deeper and more pervasive. It is a culture. Racism as a culture is a symbol system that justifies race-based disparities and shapes identity. There is a pervasive cultural stigma attached to dark skin in this country. Race then functions as a largely unconscious or preconscious frame of perception developed through cultural conditioning and instilled by socialization. Most of us are not even conscious of our racism. In a sense, it is in the air that we breathe. White Americans are ensnared, entangled, and enmeshed in a value-laden role of racial significance and meaning that is largely invisible and outside of conscious awareness.[12]

Racism by its very nature involves white privilege. Yes, racism is unjust to people of color, but white Americans derive privilege precisely because of it. White privilege involves the reality that in this country whites have many opportunities and privileges that people of color do not share. Pervasive beliefs about the inadequacies of people of color have become entrenched in our society's institutional policies, social customs, cultural media, political processes, and economic realities. With regard to the latter, Massingale cites many historical illustrations of economic injustice done to people of color. Massingale gives a poignant example of how racism and white privilege kept his own father from being employed as a carpenter even though he had received an associate's degree in carpentry. Yes, some whites denounce latent racial injustice, but they also, perhaps even unconsciously, are preserving a system of white social dominance and privilege.[13]

In two essays Massingale points out how both racism and white privilege work. For example, there is indisputable evidence that environmental hazards are not randomly or evenly distributed across population groups but rather are borne disproportionately by people of color and the poor. The Environmental Protection Agency has concluded that racial minorities and low-income populations are disproportionately exposed to lead, air pollutants, hazardous-waste facilities, contaminated fish tissue, and agricultural pesticides in the workplace.[14] Massingale also cites evidence from the US General Accountability Office and the United Church of Christ Commission for Racial Justice to support these discrepancies. White neighborhoods do not want hazardous-waste facilities in their backyard, and hence they usually do not get them. Some justify the presence of hazardous-waste sites in poor and African American areas because the industry brings substantial economic benefits to them. However, environmental justice advocates reject this argument because it amounts to extortion by taking advantage of a community's dire social and economic vulnerability.[15] Another essay deals with HIV/AIDS and black bodies. This pandemic has had a much greater impact on African Americans in this country and even more so on blacks globally.[16]

How can we struggle against and strive to overcome the realities of racism and white privilege? Massingale's earlier writings stressed the theological and rational aspects—the fundamental dignity of the human person, human rights, distributive justice, and the option for the poor.[17]

In the 2010 book, he took a different approach.[18] Reconciliation calls for justice as a spirituality. The earlier ethical and theological arguments are necessary but not sufficient. Racism engages us viscerally, and this racial injustice on the deepest level is impervious to a rational approach and logic. The Catholic tradition in its spirituality provides such an approach. Massingale focuses on two aspects: lament and compassion. Laments are cries of anguish and outrage, groans of deep pain and grief, utterances of profound protest and righteous indignation over injustice. A lament is a wail of mourning and protest, but it ends on a note of praise. This cry of lament, so prevalent in scripture, interrupts the way things are and calls for attention. The prior lament of the victims allows the privileged to engage in a lament as a forthright confession of wrongdoing. Such a lament, however, needs to become very specific, recognizing the litany of concrete realities that have been done to people of color. An honest lament gives rise to a deep sense of compassion.

Compassion is a gut-wrenching response to the anguish and suffering of racism and also identifies with the victim, which leads to action bringing about reconciliation. Compassion thus gives rise to true solidarity. Church practices that facilitate social solidarity are conversion, baptism, and the Eucharist. Conversion is a radical experience of personal and social redefinition resulting from a collapse and surrender of the old order of racism. Baptism recognizes the radical equality of all Christians. The social equalitarianism of the Eucharist is rooted in the radical and shockingly inclusive table companionship of Jesus.

Massingale also devotes a whole chapter to meditating on African American understandings of justice and hope as developed in the spirituals.[19] From this experience, Massingale came to recognize that justice is a pathos, a desire, a longing, a yearning, even a passion before it is a concept or a rational definition. This dream or vision of justice grounds the black conviction of the equal dignity of all people in the sight of God. Spirituals such as "The Wisdom Table" and the "Beloved Community" flesh out the meaning of this dream. Such a dream leads to what Catholic theology has called distributive justice. Justice rooted in the black cultural experience is accompanied by the praxis of hope. Hope refuses to accept as final the empirical evidence of injustice and tragedy, even the horrible reality of slavery. Hope cannot be proved by rational argument but only witnessed to and made present in praxis in the struggle against injustice.

Throughout his writings, Massingale employs the spirituals and how they should affect all of us today of all races and all colors. The enslaved peoples' reflection on the passion of Jesus and his relevance contrasts with the silence of so many in our society to the continuing suffering caused by racism. Resurrection faith in the spirituals should inspire all Christians to work for justice with the hope that is necessary to sustain the struggle.[20]

The generally accepted understanding of the formation of conscience in the Catholic moral theology tradition is inadequate for dealing with the reality of racism and white privilege precisely because of the scotosis, or intellectual blindness, that exists. Racism for most whites is unseen and unrecognized. Conscience formation has been seen either as acquiring sufficient information to overcome doubts about what should be done or as involving the formation of virtues and character. But, as history shows, such approaches have been inadequate to deal with the realities of racism and white privilege.[21] This is why Massingale insists in his book on the need for a spirituality that can bring about the radical conversion necessary to overcome the sin of racism. In later articles, Massingale insists that the ethical categories of structural sin and intrinsic evil do not adequately describe racism and white privilege. US and global Catholicism have been co-opted into an idolatrous belief system that the holy can be mediated only through white eyes and experiences. This is idolatry.[22]

Massingale also shows that historically Catholic moral theology in the United States has been blind to the reality of racism. He researched the recurring articles "Notes on Moral Theology" in *Theological Studies*, the premier theological publication in the United States, which started in 1940, and the *Proceedings of the Catholic Theological Society of America*, which began in 1946. "Notes on Moral Theology" after 1970 reveal virtually no mention of, and certainly no sustained attention to, racism despite all that was happening in United States society during those years. In the period from 1940 to 1970, there is some mention of racism and the moral evil of compulsory racial segregation but no call to dismantle this reality. The response to racism is not a matter of justice but charity: Whites should show courtesy and respect in their dealing with African Americans. From his historical study of these publications, Massingale concludes the issues of race relations and racial justice were not pressing or significant concerns for American Catholic ethicists. In the more general theological literature, there are some few exceptions to the pattern of omission, silence, neglect, and indifference to racial concerns by Catholic theologians.[23]

What about the response of the American Catholic bishops to racism?[24] The US bishops have issued three documents on racism since the 1950s. The first was "Discrimination and the Christian Conscience" in 1968. The bishops recognized that the heart of the race issue is religious and moral. They proposed two principles based on Catholic teaching: the equality of all people and the obligation to love others. It follows from these principles that enforced segregation is morally wrong. Massingale criticizes the document for being tardy and for the lack of specificity, especially regarding concrete steps that the Church itself should take to combat its own racism.

In their 1968 document "The National Race Crisis," the bishops recognized that their earlier statement was not enough. The historical social context for this statement included the riots of 1967, the Kerner Report with its fear that the United States was becoming two societies, and the assassination of Martin Luther King Jr. This document, unlike the earlier one, has a strong and urgent tone in the light of the crisis, acknowledges Catholic culpability with regard to racism, recognizes that the problem exists not only in hearts but in institutions, and proposes some urgent, specific steps to take. The major problem with the document is the lack of doctrinal and theological foundations and the absence of the necessary funding to implement its provisions.

In the light of further social developments and growing internal criticism from within the Church itself, the bishops issued "Brothers and Sisters to Us" in 1979. This strongly worded document, according to Massingale, acknowledges the pervasiveness of racism, the covert and subtle nature of contemporary racism, the link of racism to economic injustice, racism's institutional character, and the existence of racism in the Church and makes some specific recommendations for action. But unfortunately the document was quickly forgotten and was never implemented in the Church, either as a whole or especially on the local level.

Among the statements made by individual bishops, Massingale singles out Francis George of Chicago (2001), Dale Melczek of Gary, Indiana (2003), and Alfred Hughes of New Orleans (2006). These statements stand out because they emphasize the structural aspects of racism, address the reality of white privilege, forthrightly acknowledge the Church's complicity, and propose a wider range of specific responses to racism.

In addition to the defects already mentioned in the episcopal documents,

Massingale concludes with some further criticisms. In addition to the bishops not listening to the voices of the victims, there was a lack of sustained social analysis, resulting in an overly optimistic perspective, a failure to identify the underlying cultural reality of racism, which is impervious to moral suasion, and a lack of passion for racial justice. In reality, the Catholic Church in this country is still white, Massingale says, and needs to undergo a radical change.

Dialogue with James Cone and Malcolm X

Massingale wrote his doctoral dissertation in the late 1980s on James Cone and Gustavo Gutiérrez. His 2000 *Theological Studies* article uses the thought of Cone to criticize the approach of the American Catholic bishops. The last section of that article explains the difference that occurs if one uses Cone's approach to racism and white privilege. Cone calls for shifts that involve moving from racism to white privilege, from paranesis (exhortation) to analysis, from personal sin to structures of sin, from decency to distributive justice, from moral suasion to liberative awareness, and from unconscious racial supremacy to intentional racial solidarity.[25]

After the publication of his book, Massingale described a significant project that he planned to develop into a book involving a dialogue with Malcolm X. Previously his dialogue had been with James Cone. What would Catholic theological ethics look like if it were to engage in such a dialogue with the radical thought of Malcolm X, who opposed any possibility of blacks' fitting into the United States' culture and society? Massingale admits that his own exposure to Malcolm X's life and work has become a life-altering catalyst for his own ongoing journey into political consciousness. Malcolm X is devastating in his critique of American culture and society and the Christian religion. Christianity is a white church with a white God that brings about a dual brainwashing, rendering whites unaware of the horrors of racial oppression and black people passive in their role. Christianity is incompatible with black aspirations for freedom and equality.[26]

Malcolm X's approach calls for truly being one with the oppressed. Massingale sees in this approach a similarity with the understanding of some Christians that the voice of victims is the voice of God. Such an approach challenges us to recognize a different form of rationality and logic that subverts the common understanding of rationality in the academic world. What is logical to the oppressor is not logical to the oppressed. We have to face the limits of our own rationality. With regard to the Church, the solidarity proposed by Malcolm X differs from the solidarity of Catholic social ethics, which underestimates both the recalcitrance of the privileged and the political passivity of the dispossessed. Yes, Malcolm X proclaimed the end of white world supremacy, but in a life-changing visit to the holy sites of Islam he claimed that perhaps white Americans might accept the oneness of all human beings. In Massingale's understanding, this "perhaps" expresses the hope and the challenge for all of us.[27]

What are the practical effects of dialoguing with Malcolm X, who proposed a radical nationalistic approach? Massingale distinguishes the black nationalist pole from the integrationist pole but also recognizes that these poles are not absolute. The integrationist pole also calls for some remodeling of the existing situation if it is to truly recognize equality in our society. Also, the black nationalist pole calls for blacks to create their own social, political, and economic disengagement from the present society but not necessarily territorial and total separation. Black Catholic theology, his own work included, has generally accepted up to this time the integrationist pole, but now without spelling out all the implications Massingale, by raising questions, seems to be moving toward the nationalist pole. In fact he points out that in its beginning, contemporary black Catholic theology showed the influence of black power and black nationalism in the works of Larry Lucas, Mary Roger Thibodeaux, and the Black Catholic Clergy Caucus. In addition, black Catholic theology already has some separate institutions as exemplified by the Black Catholic Theological Symposium and the Institute for Black Catholic Studies at Xavier University. At this stage he is raising questions that need to be considered but have not been. Is the integrationist approach really working in light of the continuing racism and white supremacy in American society and in the Catholic Church, which is a white-controlled church? Black Catholic theology up to now has insisted that its approach is both authentically black and truly Catholic, but, in the light of the ongoing racism, can that understanding be the basis for black Catholic theology today? These are questions that Massingale is grappling with as a result of his dialogue with the radical black nationalism of Malcolm X.[28]

Can Catholic studies embrace a Malcolm X? By calling for a space for a Catholic Malcolm X, Massingale means a discipline wedded to a radical and deep analysis, understanding race as central to the construction of Western and global social and religious life and as fundamental to personal and cultural identities. Such an approach is not to be found outside of an encounter with radical voices in the black tradition. Black nationalists have always perceived something unmentionable about America that integrationists dare not acknowledge—that white supremacy is not merely the work of hot-headed demagogues or a matter of false consciousness but a force so fundamental to America that it is difficult to imagine the country without it. The inclusion of such voices within Catholic studies would mean a discipline that would not only celebrate the contributions of a Catholic faith sensibility but would also humbly acknowledge its constraints, omissions, and blind spots—inadequacies that stem not only from collusions with social injustices but also from a particular Catholic commitment to the force of precedent, which hinders the creative exploration of or engagement with new insights, especially those that come from the margins.[29]

Massingale is familiar with the tradition of Catholic moral theology and social ethics and has occasionally written on broader topics, but his main focus has been on racism. Since he is a moral theologian, Massingale has focused on racism and not on the broader issues of black theology. He has rightly insisted on the primary need of radical conversion to overcome racism, but he has not developed in similar depth the need for structural and institutional change in the social, political, and economic arenas. His projects at the present time include the study of Malcolm X and black bodies and sexuality. As mentioned earlier, Massingale has many demands on his time, but he has still been able to make a very significant contribution to Catholic moral theology and social ethics. Based on his past activities, one hopes that in the years ahead he will continue his exemplary service to the Church in general, the black Catholic community, and black Catholic theology.

Ada María Isasi-Díaz and Bryan N. Massingale have both written theological ethics from the margins. Their theological methods are quite different, but they have much in common. Both see themselves as activists and recognize the importance of being involved with their respective communities. They emphasize the reality of the struggle for oppressed people and with it the importance of hope to carry out the struggle. Solidarity is a very important reality and concept for both, but theirs is a radical solidarity that means the privileged must recognize their role as oppressors and undergo a radical conversion. The immediate concern of both is with their own respective communities, but they both insist that justice involves the needs of all who are marginalized.

Notes

1. Bryan N. Massingale, *Racial Justice and the Catholic Church* (Maryknoll, NY: Orbis, 2010), 162.

2. Jamie T. Phelps, ed., *Black and Catholic: Challenge and Gift of Black Folks* (Milwaukee: Marquette University Press, 1997); Cyprian Davis and Jamie T. Phelps, eds., *Stamped with the Image of God: African Americans as God's Image in Black* (Maryknoll, NY: Orbis, 2003).

3. Black Catholic Theological Symposium, "Our History," at http://black catholictheologicalsymposium.org/about-us/; C. Vanessa White, "A Portrait of Black Catholicism: Celebrating 40 Years of the Black Catholic Theological Symposium,"

America, January 9, 2018, https://www.americamagazine.org/faith/2018/01/09 /portrait-black-catholicism-celebrating-40-years-black-catholic-theological.

4. Among Diana L. Hayes's books, see her *No Crystal Stair: Womanist Spirituality* (Maryknoll, NY: Orbis, 2016); *Forged in the Fiery Furnace: African American Spirituality* (Maryknoll, NY: Orbis, 2012); *Standing in the Shoes My Mother Made: A Womanist Theology* (Minneapolis: Fortress, 2010); and *And Still We Rise: An Introduction to Black Liberation Theology* (New York: Paulist, 1996).

5. "The Catholic Reception of Black Theology," *Theological Studies* 61 (December 2000).

6. M. Shawn Copeland, *Enfleshing Freedom: Body, Race, and Being* (Minneapolis: Fortress, 2010).

7. Curriculum vitae received from Bryan Massingale.

8. The following paragraphs, unless otherwise noted, depend on Bryan N. Massingale, "The Vocation of the Black Theologian and the Struggle of the Black Catholic Community," in Massingale, *Racial Justice*, 151–74.

9. Massingale, *Racial Justice*, 80–82.

10. Ibid., 30–33.

11. Bryan N. Massingale, "Has the Silence Been Broken? Catholic Theological Ethics and Racial Justice," *Theological Studies* 75 (2014): 146; Jarvis De Berry, "Catholic Theology Professor Says Church Should Ally with 'Black Lives Matter,'" November 10, 2015, www.nola.com/opinions/index.ssf/2015/11/black_lives_mat ter_xavier.html.

12. Massingale, *Racial Justice*, 24–33.

13. Ibid., 33–41.

14. Bryan N. Massingale, "The Case for Catholic Support: Catholic Social Ethics and Environmental Ethics," in *Taking Down Our Harps: Black Catholics in the United States*, ed. Diana L. Hayes and Cyprian Davis (Maryknoll, NY: Orbis, 1998), 147.

15. Bryan N. Massingale, "An Ethical Reflection on 'Environmental Racism' in the Light of Catholic Social Teaching," in *The Challenge of Global Stewardship: Roman Catholic Responses*, ed. Maura A. Ryan and Todd David Whitmore (Notre Dame, IN: University of Notre Dame Press, 1997), 234–50.

16. Bryan N. Massingale, "HIV/AIDS and the Bodies of Black People," in *Uncommon Faithfulness: The Black Catholic Experience*, ed. M. Shawn Copeland (Maryknoll, NY: Orbis, 2009), 147–66.

17. Massingale, "Case for Catholic Support," 148–55.

18. Massingale, *Racial Justice*, 103–25.

19. Massingale, "A Dream Deferred: Meditations on African American Understandings of Justice and Hope," in Massingale, *Racial Justice*, 130–50.

20. Massingale, "HIV/AIDS and the Bodies of Black People," in Copeland, *Uncommon Faithfulness*, 154–63.

21. Bryan N. Massingale, "Conscience Formation and the Challenge of Unconscious Racial Bias," in *Conscience and Catholicism: Rights, Responsibilities, and Institutional Responses*, ed. David E. DeCosse and Kristen E. Heyer (Maryknoll, NY: Orbis, 2015), 61–64.

22. Bryan N. Massingale, "Response: The Challenge of Idolatry," in *Ecclesiology and Exclusion: Boundaries of Being and Belonging in Postmodern Times*, ed. Dennis M. Doyle, Timothy J. Furry, and Pascal D. Bozzell (Maryknoll, NY: Orbis, 2012), 130–35; Massingale, "Has the Silence Been Broken?," *Theological Studies* 75 (2014): 151–52.

23. Bryan Massingale, "The African American Experience and U.S. Roman Catholic Ethics: 'Strangers and Aliens No Longer,'" in Phelps, *Black and Catholic*, 79–101.

24. Bryan N. Massingale, "James Cone and Recent Catholic Episcopal Teaching on Racism," *Theological Studies* 61 (2000): 701–12. For an in-depth analysis and criticism of the statements by the bishops' conferences in the United States and some statements by individual bishops, see Massingale, *Racial Justice*, 50–78.

25. Massingale, "James Cone," *Theological Studies* 61 (2000): 721–30.

26. Bryan N. Massingale, "*Vox Victimarum Vox Dei:* Malcolm X as a Neglected 'Classic' for Catholic Theological Reflection," *Proceedings of the Catholic Theological Society of America* 65 (2010): 63–71.

27. Ibid., 77–88.

28. Bryan N. Massingale, "Malcolm X and the Limits of 'Authentically Black and Truly Catholic': A Research Project in Black Radicalism and Black Catholic Faith," *Journal of the Black Catholic Theological Symposium* 5 (2011): 7–23.

29. Bryan N. Massingale, "Toward a Catholic Malcolm X?," *American Catholic Studies* 125, no. 3 (2014): 8–11.

11

New Wine, New Wineskins

This book insists on the importance of the *Sitz im Leben* to understand and appreciate the work of Catholic moral theologians over time. This chapter will not focus on an individual theologian as such but on a group that calls itself "New Wine, New Wineskins." The group consists of young, pretenured Catholic moral theologians who in the summer of 2002 met for the first time at the University of Notre Dame.[1] The group has continued to meet and in 2013 developed its own bylaws and now has its own website. The group, however, is still restricted to members who are pretenured, thus the membership is constantly changing.[2] The founding group published two books, which will serve to introduce the discussion here.[3] The previous chapter focused on the single issue of racism; this chapter is limited to the narrow time frame of the first cohort of this group of young Catholic moral theologians.

The first book, *New Wine, New Wineskins*, has the subtitle *A Next Generation Reflects on Key Issues in Catholic Moral Theology*. The subtitle thus recognizes a chronological fact that this is a new generation. Earlier chapters have indicated that the realities of Vatican II (1962) and the encyclical *Humanae vitae* (1968) were the most significant factors shaping the development of moral theology in most of the latter part of the twentieth century. But this new generation represented in these two books was not even born before the 1970s.

A team of sociologists headed by William V. D'Antonio has studied and published their results about the identity and commitment of Catholics in the United States in four different periods: 1987, 1993, 1994, and 2005. These sociologists, while recognizing other important factors, rely on a chronological approach, with emphasis on the role of Vatican II. The 1987 study described the Catholic population as pre–Vatican II (31 percent), Vatican II (31 percent), and post–Vatican II (47 percent). The 2005 study described the

Catholic population as pre–Vatican II (17 percent), Vatican II (35 percent), post–Vatican II (40 percent), and millennials (9 percent).[4]

Characteristics of the New Generation

Chronology, however, is not the primary or decisive factor involved in trying to understand the contemporary generation of young US Catholic moral theologians. In a significant 2004 article, William L. Portier insists on the importance of cultural change to explain the group that he calls "evangelical Catholics."[5] Portier recognizes that the group is not and will not be a majority of Catholics but constitutes a significant minority. Rather than emphasize the focus on Vatican II, Portier focuses on the destruction of the Catholic subculture to understand and explain this new generation of Catholics. According to Portier, they are evangelical, not conservative.[6] Catholicism in the United States before Vatican II was a tightly knit cultural system. Catholicism characterized much of what Catholics thought and did. Many went to Catholic schools, where even in their early years they memorized the catechism. The Catholic Youth Organization in cities became the home for young Catholics engaged in sports. Practices such as Sunday Mass, no meat on Fridays, and the celebration of Lent helped identify Catholics. Catholics often went to Catholic doctors and Catholic lawyers. The description of the Catholic ghetto accurately describes the cultural reality.

David Cloutier and William C. Mattison III in their introduction to *New Wine, New Wineskins* accept and build on the significance of losing the Catholic subculture.[7] For pre–Vatican II Catholics, the subculture enveloped them in a thoroughly Catholic vision of life, which was quite insular. Their stance toward the world, even if engaged in, was guarded. Vatican II with its emphasis on *aggiornamento*—opening the Church to the world and bringing it up to date—became a decisive factor in future development. The Vatican II generation of young Catholic intellectuals was a transitional generation that engaged in a more liberating engagement with the world outside the Church. But this transitional generation still brought with it the Catholic understanding, training, background, and lens as they engaged with the contemporary world. The signs of the times for today's younger Catholic generation of intellectuals are not the same as for the transitional generation.

The introduction to *New Wine, New Wineskins* points out three characteristics of the present generation. First, this generation regards itself as having been poorly formed in the Catholic faith. The loss of the Catholic subculture occasions the loss of a thoroughgoing Catholic identity and formation. Andrew Greeley, the well-known Catholic sociologist (and novelist), maintained his generation had a truly Catholic imagination, but such is not the case for the new generation. A poor catechesis in the Catholic faith and living in a pluralistic culture have contributed to the fact that the new generation does not have a solid Catholic identity. Second, this generation has lived primarily in our pluralistic world and not in the Church or even in the Church trying to engage the world. Young Catholics are not trying to engage the world, since they are already living in it. They are now trying to understand better their own Catholic traditions and identity. Third, young Catholics recognize it is now their free choice to try to understand better their Catholic tradition and identity. Individual choice rather than cultural or ethnic identity is the primary source of religious commitment. Such an approach has many strengths, but such an emphasis on individual, free commitment can lack the importance of social and community relationships, which also are helpful in supporting the commitment.

The New Wine, New Wineskins group involves primarily laypeople. This development is a very radical change. The professors of moral theology at the time of Vatican II and for a number of years thereafter were priests. In the later 1970s, religious women began entering the field. Lisa Sowle Cahill was one of the first laypeople to enter the field and make important contributions to the discipline. Now the majority and even the vast majority of new Catholic moral theologians are laypeople. The religious formation of priest and religious theologians was a part of their own training, but laypeople for the most part have not had this training. The primary question for them then is "How do I live a Christian life in the circumstances of these times?" Their doctoral training has been primarily professional in terms of the intellectual understanding of the discipline. They generally appreciate this formation, but they want to recognize that they themselves are facing the personal existential question of living a Christian life as a disciple of Jesus in the world today.[8]

It follows from this that for many of them the professor of moral theology should be concerned not only about her own faith life but also the faith life of her students. An important new development in colleges involves community-based learning, or service learning. Here in Catholic colleges one puts Catholic social teaching into practice, thus bringing together faith, intellectual understanding, and practice.[9] In his own article in the book, Mattison goes further by calling for the professor in the classroom to be actively concerned about the faith formation of one's students in a Catholic college. He recognizes the problems involved in such an approach, including the pluralism of the student body, the freedom of all students, and the danger of proselytizing. He sees a good example of what he is trying to do in C. S. Lewis's approach in *Mere Christianity*. For the previous generation of moral theologians, it is safe to say it saw its role as intellectual: faith seeking understanding. How the intellectual understanding affected the faith life of the particular student was left to the individual student.[10]

One of the shifts involved in the move out of the Catholic subculture was the move from a crisis over individual liberty to a crisis over shared meaning.[11] Especially in the area of sexuality, the Church's teaching emphasized the boundaries in relationships, in bedrooms, and even in the mind, and these boundaries were enforced through the penalty of mortal sin. But this tension between freedom and Church moral teaching is not the issue today. Young students do not experience the need to be liberated from the Church's sexual teaching.

The Sitz im Leben of the teaching of these young Catholic moral theologians is the undergraduate college classroom. To their credit, they see their teaching role as intimately related to their students and their needs, but there are two other realities that enter into the discipline of moral theology. First, there are the realities and needs of the discipline itself. All who take courses in moral theology should learn what is involved in the discipline as such. In addition, there are the needs of the Church as a whole. As this group recognizes, moral theology is related to the academy, the Church, and the broader society. In my judgment, the needs of the discipline and the needs of the Church as a whole are more important on the graduate level, where the students themselves are primarily interested in these areas, but they still have some role to play even on the undergraduate level. New Wine, New Wineskins correctly points out that moral theology in the second half of the twentieth century rightly had to deal with Vatican II and *Humanae vitae*. It recognizes that the issues raised by *Humanae vitae* about norms retain their relevance for moral theology today, but they must be contextualized within larger frameworks.[12]

The New Wine, New Wineskins group, however, recognizes within the broad parameters of its Sitz im Leben that there are disagreements among members both with regard to method and on particular issues. David Cloutier, for example, follows the methodological approach of Alasdair MacIntyre.[13] Not all the theologians in this group follow this methodology. Cloutier himself points out that some, unlike himself, want to hold on to a concept of nature.[14] Likewise, within the group there is a difference of opinion on specific issues. The volume on sexuality has two contrasting essays on the issue of contraception within marriage.[15] The editor, however, has not tried to achieve a balance on particular issues. There is a strong article against homosexual relationships.[16] The editor reports that the oral presentation of this paper occasioned a great deal of intense debate, and the presence of this particular article in the book should not indicate any sort of group consensus on the issue.[17]

From a logical perspective, it is quite obvious that within groups united by an overall vision there are bound to be differences. Cloutier recognizes this among the group of Catholic moral theologians he calls proportionalists. Cloutier points out that the proportionalists constitute a loosely connected group of scholars and also that two of the leading figures do not make proportionalism all that central to their approach.[18]

The Church and Culture

New Wine, New Wineskins has raised two significant issues that should concern all moral theologians. The first issue concerns the relationship between the Church and culture, and the second involves ways to go beyond the sharp divisions between conservative and liberal Catholic moral theologians. The New Wine, New Wineskins group sees themselves unlike the previous generation as striving to discover their Catholic identity in order to oppose much of what they find in the contemporary culture. The second volume, with the title *Leaving and Coming Home*, is structured in accord with this understanding. "Home" goes beyond the personalistic approaches of the past since it describes a setting for shared practices in which identity and meaning are established and carried out through shared activity. A practice-based approach sees the theologizing about sex within larger accounts of the Christian life as a whole (the Christian story). Christians are called to live out the Christian story in the midst of the culture and world in which they find themselves. The previous generation of Catholics coming out of their subculture was more concerned about fitting into the culture, but the new generation is more concerned about standing out and establishing its identity sometimes against the culture.[19]

The first three chapters of *Leaving and Coming Home* discuss three aspects of the contemporary culture with regard to sexuality: the culture of abuse in dating, the hookup culture so prevalent in colleges and even high schools, and the pornography culture. These are huge problems in our sexual culture today.[20] It is safe to say, however, that Catholic moral theologians of all persuasions would agree in opposing such realities. David Cloutier's 2015 book *The Vice of Luxury: Economic Excess in a Consumer Age* deals with the problem of individualism, materialism, and economics in our culture.[21] Cloutier here insists on a sacramental perspective that points out the problem of the wealthy but focuses attention on the everyday choices that middle-class people make and how they can affect economic culture. In my judgment again, the vast majority of Catholic moral theologians of all stripes would be in agreement with his general approach.

From a theoretical perspective, we are here discussing the relationship between the Church and culture or what, since H. Richard Niebuhr, has been described as the relationship between Christ and culture.[22] The introduction to the first volume points out that the trajectory of the previous generation was from the Church to the world or culture, while the younger and present generation of Catholics in general and moral theologians in particular involves a turn from the culture toward the Church in the search for wisdom. This new trajectory helps explain the charge of some that this approach is sectarian—an approach that calls for one to leave the world in order to be true and faithful to the Gospel. The editors reject such a charge. The new generation is turning back to the Church in search of a more solid understanding of its members' tradition before turning back to the world in witness and service, having been nourished by that wisdom. They are not retreating from the world but want to enter into dialogue with the world on the basis of the wisdom of their own Catholic tradition.[23]

Here a question naturally arises: Does the dialogue with the world and culture involve a two-way street? The chapters in the two New Wine, New Wineskins books indicate how the Church can correct the culture. All should agree that the Church is called to transform the world. However, history shows that the Church has learned from the world on moral issues such as religious freedom, human rights, democracy, love in marriage, equality between spouses, and the evil of slavery. Such a recognition helps to explain the possibility of dissent from specific moral teachings.

Overcoming the Divisions

A second significant issue raised by New Wine, New Wineskins is to move beyond the impasse of Catholic moral theology between the so-called liberal and conservative groups that has been so obvious in Catholic moral theology since Vatican II. All have to recognize the realities of this division. In fact, the division is even greater than the New Wine, New Wineskins movement explicitly recognizes in its writings. Catholic theologians in the United States in general and not only moral theologians are seriously divided over the ecclesial issue of the legitimacy of dissent from noninfallible teaching within the Church. The preface to this volume pointed out that conservative and liberal theologians belong to different academic societies and tend to write in different journals.

The division between liberal and conservative moral theologians in the Catholic Church was hardened by the actions taken by the Congregation for the Doctrine of the Faith against revisionist Catholic moral theologians in the United States. The most serious of these was the congregation's conclusion after a seven-year inquiry that the present volume's author was neither suitable nor eligible to be a Catholic theologian because of his dissent from some noninfallible teachings, especially in the area of sexuality.[24]

Richard A. McCormick, the leading Jesuit moral theologian who wrote "Notes on Moral Theology" in *Theological Studies*, referred to the chill factor brought about by the Vatican investigations and condemnations of a number of liberal Catholic moral theologians.[25] In the late 1980s, McCormick used his discretionary funds at Notre Dame to invite about twenty-five recognized Catholic liberal moral theologians to a number of meetings there during the summers to discuss their own situations in light of the Vatican actions. It is somewhat ironic that in the early 2000s a different group of Catholic moral theologians met at Notre Dame in the summers to strengthen their bonds of scholarship and friendship among themselves. Both groups shared scholarly papers, meals, discussion, and prayer among themselves. There is no doubt the group McCormick gathered together felt they were threatened by the Vatican actions but tried to avoid succumbing to the martyr complex. The Vatican actions, however, as well as the meetings at Notre Dame, continued to accentuate the differences between liberal and conservative Catholic moral theologians.

The members of New Wine, New Wineskins did not live through this history, and many are probably not totally aware of it. They are, however, conscious of the seeming impasse between what one called "the boosters" and "the knockers." The boosters believed that *Humanae vitae* is wrong, that rules especially in conflict situations need to be nuanced, and that a primary problem is legalism. The knockers, who constitute a minority, are strongly opposed to relativism.[26] The young moral theologians are convinced that their primary goal is to overcome this division.

How can such a goal be achieved? The attendees at the first meeting in 2002 came together for two primary reasons. The first was to discuss among themselves their understanding of their vocation as moral theologians and its ecclesial dimensions. They had received an excellent academic training at their various graduate schools, but they wanted to explore how their vocation and their discipleship came together. They had their disagreements, but there was a unanimous desire to be more completely in the service of the Church in their life and vocation. "Friendship" suggests the second reason why they came. In light of the sharp divisions among Catholic moral theologians, there was hope they could embark on a career without ending up in the encamped divisions of their predecessors. The symposium explicitly attempted to nurture collegiality and friendship through prayer and socializing, as well as through formal and informal discussions. Their sense of collegiality did not result in an unwillingness to confront difficult questions and issues, but, in the setting of a common understanding of their vocations as disciples and theologians, they more easily discussed and even argued about difficult issues.[27]

There is much practical wisdom here. If people truly know and respect each other, it is easier to enter into serious discussions and disagreements. In fact, there are differences over the use of contraception among the members of New Wine, New Wineskins. On the basis of books from significant members of the group, there is strong support for the Church's teaching rejecting contraception for married couples.[28] However, two of the authors in the second volume accept the practice of contraception in marriage.[29] Thus, the New Wine, New Wineskins group show in reality how theologians could be in disagreement on issues of contraception and sexuality and still share mutual respect and friendship.

In the first book, David Cloutier sees the way forward beyond the debate between the boosters and the knockers in an approach of sapiential moral theology based on the method of Alasdair MacIntyre, with a focus on ordering desires and an emphasis on specific practices.[30] The introduction of the second volume calls for an approach beyond personalism, which had become central after Vatican II. Those arguing for change in the teaching on contraception invoked personalism, but John Paul II also used personalism to support his condemnation of contraception. The beyond-personalism approach insists on practices rather than persons. A practice-based approach thinks theologically about sex, not by abstract theologizing but by placing the practices of sex in marriage within larger contexts of the Christian life as a whole. The emphasis here is on the story or the context within which sex and marriage are going on. Another approach calls for a move from an emphasis on individual freedom to shared meaning.[31] Such approaches might help to bring about more dialogue, but, as this volume points out, the issue involves the need for dialogue among various approaches. There will never be agreement on just one approach.

Julie Hanlon Rubio has written more than any other theologian about how to find common ground even when liberals and conservatives disagree. In her contribution to *Leaving and Coming Home*, she accepts the justification of contraception. But she focuses on the experience of practices of sex in marriage and asks about the practice of self-sacrificing love. Those who advocate natural family planning such as Cloutier see in natural family planning the need for self-sacrifice by giving the gift of sex only when the woman is not fertile. Rubio insists that self-sacrifice is also present in the marriage of those who use contraception. Giving oneself to a spouse requires self-sacrifice even if every act might not reach the height of the symbol of total self-giving. Sex involves two people with different sex drives, sexual histories, preferences, and personalities. Having sex and forgoing it can be vital aspects of a self-giving love. There are many situations in married life when a couple cannot have sexual relations—for example, pregnancy, illness, travel, needs of their children, demanding jobs.[32]

In a subsequent article Rubio again finds common ground between those who practice contraception and those who practice natural family planning. Both groups seek basic common goods in their sexual married lives: self-giving, relational intimacy, mutuality, sexual pleasure, and a strong connection between sexual and spiritual experiences.[33] Her 2016 book *Hope for Common Ground* has a slightly different focus. Instead of concentrating on the sociopolitical structural area or just the level of personal conversion (without, however, abandoning these aspects), she argues for developing a third space for social action. On the local level, people of different persuasions can work more easily together for the common good. In the space between the personal and the political, common ground is possible and progress toward justice can be attained.[34]

In conclusion, the New Wine, New Wineskins movement described here did not last long because once people became tenured, they no longer belonged to the original cohort. One hopes that in the future many in this original group will make notable advances in the discipline of moral theology. Although restricted in time, this movement well illustrates a central aim of this volume in showing how the Sitz im Leben heavily influences one's approach to moral theology. I can only applaud their efforts to establish dialogue between conservative and liberal moral theologians. All moral theologians should not only applaud but work to bring about such dialogue.

Notes

1. David Cloutier and William C. Mattison III, "Introduction," in *New Wine, New Wineskins: A Next Generation Reflects on Key Issues in Catholic Moral Theology*, ed. William C. Mattison III (Lanham, MD: Rowman & Littlefield, 2005), xiii.

2. New Wine, New Wineskins, http://ycmt-newwineskins.com/wp-content/uploads/2014/11/YCMT-Bylaws.pdf.

3. The second book is David Cloutier, ed., *Leaving and Coming Home: New Wineskins for Catholic Sexual Ethics* (Eugene, OR: Cascade Books, 2010).

4. William V. D'Antonio, James D. Davidson, Dean R. Hoge, and Mary L. Gautier, *American Catholics Today: New Realities of Their Faith in Their Church* (Lanham, MD: Rowman & Littlefield, 2007), 11.

5. William Portier, "Here Come the Evangelical Catholics," *Communio* 31, no. 1 (Spring 2004): 35–66.

6. William L. Portier, "In Defense of Mount Saint Mary's: They Are Evangelical Not Conservative," *Commonweal* (February 11, 2000), 31.

7. Cloutier and Mattison, "Introduction," in Mattison, *New Wine, New Wineskins*, 3–7.

8. Ibid., 12–16.

9. William P. Bolan, "Promoting Social Change: Theoretical and Empirical Arguments for Using Traditional Community-Based Learning When Teaching Catholic Social Thought," in Mattison, *New Wine, New Wineskins*, 103–18.

10. William C. Mattison III, "Dare We Hope Our Students Believe? Patristic Rhetoric in the Contemporary Classroom," in Mattison, *New Wine, New Wineskins*, 77–101.

11. David Cloutier, "Introduction: The Trajectories of Catholic Sexual Ethics," in Cloutier, *Leaving and Coming Home*, 14–18.

12. Cloutier, "Introduction," in Cloutier, *Leaving and Coming Home*, 20.

13. David Cloutier, "Moral Theology for Real People: Agency, Practical Reason, and the Task of the Moral Theologian," in Mattison, *New Wine, New Wineskins*, 126–32.

14. Cloutier, "Introduction," in Cloutier, *Leaving and Coming Home*, 19.

15. Florence Caffery Bourg, "Multi-Dimensional Marriage Vocations and Responsible Parenthood," in Cloutier, *Leaving and Coming Home*, 147–72; Michel Therrien, "The Practice of Responsible Parenthood, NFP, and the Covenantal Unity of Spouses," in Cloutier, *Leaving and Coming Home*, 173–205.

16. Nicanor Pier Giorgio Austriaco, "Understanding Sexual Orientation as a *Habitus*: Reasoning from the Natural Law, Appeals to Human Experience, and the Data of Science," in Cloutier, *Leaving and Coming Home*, 101–18.

17. Cloutier, "Introduction," in Cloutier, *Leaving and Coming Home*, 23.

18. Cloutier, "Moral Theology for Real People, 135n5.

19. Cloutier, "Introduction," in Cloutier, *Leaving and Coming Home*, 12.

20. Cloutier, *Leaving and Coming Home*, 29–84.

21. David Cloutier, *The Vice of Luxury: Economic Excess in a Consumer Age* (Washington, DC: Georgetown University Press, 2015).

22. H. Richard Niebuhr, *Christ and Culture* (New York: Harper, 1951).

23. Cloutier and Mattison, "Introduction," in Mattison, *New Wine, New Wineskins*, 5–6.

24. For all the documentation, see Charles E. Curran, *Faithful Dissent* (Kansas City, MO: Sheed & Ward, 1986), 113–276.

25. Richard A. McCormick, "The Chill Factor in Contemporary Moral Theology," in Richard A. McCormick, *The Critical Calling: Reflections on Moral Dilemmas since Vatican II* (Washington, DC: Georgetown University Press, 1984), 71–94; Richard A. McCormick, "L'Affaire Curran," 111–30; in McCormick, Critical Calling Richard A. McCormick, "L'Affaire Curran II," in Richard A. McCormick, *Corrective Vision: Explorations in Moral Theology* (Kansas City, MO: Sheed & Ward, 1994), 110–21.

26. Cloutier, "Moral Theology for Real People," 122–23.

27. Cloutier and Mattison, "Introduction," in Mattison, *New Wine, New Wineskins*, 12–14.

28. See, for example, the following books: David Cloutier, *Love, Reason, and God's Story: An Introduction to Catholic Sexual Ethics* (Winona, MN: St Mary's, 2008); David Matzko McCarthy, *Sex and Love in the Home: A Theology of the Household* (London: SCM, 2001); and Christopher C. Roberts, *Creation and Covenant: The Significance of Sexual Differences in the Moral Theology of Marriage* (London: T&T Clark, 2008).

29. Bourg, "Multi-Dimensional Marriage," 147–72; Julie Hanlon Rubio, "The Practice of Sex," in Cloutier, *Leaving and Coming Home*, 226–49.

30. Cloutier, "Moral Theology for Real People," 126–34.

31. Cloutier, "Introduction," in Cloutier, *Leaving and Coming Home*, 2–15.

32. Rubio, "Practice of Sex," 235–43.

33. Julie Hanlon Rubio, "Beyond the Liberal/Conservative Divide over Contraception: The Wisdom of Practitioners of Natural Family Planning and Artificial Birth Control," *Horizons* 32, no. 2 (2005): 270–84.

34. Julie Hanlon Rubio, *Hope for Common Ground: Mediating the Personal and the Political in a Divided Church* (Washington, DC: Georgetown University Press, 2016).

12

James F. Keenan

This chapter deals with the work of James F. Keenan, the Canisius Professor at Boston College. My discussion of Keenan differs from all the other voices considered in this book, which were studied in light of their *Sitz im Leben*. There is no doubt that Keenan, like everyone else, is also influenced by his, but in my judgment he is unique because of his commitment to the discipline of moral theology as such. There is no doubt that others in this volume, especially Lisa Sowle Cahill, also share some concerns for the discipline of moral theology. But Keenan differs from all the others in the degree to which he has been concerned with the good of the discipline itself. Thus, Keenan is a very important, different voice in contemporary US Catholic moral theology.

Keenan, a Jesuit priest, received his doctorate in 1988 from the Gregorian University in Rome writing on the difference between goodness and rightness in Thomas Aquinas.[1] He was the last student to do a doctoral dissertation with Josef Fuchs. While studying in Rome, he was also influenced by the work of Klaus Demmer, who also taught at the Gregorian. Keenan himself first taught at Fordham University, then the Jesuit theologate at Weston before joining the faculty at Boston College.[2]

Keenan himself describes his own theological interests and research as including university ethics, fundamental moral theology, the history of theological ethics, Thomas Aquinas, virtue ethics, HIV/AIDS, and Church leadership ethics. His bibliography shows the breadth of his interests.[3] Keenan is a prolific scholar who has published much more than his contemporaries. His other academic activities in addition to publications have also made significant contributions to the discipline of moral theology.

In defending the thesis that Keenan is best understood in light of his contributions to the discipline of moral theology, this chapter will discuss his contribution to "Notes on Moral Theology" in *Theological Studies*, the history of moral theology, and method and foundational moral theology, including such issues as virtue ethics, casuistry, conscience, the role of Scripture, and the distinction between goodness and rightness. Keenan also addressed many particular issues, such as HIV/AIDS, the crisis in the Catholic Church in the United States, the ethics of those in teaching and ministry in the Church, and the ethics of the university, in addition to many other specific moral issues.

Notes on Moral Theology

From 1993 to 2017, Keenan contributed nineteen articles to "Notes on Moral Theology," now published annually in the March issue of *Theological Studies*, often in two or three sections. Recall that Richard A. McCormick's "Notes on Moral Theology" was his most significant contribution to moral theology. Keenan's articles were usually about twenty pages. Here he dealt with many different issues, including all those that were mentioned above as described as his theological interests in his curriculum vitae. These "Notes" show his scholarly research and interest in many areas of the discipline of moral theology.

Keenan's approach and method in the "Notes" was mainly bibliographical. His 2010 "Notes" titled "Contemporary Contributions to Sexual Ethics" well illustrates this bibliographical approach, as Keenan reports on recent writings, including books and articles, responding to contemporary needs; the Church and sexual ethics; eros, pleasure, and the body; justice; sin; and HIV/AIDs. Keenan's own voice appears only in the short conclusion. He comments that these writings, even coming from different perspectives and attitudes, emphasize the role of experience. Even those who lament the critical reaction to *Humanae vitae* turn to experience. He sees this move as coming from the fact of the ever-growing presence of laypersons in the ranks of moral theologians. Such an emphasis will undoubtedly become even more prevalent in the future.[4]

Sometimes in the "Notes," Keenan follows a somewhat different approach of using the writings of others to support his own thesis. His "Vatican II and Theological Ethics" in 2013 illustrates such an approach by developing the centrality of conscience found in his history of contemporary moral theology.[5] European theologians, especially after World War II, turned to conscience as foundational for the moral life. The role of the moral theologian thus is to inform the consciences of the baptized. Such an approach contrasts with the manuals of moral theology. In the United States in the post–World War II period, Catholic manualists John Ford and Gerald Kelly were even more rigid, authoritarian, and intolerant than their manualistic predecessors.

Vatican II, based on the European writings, insisted on the role of conscience. As a result, Keenan maintains that revisionist theologians universally made conscience their starting point. An important event in this consensus was the fact that Josef Fuchs, in the course of listening to the lay members of the papal birth control commission, changed his approach and recognized that contraception for spouses could be morally acceptable and good. Keenan here accepts Demmer's view that conscience is at the origin of every decision.[6]

In the 1998 "Notes," Keenan and Thomas Kopfensteiner published "Moral Theology out of Western Europe." With this topic they were carrying out the policy of giving a more international character to the "Notes." They covered material published in the previous five years, especially in Austria, Belgium, France, Germany, Italy, and Spain. They discovered an emerging consensus in developing an autonomous ethic in the context of faith but not in the sense that autonomy is the end toward which everything moves. This approach calls for the responsible self-determination of a relational subject living in solidarity with God, neighbor, and nature.

In his subsequent "Notes," Keenan continued to develop the international flavor but also brought in South America, Africa, and Asia.[7] His "Notes" enabled moral theologians in the United States and elsewhere to become conscious of and engage in dialogue with moral theologians throughout the world. The massive footnotes indicate that he read voraciously in these many languages.

Richard McCormick used the "Notes" to enter into dialogue with the authors cited, to criticize them, and to develop his own position. Keenan, as described above, employs a different approach. Very seldom indeed, and then in a brief way, does Keenan disagree with the authors whose positions he describes. For example, he explicitly disagrees with one author's understanding of sins as materially wrong actions.[8]

Importance of History

Keenan's concern for the discipline of moral theology comes through in his emphasis on the importance of historical study for the discipline. Although he is not primarily a historian, he has both examined the contributions that history makes to moral theology and also done historical research in his own writings.

With regard to how history has contributed to the discipline of moral theology, Keenan has pointed out six significant ways. History validates what seems to be innovative by showing what has been present in the past, showing the role of development and progress in moral truth, serving as a correction to what might be wrongly emphasized today, helping to ascertain critical identity for moral theology, and helping to direct future discourse in moral theology, either by recalling important aspects of the past or trying to make up for some of the lacunae of the past.[9]

Keenan himself has done important historical research in three contexts: his doctoral dissertation, moral theology in the twentieth century, and the importance and role of casuistry. His revised published doctoral dissertation studies the *Summa Theologiae* of Aquinas to see if Aquinas recognized the contemporary distinction between the goodness and rightness of human acts.

Keenan accepts and defends the distinction between goodness and rightness proposed by Fuchs and other contemporary Catholic revisionist theologians. Recall Fuchs's development of this distinction in chapter 3. An act can be morally disordered and wrong but still good if the person is truly striving to do what is right. Such an actual striving, however, can never be known simply by looking at the act itself since it involves the disposition of the subject.[10]

Keenan investigated Aquinas's teaching in the *Summa Theologiae* to determine if there is any basis for this distinction in Aquinas. Keenan studied Aquinas in depth on the moral act and especially on the virtues but found no basis for this distinction between goodness and rightness. Aquinas often uses goodness and rightness as synonymous. In Aquinas's discussion of charity, Keenan finds some basis for this distinction between goodness and rightness, but the full distinction does not permeate his approach to moral theology. Aquinas in his discussion of sin does not recognize this distinction between goodness and rightness. The most that Aquinas proposes is that a morally wrong act might be excused by the subjective disposition of the person acting, but it is not a good act. However, Keenan's study of Aquinas gave insight to his future work, such as that the virtues deal with the right ordering of the person and her acts.[11]

In an article written after his dissertation, Keenan puts the question of erroneous conscience in a broader historical perspective: Can a wrong action be good? In studying the broader context of this question, he shows developments that have occurred. In this context, on some aspects Aquinas disagreed with Peter Lombard; the Council of Sens rejected Abelard's position; Pope Alexander VIII repudiated Saint Bernard's position; William of Ockham reformed Abelard's understanding. Aquinas firmly pointed out that one is obliged under sin to follow one's conscience. But if the conscience is erroneous through no fault of the person, the act is excused from being sinful, but he does not say it is a good act. However, Alphonsus Liguori, later proclaimed the patron of confessors and moral theologians, went beyond Aquinas. If the person acted out of love or charity when committing the error, the erroneous act is not excused but is good. Subsequent moral theologians in the nineteenth and twentieth centuries generally follow Alphonsus's position, thus paving the way for the contemporary distinction between goodness and rightness.[12] This distinction is important to Keenan because it reinforces the centrality of conscience in Catholic moral theology. Keenan here uses history to show the progress of moral truth.

Keenan's major contribution in the area of history is his 2010 monograph *A History of Catholic Moral Theology in the Twentieth Century: From Confessing Sins to Liberating Consciences*.[13] The subtitle well illustrates the thesis that Keenan tries to prove in the book. Here again his historical work shows the progress and the development of moral truth now with regard to the primacy of the role of conscience in moral theology.

Half of the book deals with the developments in moral theology from the approach of the manuals to Vatican II, although he does not devote a specific chapter to Vatican II.[14] These chapters show how the trajectory toward liberating consciences developed. Chapter 3 deals with the work of the Belgian Benedictine Odon Lottin (1880–1965), whose contribution involved recovering history and the recognition of the developments that have occurred in history, especially in his multivolume *Psychologie et morale aux XIIe e XIIIe siècles*.[15] In his book *Morale fondamentale*, he strongly criticized the manuals, made conscience foundational to the moral life, and, by emphasizing the role of prudence, freed conscience from docility to the confessor.[16] Chapter 4 considers the work of Fritz Tillmann (1874–1953), who recognized the fundamental importance of scripture for moral theology, and Gérard Gillemann (1910–2002), who insisted on the primacy of charity. Chapter 5 treats Bernhard Häring (1912–98), whose three-volume *Law of Christ: Moral Theology for Priests and Laity* was originally published in German in 1954 and translated into more than a dozen languages.[17] Here Häring produced a synthesis of fundamental moral theology rooted in theology, scripture, and spirituality that highlights human freedom as foundational for goodness. Keenan ends each of these chapters, as he does all the chapters in this book, with a discussion of a contemporary work or author dealing with the issues raised in the chapter.

The second half of this history deals with the period from about 1960 through the beginning of the twenty-first century.[18] Keenan summarizes the period of the second half of the twentieth century as the difference between the classicist and historically conscious approaches. The Americans John Ford and Gerald Kelly and especially the hierarchical magisterium illustrate the classicist approach. The historically conscious approach played out in the work of many European and US moral theologians, with the Europeans especially building on the autonomous-ethic approach with a relational anthropology in a theonomous context to highlight the fundamental role and importance of conscience. The final chapter, "Toward Global Discourse on Suffering and Solidarity," highlights especially the work of Latin American, African, and Asian moral theologians, as well as the influence of liberation theology on Catholic ethicists in the United States.

As the title indicates, Keenan sees this history as showing the movement from the confessing of sins to the liberation of consciences. Keenan points out that after Pope John Paul II's encyclical *Veritatis splendor* (1993), many Catholic ethicists realized they had achieved a consensus in terms of revisionism in general. They stood together on the importance of conscience and the notion that moral truth is articulated in the judgment of the agent who has adequately considered all moral claims.[19]

Keenan's history in the post–Vatican II period does not consider in any depth what can be called the conservative Catholic moral theologians who have in various ways strongly supported the general thrust of the teaching of the hierarchical magisterium. Such an approach exists throughout the world and underscores the existing tension in the discipline today. Keenan has marshaled the historical evidence to show the movement toward the liberation of consciences. There is no doubt that the revisionist position supports this thesis, but there is still a strong minority voice among Catholic ethicists throughout the world today who reject the revisionist approach.

Keenan's *History* is his most important monograph, but his recognition of the importance of the history of moral theology also comes through in his extended treatment of casuistry. Keenan was most impressed by the historical work of Albert Jonsen and Stephen Toulmin, who described the high casuistry of 1550–1660 on the continent as involving an inductive method based on paradigmatic cases and not a deductive method applying principles. The deductive method was the one used in later Catholic casuistry in the nineteenth- and twentieth-century manuals of moral theology.[20]

To further the historical study of casuistry, Keenan did original historical research on three significant figures: John Mair (sometimes John Major, 1467–1550), Francesco de Toledo (1532–96), and William Perkins (1558–1602). The extensive footnotes in these studies show the depth and breadth of Keenan's historical research.

Keenan examined two cases explored by Mair, a significant professor at the University of Paris, dealing with maritime insurance and a lending exchange (*cambium bursae*). His casuistry, in the period just before that studied by Jonsen and Toulmin, was not the geometric application of a principle to a case but rather a taxonomic comparison of the congruences between one controlling insight or case and another. The standard was an acceptable form of behavior and not a principle. Mair's casuistry, however, did not make the conscience of the individual the arbiter of what was right or wrong.[21] Keenan studied the birth of Jesuit casuistry in the work of Francesco de Toledo summarizing in some detail Toledo's approach. Unlike the manuals of moral theology, Toledo was concerned also with social matters and institutional concerns, not just individual concerns.[22]

The third casuist Keenan studied was William Perkins, the Puritan father of British casuistry. Perkins's book *The Whole Treatise of Cases of Conscience* considered 148 cases. The cases, however, formed the point of departure for his further development and thus differed considerably from the understanding of the case in either inductive or deductive casuistry. His approach emphasized scripture, conscience, and law, as well as the use of reason, to aid the self-governance and conscience of the reader. Here he brought together both morality and spirituality, thus differing from the Catholic approach with its emphasis on sin and its avoidance.[23] A number of commentators maintain that British Puritan casuistry in the seventeenth century had its roots in Jesuit casuistry but with the important difference of putting spirituality into the casuistic method. Keenan argues that the roots of Puritan casuistry were in Jesuit devotional literature (e.g., the works of Gaspar Loarte and Robert Persons) and not in Jesuit continental casuistry.[24]

Keenan's Basic Approach to Moral Theology

Keenan has not written a monograph on his approach to moral theology and his method, but he has published many articles and essays dealing with the important issues involved in doing fundamental moral theology. He has often written on virtue and virtue ethics, casuistry, the need for moral theology to include spirituality (he often uses the term "ascetical theology"), the role of scripture in moral theology, and especially the role of conscience. In my judgment, he has given some indication in his many writings how all these pieces fit together.

Conscience

His historical monograph stresses the fundamental importance of conscience and traces the historical developments in the twentieth century moving toward the liberation of consciences. Keenan's specific writings on conscience often overlap with and repeat what is in his book on the history of moral theology in the twentieth century. His basic thesis is the primacy of conscience and the individual Christian's responsibility to form it. The role of moral theology consequently cannot be found primarily in specific moral teachings but in the protection and promotion of the personal conscience where God awakens the person to follow Christ. The primacy of conscience has to be protected from being overthrown by any outside authority in general or even by the magisterium in particular. The Church's teaching must be made plausible by dialogue and rational arguments with all people of good will.[25] On more than one occasion, Keenan has quoted his teacher and friend in Rome, Klaus Demmer, as maintaining that the primary charge of bishops in the Church is to remind all Christians that they have a conscience to be followed. The second task of bishops is to instruct Christians, knowing they have to follow their consciences, about the need to inform their consciences.[26]

Keenan often uses a historical approach in dealing with conscience and blames the manualists of moral theology for not promoting the primacy of conscience. The manuals focused only on what acts were sinful. Conscience needed moral certitude in order to act properly. The conscientious but doubtful Catholic, consequently, had to search for certitude and often "needed to consult an expert: the parish priest." The manualists often discussed problematic consciences such as the false, doubting, perplexed, scrupulous, and lax consciences and described a host of nervous and psychological conditions that diminish the agent's responsibility. The twentieth-century manuals gave great importance to the moral and canonical teachings of the Roman congregations and insisted on the need of obedience to these directives. Thus, the manuals did not recognize and develop the primacy of conscience.[27]

Moral theologians in Europe after World War II repudiated the manuals with their narrow scope and called for a new approach to moral theology. An important factor in this repudiation was the recognition that many Catholics had blindly submitted to authoritarian political regimes, but some also had courageously stood up in opposition. Bernard Häring experienced the bravery, solidarity, and truthfulness of many people struggling against Hitler, as well as the absurd obedience of many Christians to a tyrannical regime. This experience helped Häring to see conscience as foundational for a Christocentric moral theology. Häring was most influential in the understanding of conscience developed in the Pastoral Constitution on the Church and the Modern World (*Gaudium et spes*) of Vatican II as the place where the Christian hears the call of God with its twofold command to love God and neighbor. In fidelity to conscience, Christians are joined with the rest of humanity in the search for truth.[28]

US moral theologians after World War II, unlike the Europeans, still basically defended the manualist approach and saw the need for the magisterium, moral theologians, and confessors to instruct the laity in what is sinful and therefore what they cannot do. Keenan here is once again very negative on the work of John Ford and Gerald Kelly.[29]

After *Humanae vitae* in 1968, US moral theologians abandoned the manualistic approach and recognized the importance of conscience as illustrated in opposition to the Vietnam War as well as to *Humanae vitae*, but even here there was a difference with the European approach. The Americans appealed to conscience in these cases to recognize the right of the individual to disagree, whereas the European understanding arose out of the need to be collectively accountable for problems associated with the war. The European emphasis was on collective solidarity and not on just the individual conscience. In the United States, the acceptance of slavery and racism greatly corrupted the US collective conscience and left it without the capacity for creative vigilance, hospitable solidarity, and an honest sense of collective remorse. More recently contemporary moral theologians such as Shawn Copeland, Bryan Massingale, Alex Mikulich, and Maureen O'Connell have made us aware of our collective solidarity in the evil and the injustice of racism and the need for active moral agency to overcome the existing evil.[30]

Keenan also sees many other factors contributing to the primacy of conscience in moral theology today. In his opposition to the manualist approach, he has strongly supported the need for moral theology to bring spirituality and morality together. Moral theology thus calls for the Christian to live out the fullness of Christian discipleship and not just to avoid evil acts. Christians are called to holiness. As a result, it is the role of conscience to strive to respond as fully as possible to that call. The role of moral theology is to contribute to the formation of conscience so that Christians can strive for holiness in their daily lives. The manuals told Catholics what they could not do, but moral theology today must enable Christians to creatively live out their call to holiness. Ascetical writings from the seventeenth century until Vatican II too often were affected by the approach of the manuals of moral theology insisting on obedience as the primary virtue and pointing out the dangers of the passions. But today's moral theology should show the importance of the virtues in helping the Christian person to determine in conscience how best to grow in faith, hope, and love.[31]

In "Notes on Moral Theology" in 1998, Keenan and Thomas Kopfensteiner, in dealing with moral theology out of Western Europe, discussed European contributions to the primacy of conscience as the privileged point of departure for determining right conduct and an autonomous ethic.[32] Later Keenan stated that the most important contribution out of Europe in the last twenty years has been the autonomous ethic in the context of faith. As first articulated by Alfons Auer, this approach rests on a theological claim that the specificity of Christian ethics cannot be found primarily in specific moral teaching but rather in its promotion of the personal conscience wherein God animates the person to follow Christ. Autonomous ethics, however, has undergone a significant shift in later years. The danger in such an approach is a too individualistic understanding of the human person seen as completely independent. Supporters of an autonomous ethic now insist that the person is constitutively relational and that this relationship involves God, other human beings, and nature. We are images of God, whose Trinitarian nature is itself essentially relational. Our relationship with others is well illustrated by the virtues. Our relationship with neighbors reflects both our responsibility for nature, of which we are a part, and our ability to mold nature in light of true human purposes. Thus, the autonomous ethic underscores the primacy of conscience in the search for moral truth.[33]

Another factor Keenan notes as supporting the primacy and fundamental importance of conscience in Catholic moral theology is liberation ethics, with its emphasis on an option for the poor. This option is an important value and virtue, illustrating the solidarity and relational anthropology that should support the primacy of conscience. The same basic liberationist approach should be used against the violence and the abuse against women today. All, especially men, have to recognize their complicity and be remorseful over their failure to speak out and work against such abuse.[34] In concluding this section, there is no doubt that for Keenan the primary source for discovering moral truth is the conscience of the Christian who lives in solidarity and relationships with God, neighbor, and nature. The next section will discuss virtue, the primary way of forming a good conscience.

Virtue Ethics

Keenan has written often and in depth on virtue ethics, although he recognized that Jean Porter and William Spohn addressed virtue ethics before he did.[35] Virtue ethics describes the well-ordered person, who as an agent will then do rightly ordered actions.[36] The moral virtues dispose the person to well-ordered acts. Virtue ethics is opposed to quandary- or dilemma-oriented ethics, which have too often characterized much of contemporary theological and philosophical ethics. Keenan puts proportionalism in this category. Proportionalism was a transitional phase in Catholic theological ethics trying to establish a method for moral judgment as an alternative to the moral manuals, but it was simply the logic of the moral manuals without the overriding absolute moral norms. Its focus was primarily on dilemmas and quandaries. It never developed a positive agenda that could be seen as recognizing the fact that moral theology and spirituality must be seen together. Also, proportionalism did not have any context to weigh the premoral values involved. In time most theological ethicists moved on in search of a context for developing arguments on moral reasoning and moral living in all its dimensions.[37] Today we recognize that moral dilemmas are not based primarily on the opposition of good and evil but on the clash of various goods. In addition, McCormick saw virtues as descriptive of personal goodness rather than right action. This indicates the assumption coming from act-oriented ethics that anything pertaining to the agent belongs to moral goodness instead of moral rightness.[38]

Virtue ethics deals with the ordinary life of people and not esoteric or hard cases. Every truly human act is a moral act, and ethics should deal with all that transpires in ordinary life using ordinary language and not the esoteric language often used by other approaches to ethics. Some ethicists see a place for virtue ethics as a supplement to deontological or teleological ethics, but the Boston College professor insists that virtue ethics aims to construct a coherent system of ethics that is not merely supplemental but rather stands on its own and replaces the other approaches to ethics.

The primary ethical question is not "What should I do?" but "What should I become?" Three further questions expand this basic question of who I should become. The first question is "Who am I?" The standards I measure myself against are the moral virtues. My actions tell me if I measure up to these standards. The second question is "Who ought I to become?" Just as the cardinal moral virtues (prudence, justice, fortitude, and temperance) help us to discover who we are, they also set the goals or ends that we ought to seek. The fundamental task of the moral life is to develop a vision and strive to attain it.

The third question is "How do I get to the end?" To strive for the end is the work of prudence. Prudence has too often been associated with caution and timidity, but the prudent person knows how to set realistic goals and how to grow toward them. Prudence must be attentive to detail, anticipate difficulties along the way, and measure rightly. Prudence strives to get to the mean or middle point between the extremes of excess or defect. Finding the mean is not easy and differs from person to person. The good parent appreciates the significance of each child and tries to address each child as unique. Virtue ethics is a proactive system inviting all people to see themselves as they are, assess themselves, and see who they can actually become. It deals with the ordinary and all-encompassing, with emphasis on the person. Quandary ethics does not consider the person but merely somewhat esoteric cases of particular acts. The moral virtue of prudence makes one a well-ordered person. Such a person does right actions, and their actions in turn cause the person to grow as a virtuous person. In this whole process, prudence is the most important of the virtues.

Keenan has studied the importance and role of prudence in the thought of Aquinas. For Aquinas, prudence is right reason about things to be done.

Prudence recognizes the ends of the moral virtues, appraises the means to attain the ends, and directs the right realization of these means. Thomas thus gives to prudence this integrating and directive function through which the person as agent moves toward the right realization of the actions, which themselves transform the person.[39]

Keenan uses ordinary language and sources in explaining the role of prudence as seeking the mean. This seems to be very much in keeping with his insistence that the virtues deal with the ordinary life of ordinary people. The prudent drinker knows how to avoid the excessive use of alcohol while appreciating an occasional drink; the prudent person who has a fear of heights does not try to overcome the fear by going to the observation platform of the World Trade Center, which would only intensify her problem, but instead goes to a second-floor balcony as a first step of overcoming the problem. The prudent weight lifter knows how to find the medium, avoiding what is too much or what is too little weight. Virtue ethics deals with direct, plain talk. It is used in the home, at school, in houses of worship, in civic centers, in sports arenas, in the media, in cross-cultural discourse, and in interreligious dialogue. One does not have to be a philosopher or a professor to justify what is the right action.[40]

Note the teleological or goal-oriented character of virtue ethics. The more we grow in virtue, the more we recognize our need for further growth. The nature of virtue is historically dynamic. Virtues require being continually considered, understood, acquired, developed, and reformulated.[41]

Virtue ethics also has an important cross-cultural dimension. The cardinal virtues do not purport to offer a portrait of the ideal person or exhaust the entire domain of virtue. The cardinal virtues are hinges and provide the bare essentials or skeleton. In particular cultures, these virtues are thickened and given flesh. Thus, virtue ethics recognizes a broad universal agreement but also the different particularities in different cultures and times. The Christian culture itself also thickens these cardinal virtues by bringing in the important role of mercy. Mercy, for example, thickens justice by taking into account the chaos of the most marginalized.[42] Keenan also has written a more popular book on the important role of mercy for the Christian.[43] Notice that his emphasis on mercy for the Christian antedates the same emphasis by Pope Francis.[44]

Virtue ethics recognizes that principles and norms can be helpful in prudence discerning what is right action. However, virtue ethics itself generates its own principles, norms, and rules. These practices, principles, and norms are derived inductively in particular cultures and times. Relevant norms find their ground and origin in a virtue ethic. Thus, they are open to change and development. Keenan uses the rules of parenting to illustrate this point.[45] In two places, he deals with the objection that virtue ethics cannot deal with specific, practical issues. In a one-paragraph response, he simply asserts that a variety of writers have shown that it can give specific advice, that it can improve our ability to know the right and to do it, that it can give us new issues to address, and above all that it can make us better and our actions morally right.[46] In another place he points out that he has insisted on the role of prudence as providing normative guidance.[47]

Keenan has been recognized for his expertise in Thomas Aquinas's approach to virtue. He wrote the article "Virtues" in the *Cambridge Companion to the Summa Theologiae*.[48] Recall that his published doctoral dissertation examines Aquinas's approach to the virtues.

Keenan, however, disagrees with Aquinas, who saw the four cardinal virtues as perfecting the four basic powers of the human person: prudence (the intellect), justice (the will), fortitude (the irascible appetites), and temperance (the concupiscible appetites). Keenan calls for a more relational understanding of the human person. Our identity is relational in three ways: generally, specifically, and uniquely. Each of these relational ways of being human calls for a cardinal virtue. As a related being in general, we are called to justice, which is directed to the common good in which we treat all others as equal. As a relational being specifically, we are called to fidelity, which nurtures and sustains the bonds of our particular relationships whether based on blood, marriage, love, sacraments, and so forth. As a relational being uniquely, we are called to love our neighbor as ourselves and thereby directed to self-care. Finally, as in the Thomistic scheme, prudence integrates all the other three virtues composing the moral aspects for growing in the virtues and doing virtuous deeds.[49]

For Keenan the moral virtues thus form the well-ordered conscience, which itself calls for well-ordered human acts. But virtue ethics also deals with the person existing in a multiplicity of relationships. Virtue ethics restores moral theology to its full dimensions by building bridges between moral theology and scripture, ascetical theology, liturgy, and Church life.[50]

Keenan has also coauthored two books with his scripture-scholar colleague Daniel Harrington dealing with Jesus and virtue ethics and Paul and virtue ethics.[51] These books are the fruit of courses Keenan and Harrington taught together at Boston College. Harrington contributed the biblical section of each chapter, while Keenan gave the moral theology perspective. Chapters 3 to 5 of the book on Jesus develop the teaching of Jesus on the three basic questions developed in virtue ethics: Who are we? Who ought we to become? How do we get there?[52] These volumes treat the theological virtues of faith, hope, and love, the virtue of justice, and also important themes such as sin, the Eucharist, and virtues. The final section in each volume briefly discusses the virtues and societal and sexual issues. In his contribution, Keenan often relies on ideas he has developed in his other writings.[53]

Casuistry

The role of casuistry constitutes another important aspect of Keenan's work in method and fundamental moral theology. He incorporates casuistry into a broader approach, seeing its relationship both to virtue theory and to conscience. The work of Albert Jonsen and Stephen Toulmin, *The Abuse of Casuistry*, had an important influence on Keenan.[54] Jonsen and Toulmin disagreed with the emphasis on universal principles in ethics. In their experience working on a national presidential commission dealing with biomedical research on human subjects, they discovered that a casuistic approach was the most helpful in focusing the discussion of the commissioners with their different backgrounds to enable them to arrive at consensus. Such a method fits well in the morally pluralistic society in which we live. Their historical research shows that the seventeenth-century attack of Blaise Pascal had given casuistry a bad name. But in the period from 1556 to 1656, a high casuistry flourished in Catholic ethics, strongly influenced by the Jesuits. This casuistry did not follow the approach of the manuals of moral theology that saw casuistry in a deductive way, applying moral principles to particular cases, but insisted on an inductive approach, beginning with paradigmatic cases that were then compared with the new issues and questions that were arising. Such casuistry involves a careful analysis of the new circumstances in light of paradigmatic cases. As mentioned earlier, Keenan did some historical research of his own in the casuistry of John Mair, Francesco de Toledo, and William Perkins.

On these building blocks, Keenan developed his approach to casuistry with emphasis on an inductive approach, realistically assessing the existing circumstances and emphasizing the role of the paradigmatic case for the guidance of the individual person. Such a casuistry enables the individual person to form her own conscience and make her own decisions in all aspects of the moral life. Conscience here becomes the primary authority for directing the moral life. While greatly influenced by Jonsen and Toulmin, Keenan makes an important addition to their approach. *The Abuse of Casuistry* does not really provide an objective method for moral deliberation. They maintain that casuistry is context-independent, but casuistry is not context-free. It is equally effective in the hands of a tutiorist or a laxist. Casuistry needs a vision or context to ensure objective moral deliberation. It seems that Jonsen and Toulmin's use of casuistry was successful because the commissioners, despite differences, shared a basic common context. Casuistry needs a vision or a telos to ensure objective moral deliberation.[55]

For Keenan, Christian ethics today should avoid the extremes of ahistorical, acontextual universal moral principles and relativism. Here Keenan proposes a marriage between virtue ethics and high casuistry. This casuistry applies to all aspects of the moral life, from the minimum of avoiding wrongdoing to striving to grow as disciples of Jesus. Virtue theory provides the vision or telos to make sure that casuistry involves objective moral deliberations. Virtue ethics deals with the rightly ordered person disposed to perform rightly ordered acts. The integrating role of prudence and virtue ethics finds in casuistry an attentiveness to detail that appreciates the uniqueness of the situation and the circumstances in order to find a right resolution. The virtuous context provides casuistry with an objective foundation for its method. Virtue ethics, on the other hand, is in need of an objective moral reasoning that high casuistry can provide. Keenan, in the casuistry book published in 1995, recognizes that such an approach is "nascent."[56] However, he never subsequently developed in a deeper and more systematic way his understanding of the marriage of casuistry and virtue ethics. For example, he has never explored in depth the important relationship between prudence and conscience.

Such a virtue-grounded approach to high casuistry recognizes the existence and role of principles, but they are arrived at inductively, not deductively; do not claim certitude; and thus are open to revision in the light of newer developments. In this context, he has discussed the principle of double effect, maintaining that it owes its origin to such an inductive approach and also is open to change in light of new understandings and developments.[57]

Practical Issues

In addition to the interest in theory and areas of fundamental moral theology, Keenan has also considered a number of specific, practical issues. This section will first consider the issue that has received most of his attention: the HIV/AIDS pandemic. The other issues discussed in this section are the application of virtue ethics to specific issues and especially his pioneering work on institutional ethics.

HIV/AIDS Prevention

James Keenan has paid more attention to HIV/AIDS in his writing, teaching, lecturing, and leadership than any other Catholic moral theologian, not only in the United States but also in the world. He returned from doctoral studies in Rome in the late 1980s just as the discussion of the prevention of HIV was beginning to occur. The administrative board of the National Conference of Catholic Bishops in December 1987 issued "The Many Faces of AIDS," which justified the Church's toleration of public educational programs that included accurate information on condoms for the prevention of HIV/AIDS.[58] Keenan published an article in 1988 appealing to the traditional Catholic teaching on cooperation as the more appropriate moral principle in this case.[59] In a 1995 article, Keenan pointed out that his recommendation for the use of condoms to prevent HIV was an endorsement of prophylaxis and not contraception.[60] In a 1999 article, Keenan applied seventeenth-century casuistry to show that the use of condoms for prevention could be justified without in any way challenging the magisterial teaching on contraception.[61] Meanwhile, there was opposition among some American bishops to the 1987 statement of the administrative board that tolerated public policies endorsing the use of condoms for prevention. Cardinal Joseph Ratzinger intervened in this discussion and stressed the importance of unity in the teaching of all the bishops. A 1989 document from the bishops, without explicitly denying the former statement, was basically in tacit opposition to the use of condoms for prevention.[62]

At that time, Keenan had been working with other moral theologians in this country and abroad and especially with Jon D. Fuller, a Jesuit physician who had been working with HIV/AIDS patients. A result of this consultation and work was the 2000 book *Catholic Ethicists on HIV/AIDS Prevention*, which is the first book in moral theology engaging Catholic ethicists from around the world addressing a particular moral issue. In addition, the book responds to the important concern of beginning from and respecting local cultures but integrating them into a transglobal discussion. The first part of the book presents twenty-six cases from moral theologians around the world dealing with the particular local realities and showing how Catholic theologians in these different circumstances have defended HIV/AIDS prevention by the use of condoms. A second part of seven essays addresses the issue of prevention transglobally. Facing the second generation of HIV/AIDS, Keenan, in introducing the book, recognized that HIV prevention can be helped by condoms, but there is need to address the social problems that inhibit the prevention of HIV/AIDS. Primary among the social problems is the powerlessness and vulnerability of women and children. In addition to the condom issue, the book also discusses needle-exchange programs, which also can be justified by the same moral arguments.[63]

Keenan is the leading theologian in this area working to get Catholic bishops to accept the need for condoms as part of the prevention of HIV/

AIDS. In a 2001 article, he discusses the various casuistic moral principles (lesser evil, double effect, cooperation) to justify the compatibility of the teaching of *Humanae vitae* with effective HIV/AIDS prevention methods. This approach was based on the fact that the AIDS pandemic was so vast that Catholic bishops were needed to promote Catholic involvement in the work of prevention. All those involved in the work of prevention knew that Catholic bishops were not going to publicly challenge the teaching of *Humanae vitae* on contraception, so Keenan and the others tried to present them a way to support HIV prevention without having to accept contraception.[64] Twenty years after first broaching such an approach, Keenan, like many others, is confounded that bishops continue to oppose condom usage by invoking the immutability of the teaching on contraception. The issue of protecting life does not seem to be in the forefront of their priorities.[65] I think that on almost all other issues the bishops would be willing to accept the casuistry proposed here by Keenan and others.

On the other hand, Keenan insists that the prevention of HIV/AIDS involves much more than the condom issue, especially the need to deal with the social structures and institutions that help to spread the disease and obstruct its prevention. Here he urges theologians to bring into their discourse the Catholic teaching on the common good, social justice, human rights, solidarity, and the option for the poor to help dismantle the existing negative social structures.[66]

Application of Virtue Ethics to Specific Issues

Keenan has applied his virtue ethics to a number of significant areas in the moral life. In these essays and articles, he usually summarizes his approach to virtue ethics before discussing how virtue ethics deals with these specific moral realities. With regard to sexuality, he shows how the four cardinal virtues—justice, fidelity, self-care, and prudence—in addition to chastity pose who the well-ordered sexual person is and the type of person one strives to become. In the Catholic tradition, mercy again adds depth to all these other virtues.[67]

The structure of the usual discourse on the consistent ethic of life goes in the wrong direction by beginning with principles or norms. Rather, we need to begin with the constellation of virtues and practices disposing us to appreciate the sanctity of life. In this context, Keenan mentions the virtues of mercy, vigilance, and humility, as well as some practices that encapsulate these virtues.[68]

With regard to genetics, virtue ethics brings to the discussion its relational anthropological approach, which differs from the usual individualistic approach found in approaches to genetics in the United States. In this context, Keenan criticizes some papers commissioned by the National Institutes of Health to study embryo research. Those justifying such research insist on "respect" for human embryos and are opposed to demeaning research. These respectful dispositions, however, do not lead to any guidance for such embryonic research and in reality have no effect on the fact that these authors accept that human embryos can be produced, cloned, manipulated, and discarded. But virtue theory must provide positive guidelines toward becoming the type of people we should be. In this context, prudence again helps us to articulate the demands of justice and equality (especially the extent that human embryonic life participates in basic human equality), fidelity, and self-care. Keenan is opposed to producing embryos for research, but in this essay he challenges proponents to truly propose ethical arguments to sustain their position.[69]

Institutional Ethics

Keenan has shown great creativity and initiative in discussing an issue that has been mostly ignored before his own work. The issue concerns the ethics of the two institutions with which he has been associated: the Church and the university. Ironically, while the Church and the university both teach ethics for how others should live, they have paid practically no attention to the ethical content that should be present in the lives of these two important institutions and their leadership.

In dealing with ethics in the Church, he has followed the process also used with regard to his work on HIV/AIDS prevention by bringing together a large number of other scholars to deal with this issue in an edited book. In 1990, he and Joseph Kotva, a Mennonite pastor, coedited *Practice What You Preach: Virtue, Ethics, and Power in the Lives of Pastoral Ministers and Their Congregations*. The editors brought together over twenty ethicists from various churches to write about a particular case of ethics involving how the church and its leadership functioned. In almost all these cases, the authors wrote as observers; they were not asked by church officials for their expert ethical advice about what should be done. For all practical purposes, their churches had no professional guidelines for church leaders to follow.[70]

In this book, Keenan himself addressed the ethical issue of testing religious-order candidates for HIV. He begins by presenting the general reasons for and against such testing without choosing sides. Often such testing is done to exclude those who have HIV. Keenan insists that generic arguments pro and con need to be supplemented by recognizing the virtues involved as well as other considerations such as the individual candidate, the nature of the religious order (many were founded with a special charism for the marginalized), the people the order serves, and the resources of the order to support people with chronic illness. Also, today people who have AIDS are living much longer than previously. Religious, testing to exclude candidates, must ask themselves what this policy says about who they are and who they want to become. In light of all these factors, Keenan agrees with those who oppose the general policy of excluding people with AIDS from religious orders.[71]

For over three years, what was called the Church Twenty-One Project at Boston College held lectures, panels, forums, and meetings to better understand and respond to the pedophilia crisis in the Catholic Church. As part of this project, Keenan and two others in 2006 edited *Church Ethics and Its Organizational Context: Learning from the Sex Abuse Scandal in the Catholic Church*, which brought together sixteen essays dealing with the crisis.[72]

In his own writings, Keenan points out that professions such as law and medicine have very definite ethical standards that help to shape the ethos of these professions, but the Church and the university do not have such standards. With regard to the Church, the crisis experienced in the last decades reminds us of the lack of such standards and the need to establish them.[73] The fact is that clerical culture, episcopal culture, and the culture of religious life do not regularly show an awareness of the ethical virtues and norms with regard to routine decision-making. A primary reason for this failure comes from the fact that those exercising such roles have not been trained in the ethical issues in how they carry out their responsibilities. He makes the case for professional ethics in Church leadership by considering three issues illustrating the need for such training: confidentiality in religious life, due process in priestly life, and the ethics of discourse and open dialogue in episcopal life.[74]

With regard to the crisis and need for Church institutional ethics, Keenan emphasizes especially the role of priests. While priests are generally happy in their ministry, they have been deeply affected by the pedophilia scandal. There is also a sharp division between older priests following a servant-leader model and younger priests following a cultic model. A pervasive clerical culture, including denial and silence, forms an unhealthy culture. There is a need today for a more open professional culture that can be shaped by a professional ethics of the priestly minister.[75] In developing the professional ethics of priests, Keenan describes some moral rights of priests—the right to share in the ministry of the local bishop, the right of association, the right to their personal development, the right to privacy, and the right to fair treatment.[76]

The university is the second institution that, according to Keenan, lacks an institutional ethics despite the fact that within the university ethics courses deal with many other professions and institutions. His approach to university ethics differs from his approach to Church ethics in two significant ways. First, he uses a very different format. In dealing with the Church, he coedited two different books bringing together many different Christian ethicists to address the issues. With regard to the university, he wrote his own monograph on the subject.[77] Here he also uses a very different method. He is not writing for only Catholic or Christian universities but for all universities. Thus, he does not write from the discipline of Christian ethics but from the broader ethical perspective of using only human sources of wisdom and knowledge.

His book on university ethics constitutes a very creative initiative since for all practical purposes it is the first book that has been written on this very important but neglected topic. This book shows his scholarly approach, but now he has researched deeply and broadly in an entirely new area. The forty-five pages of endnotes testify to the depth and breadth of his research.[78]

His book shows that universities, unlike many other institutions and professions, lack an ethical culture permeating the whole. He devotes individual chapters to seven important topics that cry out for ethical consideration: the treatment of adjunct faculty (chapter 4); cheating (chapter 6); bad undergraduate behavior with drinking, partying, and so forth (chapter 7); gender inequity (chapter 8); ethnic and racial inequity (chapter 9); the commodification of higher education (chapter 10); and athletics (chapter 11).

The seven different chapters showing seven areas needing ethical considerations illustrate a fundamental problem he sees in the contemporary university. The fragmented nature of the university's geography involves many different silos that are basically independent from one another. He refers to these different silos as "fiefdoms" and "organized anarchies." Keenan indicates, perhaps without emphasizing it strongly enough, the culture that seems to have a significant influence on all these different fiefdoms that constitute the contemporary university: the culture of commodification. The absence of an identifiable ethical culture is seen today in the creeping growth of commodification, which affects the entire undefended mission and integrity of the university. Naive market strategies (in my words, the capitalistic business model) override all other concerns about the mission of the university. There is simply nothing to check the growing claims of commodification.[79]

Values that should direct the entire life of the university include the dignity of the human person, social justice, the common good, equity, accountability, transparency, fairness, nondiscrimination, honesty, consent, and other important ethical values.[80] For these values to permeate the whole university, it is necessary to connect the dots. Since the contemporary university is siloed, so are the ethical issues. The student affairs department is familiar with sexual assault and binge drinking, the faculty are more familiar with cheating, but neither knows what athletics is really doing and the role it is playing. Only deans and department chairs know about adjunct faculty, and few dare to address the responsibility of post-tenured faculty. All these realities are ethically related and show the need for an ethical culture affecting the entire university.[81]

Keenan has been criticized for not proposing better positive pathways for ethically improving the university. He responds that he is more interested in trying to create a culture for ethics than in trying to articulate the direction a university ought to take to improve ethically.[82] At the end of his final chapter in the book, he points out what he would do if he were president to create a culture of ethics. He is not interested in promoting a code of ethics. Codes are meaningless without a culture of ethics, its virtues, and its practices. He then describes the process he would use to help bring about such a culture throughout the whole campus. Such a culture cannot be imposed from the top down but must be enkindled in all parts of the university. The role of the president is to stimulate and try to find the ways in which such a culture can truly grow and develop.[83]

Two Significant Involvements

Every moral theologian is affected by one's own Sitz im Leben; Keenan is no exception. His creative attempts as an ethicist to respond to the lack of an institutional culture of ethics in the Church and the university today well illustrate such an influence, but in my judgment his many writings are so extensive in covering so many different areas that his characteristic contribution can best be described as a contribution to the discipline of moral theology as such. His two outstanding works on behalf of the discipline of moral theology in addition to his writing supply further proof for my thesis. These two involvements are his work as editor of the monograph series Moral Traditions from Georgetown University Press and his work as the founder, organizer, and chief animator of the group called Catholic Theological Ethics in the World Church.

From 1993 to 2013, Keenan served as editor of Moral Traditions, which he made the premier academic publishing series in Catholic moral theology. Moral Traditions contains over forty-five volumes that touch on all aspects of moral theology. This series has published the work of older scholars but also, under Keenan's guidance, the work of younger scholars, thus contributing to the growth of the discipline itself. The topics include all the areas of moral theology. The work involved in editing such a large series is most extensive. The help that Keenan provided the authors shows his broad and deep knowledge in all areas of moral theology.[84] If this were his only contribution to moral theology, it would stand as a lasting and significant addition to the work of this discipline.

Keenan's incomparable achievement has been to bring into existence and direct the coming together of the organization Catholic Theological Ethics in the World Church (CTEWC). This chapter has pointed out how he brought together moral theologians from all parts of the globe to respond to the HIV/AIDS pandemic in the 1990s. In 2003, with funding from a European foundation, Keenan gathered eight moral theologians from seven countries at a meeting in Leuven University in Belgium to discuss organizing an international conference of Catholic moral theologians. This was the beginning of what became CTEWC.[85] Its mission is to bring about an exchange of ideas in Catholic theological ethics by appreciating the challenge of pluralism, dialoguing from and beyond local cultures, and interconnecting with the world Church not dominated by the Northern Hemisphere. Too often the tendency has been for the Northern Hemisphere to see its role as teaching the Southern Hemisphere. In reality, the Northern Hemisphere has much to learn from the Southern Hemisphere.[86]

A major aspect of this organization's work has been the holding of international conferences. In Padua, in July 2006, nearly four hundred Catholic moral theologians from sixty-three countries participated in the First Cross-Cultural Conference on Catholic Theological Ethics. In July 2010, six hundred Catholic ethicists from seventy-three countries participated in the second international conference, in Trent. In July 2018, the third international conference at Sarajevo discussed the climate crisis and the problem of political leadership in many countries. In addition to these international conferences, regional conferences in Manila (2008), Bangalore (2012), Nairobi (2012), Berlin (2013), Krakow (2014), Bangalore (2015), and Bogota (2016) have carried on the discussions, with particular emphasis on theologians in the developing world. Books have been published based on the work of these conferences. With more than fourteen hundred moral theologians, CTEWC facilitates forums in Africa, Asia, Europe, Latin America, and North America. A monthly newsletter keeps all participants informed of the developments. Grants and fellowships have been provided for individuals to study moral theology in developing countries.[87]

There has been no instrumentality that has even come close to the work of CTEWC in the development of contemporary Catholic moral theology in all parts of the globe. Through his creative thinking, fundraising skills, and great organizational abilities, Keenan has made all this possible.

This chapter has discussed Keenan's major scholarly writings. One exception is the area of bioethics. In his early writings, he often published in this area but has not done so for the last two decades. In addition to his scholarly writings, Keenan has also published four books of a more popular nature, which still show his theological understandings and approaches. Three of these books were originally published as columns in *Church* magazine.[88] The fourth book, *Moral Wisdom*, was originally a series of eight lectures given at the Church of St. Ignatius Loyola in New York City.[89]

In conclusion, on the basis of his contribution to the discipline of moral theology as evidenced in his very extensive scholarly writings, his work in editing the Moral Traditions series, and in giving birth to CTEWC, James F. Keenan has made a singular contribution to contemporary Catholic moral theology in the United States and in the world.

Notes

1. James F. Keenan, *Goodness and Rightness in Thomas Aquinas's Summa Theologiae* (Washington, DC: Georgetown University Press, 1992).

2. Keenan provides many details of his life in James F. Keenan, *Ethics of the Word: Voices in the Catholic Church Today* (Lanham, MD: Rowman & Littlefield, 2010).

3. "James F. Keenan," https://www.bc.edu/bc-web/schools/mcas/departments /...james-keenan-sj.html.

4. James F. Keenan, "Notes on Moral Theology: Contemporary Contributions to Sexual Ethics," *Theological Studies* 71 (2010): 148–67.

5. James F. Keenan, *A History of Catholic Moral Theology in the Twentieth Century: From Confessing Sins to Liberating Consciences* (New York: Continuum, 2010).

6. James F. Keenan, "Notes on Moral Theology: Vatican II and Theological Ethics," *Theological Studies* 74 (2013): 162–90.

7. E.g., James F. Keenan, "Notes on Moral Theology: What Happened at Trento 2010?," *Theological Studies* 72 (2011): 131–49; James F. Keenan, "Notes on Moral Theology: Receiving *Amoris Laetitiae*," *Theological Studies* 78 (2017): 193–212.

8. James F. Keenan, "Notes on Moral Theology: Raising Expectations on Sin," *Theological Studies* 77 (2016): 135–36.

9. James F. Keenan, "Notes on Moral Theology: Moral Theology in History," *Theological Studies* 62 (2001): 86–104.

10. For Keenan's understanding of this distinction, see Keenan, *Goodness and Rightness*, 3–20.

11. Ibid., 65–182.

12. James F. Keenan, "Can a Wrong Action Be Good? The Development of Theological Opinion on Erroneous Conscience," *Église et théologie* 24 (1993): 205–19.

13. Keenan, *History*.

14. Ibid., 35–110.

15. Odon Lottin, *Psychologie et morale aux XIIe et XIIIe siècles* (Gembloux, Belgium: J. Duculot [vol. 1, 1942; vol. 2, 1948; vol. 3, 1949; vol. 4, 1960]).

16. Odon Lottin, *Morale fondamentale* (Tournai, Belgium: Desclée, 1954).

17. Bernard Häring, *The Law of Christ: Moral Theology for Priests and Laity*, 3 vols., trans. Edwin G. Kaiser (Westminster, MD: Newman Press, 1960, 1963, 1966).

18. Keenan, *History*, 111–239.

19. Ibid., 173.

20. Albert R. Jonsen and Stephen Toulmin, *The Abuse of Casuistry: A History of Moral Reasoning* (Berkeley: University of California Press, 1988).

21. James F. Keenan, "The Casuistry of John Mair, Nominalist Professor of Paris," in *The Context of Casuistry*, ed. James F. Keenan and Thomas A. Shannon (Washington, DC: Georgetown University Press, 1995), 85–102.

22. James F. Keenan, "The Birth of Jesuit Casuistry: *Summa casuum conscientiae, sive de instructione sacerdotum, libri septem* by Francesco de Toledo (1532–1596)," in *The Mercurian Project: Forming Jesuit Culture, 1573–1580*, ed. Thomas McCoog (Rome: Institutum Historicum Societatis Iesu, 2004), 461–82.

23. James F. Keenan, "William Perkins (1558–1602) and the Birth of British Casuistry," in Keenan and Shannon, *Context of Casuistry*, 105–30.

24. James F. Keenan, "Jesuit Casuistry or Jesuit Spirituality: The Roots of Seventeenth-Century British Puritan Practical Divinity," in *The Jesuits: Culture, Sciences, and the Arts, 1540–1773*, ed. John W. O'Malley et al. (Toronto: University of Toronto Press, 1999), 627–40.

25. James F. Keenan, "Fundamental Moral Theology in the New Millennium," in *Ethical Dilemmas in the New Millennium*, ed. Francis Eigo (Villanova, PA: Villanova University Press, 2000), 14–16.

26. James F. Keenan, "To Follow and Form over Time: A Phenomenology of Conscience," in *Conscience and Catholicism: Rights, Responsibilities, and Institutional Responses*, ed. David E. DeCosse and Kristen E. Heyer (Maryknoll, NY: Orbis, 2015), 13.

27. Ibid., 3–4; Keenan, "Vatican II and Theological Ethics," 175–76.

28. Keenan, "Vatican II and Theological Ethics," 169–74; Keenan, "To Follow and Form over Time," 5–8.

29. Keenan, "Vatican II and Theological Ethics," 174–76.

30. James F. Keenan, "Notes on Moral Theology: Redeeming Conscience," *Theological Studies* 76 (2015): 133–38.

31. James F. Keenan, "Spirituality and Morality: What's the Difference?" in *Method in Catholic Moral Theology: The Ongoing Reconstruction*, ed. Todd A. Salzman (Omaha, NE: Creighton University Press, 1999), 87–102; Keenan, "Fundamental Moral Theology," 1–13.

32. James F. Keenan and Thomas R. Kopfensteiner, "Notes on Moral Theology: Moral Theology out of Western Europe," *Theological Studies* 89 (1998): 115–25.

33. James F. Keenan, "The Moral Agent: Actions and Normative Decision Making," in *A Call to Fidelity: On the Moral Theology of Charles E. Curran*, ed. James J. Walter, Timothy E. O'Connell, and Thomas A. Shannon (Washington, DC: Georgetown University Press, 2002), 45; Keenan, "Fundamental Moral Theology," 15–16.

34. Keenan, "Fundamental Moral Theology," 18–20.

35. Keenan, "Vatican II and Theological Ethics," 186.

36. For his first article that expresses his basic understanding of virtue ethics, see

James F. Keenan, "Virtue Ethics: Making a Case as It Comes of Age," *Thought* 67, no. 265 (June 1992): 115–26. Subsequent articles repeat and develop somewhat the basic thesis of the original essay. See, e.g., James F. Keenan, "Virtue Ethics," in *Christian Ethics: An Introduction*, ed. Bernard Hoose (Collegeville, MN: Liturgical, 1998), 84–94; James F. Keenan, "Virtues and Identity," in *Creating Identity*, ed. Hermann Häring, Maureen Junker-Kenny, and Dietmar Mieth (London: SCM, 2000), 69–77; and James F. Keenan, "Seven Reasons for Doing Virtue Ethics Today," in *Virtue and the Moral Life: Theological and Philosophical Perspectives*, ed. William Werpehowski and Kathryn Getek Soltis (Lanham, MD: Lexington, 2014), 3–17. The following paragraphs in the text will be based on these publications. Specific references will be given when an aspect is more developed in one of these.

37. Keenan, *History*, 158.

38. Keenan, "Virtue Ethics: Making a Case," 118.

39. James F. Keenan, "The Virtue of Prudence (IIa IIae, qq. 47–56)," in *The Ethics of Aquinas*, ed. Stephen J. Pope (Washington, DC: Georgetown University Press, 2002), 259–71.

40. James F. Keenan, "The Style of Virtue Ethics," in *Performing the Word: Festschrift for Ronan Drury*, ed. Enda McDonagh (Dublin: Columba, 2014), 215–21.

41. James F. Keenan, "Virtue Ethics and Sexual Ethics," *Louvain Studies* 30, no. 3 (2005): 180.

42. James F. Keenan, "What Does Virtue Ethics Bring to Genetics?," in *Genetics, Theology, and Ethics: An Interdisciplinary Conversation*, ed. Lisa Sowle Cahill (New York: Crossroad, 2005), 104.

43. James F. Keenan, *The Works of Mercy: The Heart of Catholicism* (Lanham, MD: Rowman & Littlefield, 2005).

44. Pope Francis, *The Name of God Is Mercy: A Conversation with Andrea Tornielli* (New York: Random House, 2016).

45. Keenan, "Seven Reasons," 10–11.

46. Keenan, "Virtue Ethics," in *Christian Ethics*, 46.

47. Donald J. Harrington and James F. Keenan, *Paul and Virtue Ethics: Building Bridges between New Testament Studies and Moral Theology* (Lanham, MD: Rowman & Littlefield, 2010), 11–12.

48. James F. Keenan, "Virtues," in *Cambridge Companion to the Summa Theologiae*, ed. Philip McCosker and Denys Turner (New York: Cambridge University Press, 2016), 194–205.

49. James F. Keenan, "Proposing Cardinal Virtues," *Theological Studies* 56 (1995): 709–29.

50. Daniel J. Harrington and James F. Keenan, *Jesus and Virtue Ethics: Building Bridges between New Testament Studies and Moral Theology* (Lanham, MD: Sheed & Ward, 2002), 24–30.

51. Harrington and Keenan, *Jesus and Virtue Ethics*; Harrington and Keenan, *Paul and Virtue Ethics*.

52. Harrington and Keenan, *Jesus and Virtue Ethics*, 35–75.

53. In addition to these two volumes, Keenan has also coedited a significant vol-

ume on the Bible and ethics. See Yiu Sing Lúcás Chan, Ronaldo Zacharias, and James F. Keenan, eds., *The Bible and Catholic Theological Ethics* (Maryknoll, NY: Orbis, 2016).

54. Jonsen and Toulmin, *Abuse of Casuistry*.

55. James F. Keenan and Thomas A. Shannon, "Contexts of Casuistry: Historical and Contemporary," in *Context of Casuistry*, 226–27.

56. Ibid., 226–30. See also James F. Keenan, "Notes on Moral Theology: The Return of Casuistry," *Theological Studies* 57 (1996): 123–39.

57. Keenan, "Return of Casuistry," 134–39.

58. Jon D. Fuller and James F. Keenan, "Church Politics and HIV Prevention: Why Is the Condom Question So Significant and So Neuralgic?," in *Between Poetry and Politics: Essays in Honor of Enda McDonagh*, ed. Linda Hogan and Barbara FitzGerald (Dublin: Columba, 2003), 161–62.

59. James F. Keenan, "Prophylactics, Toleration, and Cooperation: Contemporary Problems and Traditional Principles," *International Philosophical Quarterly* 29, no. 2 (1998): 205–21.

60. James F. Keenan, "Living with HIV/AIDS," *Tablet* (June 3, 1995): 701.

61. James F. Keenan, "Applying the Seventeenth Century Casuistry of Accommodation to HIV Prevention," *Theological Studies* 60 (1999): 492–512.

62. Fuller and Keenan, in *Between Poetry and Politics*, 167–69.

63. James F. Keenan, "About the Book," in *Catholic Ethicists*, 13–19.

64. Jon D. Fuller and James F. Keenan, "Condoms, Catholics, and HIV/AIDS Prevention," *The Furrow* 52 (2001): 45–67.

65. James F. Keenan, "HIV/AIDS: The Expanding Ethical Challenge," in *Beauty, Truth and Love: Essays in Honor of Enda McDonagh*, ed. Eugene Duffy and Patrick Hannon (Dublin: Columba, 2009), 139–40.

66. Ibid., 138–42.

67. Keenan, "Virtue Ethics and Sexual Ethics," 183–203.

68. James F. Keenan, "Virtues, Principles, and a Consistent Ethic of Life," in *The Consistent Ethic of Life: Assessing Its Reception and Relevance*, ed. Thomas A. Narin (Maryknoll, NY: Orbis, 2008), 48–60.

69. James F. Kennan, "Casuistry, Virtue, and the Slippery Slope: Moral Problems with Producing Human Embryonic Life for Research Purposes," in *Cloning and the Future of Human Embryo Research*, ed. Paul Lauritzen (New York: Oxford University Press, 2001), 67–81.

70. James F. Keenan and Joseph Kotva Jr., *Practice What You Preach: Virtues, Ethics, and Power in the Lives of Pastoral Ministers and Their Congregations* (Franklin, WI: Sheed & Ward, 1999).

71. James F. Keenan, "Testing Religious Order Candidates for HIV," in Keenan and Kotva, Practice What You Preach, 29–41.

72. Jean M. Bartunek and James F. Keenan, "Introduction," in *Church Ethics and Its Organizational Context: Learning from the Sex Abuse Scandal in the Catholic Church*, ed. Jean M. Bartunek, Mary Ann Hinsdale, and James F. Keenan (Lanham, MD: Rowman & Littlefield, 2006), xiii–xv.

73. James F. Keenan, "Notes on Moral Theology: Ethics and the Crisis in the Church," *Theological Studies* 66 (2005): 135–36.

74. James F. Keenan, "Toward an Ecclesial Professional Ethics," in Bartunek, Hinsdale, and Keenan, *Church Ethics and Its Organizational Context*, 83–96.

75. Keenan, "Ethics and the Crisis in the Church," 121–27.

76. James F. Keenan, "The Moral Rights of Priests," in *Priests for the Twenty-First Century*, ed. Donald J. Dietrich (New York: Crossroad, 2006), 77–90. See also James F. Keenan, "Framing the Ethical Rights of Priests," *Review for Religious* 64, no. 2 (2005): 135–51.

77. James F. Keenan, *University Ethics: How Colleges Can Build and Benefit from a Culture of Ethics* (Lanham, MD: Rowman & Littlefield, 2005). For an article discussing some ideas found in this book, see James F. Keenan, "Notes on Moral Theology: Coming Home: Ethics and the American University," *Theological Studies* 75 (2014): 155–69.

78. Keenan, *University Ethics*, 219–64.

79. Ibid., 195–96.

80. James F. Keenan, "Author's Response," *Horizons* 44 (2017): 197.

81. Ibid., 193.

82. Ibid., 196.

83. Keenan, *University Ethics*, 213–17.

84. James F. Keenan, curriculum vitae, http://www.bc.edu/content/dam/files/schools/cas_sites/theology/pdf/keenan.cv.pdf.

85. Keenan, *Ethics of the Word*, 62–64.

86. Mission of Catholic Theological Ethics in the World Church, www.catholicethics.com.

87. Conferences, programs, and forums of Catholic Theological Ethics in the World Church, www.catholicethics.com.

88. James F. Keenan, *Virtues for Ordinary Christians* (Kansas City, MO: Sheed & Ward, 1996); James F. Keenan, *Commandments of Compassion* (Lanham, MD: Sheed & Ward, 1999); James F. Keenan, *The Works of Mercy: The Heart of Catholicism* (Lanham, MD: Sheed & Ward, 2005).

89. James F. Keenan, *Moral Wisdom: Lessons and Texts from the Catholic Tradition* (Lanham, MD: Sheed & Ward, 2004).

Conclusion

I started teaching moral theology at St. Bernard's Seminary in Rochester, New York, in 1961. The textbook assigned for the course was the moral manual written in Latin by the Austrian Jesuit Hieronymus Noldin (1838–1932). The manual was subsequently brought up to date by two of his successors teaching moral theology at Innsbruck. I used the thirty-second edition, published in 1959.[1] Many of the additions made to the original related to developments in canon law and the official documents from the Roman Curia, especially the Holy Office, which was later called the Congregation for the Doctrine of the Faith. According to a study in 1962, the Noldin manual was used in more Catholic seminaries in the United States than any other manual.[2]

Thanks especially to the influence of Bernard Häring when I was studying for a doctorate in moral theology at the Alfonsian Academy in Rome, I was dissatisfied with the approach of the manuals because it was too minimalistic and legalistic. I produced my own notes for the students as an introduction to moral theology. One year I went to the textbook only on the first of March of the second semester.

This volume has indicated that the manuals continued in existence even for a time after Vatican II because there were no other texts available. The pre–Vatican II Roman Catholic Church emphasized its catholicity or universality. It was the same Church in all parts of the world and also throughout history. The best illustration of this catholicity was the use of Latin in the liturgy. The Eucharist, which then was often called the Mass, was exactly the same in every country of the world. The teaching of theology in Catholic seminaries reflected the same universalism. The language of theology was Latin. The textbooks were the same textbooks used everywhere in the world. No one was surprised that a text for the practical discipline of moral theology in seminaries in the United States was written in Latin by an author living in a different country and culture.

The narrative developed in this volume shows the dramatic contrast between the situation of moral theology today and what existed just a little more than fifty years ago. What explains such a turnabout? In my judgment, Bernard Lonergan, the Canadian Jesuit theologian who himself taught in Latin in Rome (I was privileged to have classes with him), put his finger on what happened. According to Lonergan, the most significant change that occurred as a result of Vatican II was the move from classicism to historical consciousness. Classicism looked at the world in terms of the eternal, the immutable, and the unchangeable. Historical consciousness gives greater importance to the particular, the contingent, and the historical. Historical consciousness also recognizes that the human subject who is a knower and author is also embedded in and influenced by his or her own history and culture.[3]

The shift to historical consciousness explains the diversity and pluralism of Catholic moral theology today and the importance of *Sitz im Leben*. John C. Ford was one of the last manualists. Bernard Häring, Josef Fuchs, Richard A. McCormick, Germain G. Grisez, and to an extent Romanus Cessario responded to the changes of Vatican II and the discussions brought about by *Humanae vitae*. In addition, Cessario brought his Dominican and Thomistic perspective to his work. Feminism strongly influenced the approach of Margaret A. Farley and Lisa Sowle Cahill, as did their respective perspectives of a religious sister and a married laywoman. Ada María Isasi-Díaz and Bryan N. Massingale brought their ethnic and racial backgrounds and perspectives to their work. The experience of young Catholic moral theologians at the beginning of the twenty-first century helps to explain the approach taken by the New Wine, New Wineskins group. James F. Keenan's broad interest in many aspects of moral theology and his commitment to recognizing the work of moral theologians throughout the world comes through in many of his writings and his work with the CTEWC.

This diversity and pluralism, however, raises the question of whether an identifiable Catholic moral theology still exists today. All Catholic theologians today are heavily involved in ecumenical dialogue as well as a growing interreligious dialogue. What stands out in this volume is the agreement among all the authors on what they oppose. They strongly object to an anthropology that sees the human person as an isolated individual who is free to do whatever one wants. This individualism is especially present in US culture, which insists that one can pull oneself up by the bootstraps and become whatever one wants to become. Success in this country is often understood in economic terms. The Roman Catholic tradition, however, has always insisted on the social nature of the human person. We are not individual monads. Rather, we exist in and depend on many different relationships with God and others.

A fundamental characteristic of Catholic understanding in general and moral theology in particular is the principle of mediation, also called the incarnational or sacramental principle. The divine is mediated in and through the human. Catholic ecclesiology well illustrates this approach. God comes to us, and we go to God in and through the Church as the community of the disciples of Jesus. The whole sacramental system is based on such an understanding. Thomistic natural law also illustrates the role of mediation. To know what God wants us to do, one does not go immediately to God and ask. Rather, our God-given human reason reflecting on what God has made can tell us how God wants the creation to be used. The diverse approaches in this volume well illustrate the Catholic notion of mediation.

As pointed out, pre–Vatican II Catholicism gave great importance to universality. Universality, however, still remains an important characteristic of Roman Catholicism. The authors discussed in this volume obviously stress the particular and the changing, but they still hold on to a chastened universality. For example, feminists and minority groups want equality and dignity for themselves and for all human beings.

Mediation and some universality have also contributed to the Catholic emphasis on "both-and" approaches rather than "either-or" approaches. The Catholic tradition has insisted on scripture and tradition, faith and reason, grace and work, Jesus and the Church. There have been differences and problems as to how the two parts in the both-and approach fit together, but such an approach continues to be characteristic of the Catholic method and is well illustrated by the chapters in this book.

The negative criticism of individualism pointed out earlier that the Catholic approach to anthropology emphasizes the social aspect of the human person based on both scripture and reason. In accordance with such an anthropology, the Catholic tradition has given importance to the common good, solidarity, human rights, and an understanding of justice that also includes the relationship of the individual to society and society's relationship to the individual.

The tradition of Catholic moral theology and the authors studied here also recognize the importance of the ecclesial dimension of moral theology. Many of the authors in this volume have dealt with the teaching office of the Church in moral matters. There are, however, many ways in which the Church should carry out its teaching mission, which because of baptism should always involve all those who are members of the Church. The Catholic tradition has insisted on the social mission of the Church, but how this mission is carried out in different situations continues to be an important consideration. Moral theology will always experience the tension between the prophetic role of the Church and its openness to all. The Catholic approach also recognizes that Catholics belong to many other communities and societies, and moral theology needs to address the role of Catholics in these different communities and in different circumstances.

Thus, without going into greater detail, there are characteristic aspects of the Catholic moral tradition that are found in the different authors considered in this volume. The Catholic tradition in moral theology is truly a living tradition that involves both continuities and discontinuities. In the future, there will continue to be diverse approaches, especially in light of the Sitz im Leben, but all these approaches will be influenced and affected by the continuing living tradition of Catholic moral theology.

Notes

1. Hieronymus Noldin, *Summa Theologiae Moralis*, vol. 2, *De Praceptis*, 32nd ed. (Innsbruck: F. Rauch, 1959).

2. John C. Boere, "A Survey of the Content and Organization of the Curriculum of the Theological Departments of Major Seminaries in the United States of America" (MA diss., Catholic University of America, 1963), 73.

3. Bernard Lonergan, "The Transition from a Classicist World-View to Historical Mindedness," in *Law for Liberty: The Role of Law in the Church Today*, ed. James E. Biechler (Baltimore: Helicon, 1967), 126–33.

Index

Fuchs, Joseph, ix, xii, 39–60, 224; absolute norms in, 51–53; Aquinas and, 49;
background of, 39; Christian morality
in, 46–48, 53; conscience in, 54–57,
57–58; contraception in, 41–42, 48–
57; contributions of, 57–58; criticism
of, 57; early writings of, 40–42; fundamental option and, 42–46; Häring
and, 41; *Humanae vitae* and, 39–40, 48;
as Jesuit, 39; magisterium in, 53–54;
manualism and, 40–41; natural law
in, 48–51; in Pontifical Commission
on Population, Family, and Birth,
41–42; positions of, 40–42; power in,
40; Rahner and, 42–48; sexuality in,
41; sin in, 44; *Sitz im Leben,* 39, 57;
subjectivism and, 56; Vatican II and,
39–40, 56
*Fulfillment in Christ: A Summary of Chris-
tian Moral Principles* (Grisez and Shaw),
93, 99
Fuller, Jon D., 236
fundamental option, 42–46, 124

*Galilean Journey, The: The Mexican Ameri-
can Promise* (Elizondo), 178
Gandhi, Mahatma, 34
Gaudium et spes, 27, 63, 71, 228
Geinzer, John A., 92
gender, 132, 139, 156, 167
George, Francis, 203
Georgetown University, 56, 61, 66, 85
Gillemann, Gérard, 225
*Global Justice, Christology, and Christian
Ethics* (Cahill), 157–58, 171, 173n7
God: freedom and, 43; image of, 112,
118; moral virtues and, 113; responsi-
bility and, in Häring, 20; and scripture,
in Häring, 22; values and, in Häring,
21; virtues and, in Häring, 21; will
of, 53
*Godly Image, The: Christ and Salvation in
Catholic Thought from Anselm to Aquinas*
(Cessario), 108
Gramsci, Antonio, 182

gratia operans, 116
Greeley, Andrew, 210–11
Gregorian University, 39, 40, 61
Gregory the Great, 113
Grisez, Germain, xii, 85–106; abortion
in, 92, 101–2; background of, 85; basic goods theory in, 94–95, 103, 119;
Cessario and, 124; consequentialism
in, 96–97; contraception in, 85–91,
93–95; double effect in, 97, 102; euthanasia in, 103–4; faith in, 95–96;
Ford and, 90–91, 98; gospel in, 95–96;
homosexuality in, 98, 101; *Humanae
vitae* and, 85, 91, 98; infallibility and,
98–99, 100; later writings, 91–95; law
of love in, 95–96; masturbation in, 98;
McCormick and, 97; natural law in,
85–91, 93–95; nuclear deterrence in,
102–3; overview of moral theology
of, 100–101; as philosopher, 91–92;
proportionalism in, 96–98; and radical
dissent, 99–100; reason in, 87–89; responsibility in, 94, 96, 97–98; rhythm
method in, 89–90; sexuality in, 98;
Sitz im Leben, 85; Vatican II and, 95,
98–99
Grisez, Jeannette, 92
Grisez-Boyle theory, 92
Grisez-Finnis theory, 92
Gustafson, James M., 67, 129, 130, 138,
151–52
Gutíerrez, Gustavo, 180, 182, 204

habitus, 112–13
Hamel, Ron, 31
Häring, Bernard, ix, xii, 19–36, 249; emphasis on person, 24–25; evaluation of,
26–27; Fuchs and, 41; *Humanae vitae*
and, 27–29; in Keenan, 225; loving
criticism of Church by, 34–36; manualism *vs.,* 22–24; medical ethics in,
30–31; moral virtue in, 21; peace in,
33–34; power in, 33–34; *Sitz im Leben,*
20, 29; Vatican II and, 27–29
Harrington, Daniel, 233–34

About the Author

Charles E. Curran is the Elizabeth Scurlock University Professor of Human Values at Southern Methodist University. He has served as president of three national professional societies: the American Theological Society, the Catholic Theological Society of America, and the Society of Christian Ethics. Curran also was the first recipient of the John Courtney Murray Award of the Catholic Theological Society of America and received the Lifetime Achievement Award of the Society of Christian Ethics. He has published over fifty books, including nine in the Moral Traditions series of Georgetown University Press, and edited or coedited the eighteen volumes in the series Readings in Moral Theology. Curran has also been named the *New York Times* "Man in the News" and the ABC TV "Person of the Week."